Serving Those Who Served

D0754186

Serving Those Who Served

Librarian's Guide to Working with Veteran and Military Communities

SARAH LEMIRE AND
KRISTEN J. MULVIHILL

LIBRARIES
UNLIMITED™
An Imprint of ABC-CLIO, LLC
Santa Barbara, California • Denver, Colorado

Serving Those Who Served: Librarian's Guide to Working with Veteran and Military Communities
Library of Congress Cataloging in Publication Control Number: 2016039278

ISBN: 978-1-4408-3432-5
EISBN: 978-1-4408-3433-2

21 20 19 18 17   1 2 3 4 5

This book is also available as an eBook.

Libraries Unlimited
An Imprint of ABC-CLIO, LLC

ABC-CLIO, LLC
130 Cremona Drive, P.O. Box 1911
Santa Barbara, California 93116-1911
www.abc-clio.com

This book is printed on acid-free paper ∞

Manufactured in the United States of America

To our husbands, for their endless support.

Contents

Acknowledgments

We would like to thank all of our friends, family, and colleagues who have kindly provided feedback on parts of this book, including Stacey Aldrich, Catherine Blansett, Jim Blansett, Marta Brandes-Miesner, Jacquie Brinkley, Jason Broughton, Chris Brown, Sean Buckner, Dan Cisco, Karen Bosch Cobb, Rob Coppo, Jason Deitch, Michelle Donez, Lise Dyckman, April Evans, Lisa Foster, Margaret Foster, SGM Donald Freeman (Ret.), Harlynne Geisler, Christine Gonzalez, Stephanie Graves, Derek Halling, Susan Hanks, Mark Harryman, John "Buzz" Kraft, MAJ Nick Long, Patrick MacInerney, Brenda Magente, Hollie May, Kenny Mintz, Sandi Mintz, Lynne Muller-McIntyre, Nellie Moffitt, Marilyn Mulvihill, Patrick Mulvihill, Carol Naegele, Sylvia O'Hara, Cindy Olney, Frances Rickard, Erin Ropposch, Loriene Roy, Ingrid Ruffin, Lorelei Rutledge, Michelle Simmons, Vera Skop, Cynthia Smith, Mary Somerville, Lorraine Stein, Elizabeth Stevens, Ray Stevens, Robert Stevens, Shelley Stevens, Jennifer Taft, Diane Walden, and Betty Waznis.

Additionally, we would like to thank all of those who have shared their stories and experiences with us, including those who are not named on this page.

A special thank you is included for Sean Buckner, who contributed great time and effort to many aspects of the project, from proofreading to offering advice on how to organize its content.

Finally, we'd like to express our gratitude to those who are serving or have served in the military and to those of you who are the family members, spouses, partners, and caregivers of those who serve or have served.

Introduction

Veterans, service members, and their families are not new to library communities. Librarians have served the veteran and military communities in peacetime and in war, as well as in the transitionary periods between. Library literature as early as the World War II era recognized the need for librarians to adapt their wartime services to focus on helping returning troops readjust to civilian life (Merrill, 1944). However, librarian focus on veterans and service members as a special patron population has not remained consistent over the years. Recently, in the aftermath of the wars in Iraq and Afghanistan, librarians have become increasingly interested in library outreach to and services for the veteran and military communities. Efforts in the last few years include the following:

- National library conferences have featured discussions of library outreach to veteran and military-affiliated patrons (e.g., Roy, Mulvihill, Rickard, Taft, & Olney, 2016; Tinoco & Hoppenfeld, 2015; LeMire, 2015; Blansett & Blansett, 2012).

- "Community-based solutions for veterans and military families" are one of the highest priorities of the Institute of Museum and Library Services' (IMLS) fiscal year 2017 budget request (Institute of Museum and Library Services, 2016).

- ALA sponsored a 2015 diversity research grant, "Facilitating the Learning and Academic Performance of Student Veterans" (American Library Association, 2015).

- Several research articles have been published that begin to delve into the unique characteristics and needs of veterans and service members and how libraries can contribute to their success (e.g., Fawley & Krysak, 2013; Mills, Paladino, & Klentzin, 2015; Taft & Olney, 2014).

- IMLS has sponsored projects such as War Ink and California's Veterans Connect @ the Library program ("War Ink," 2014; "Veterans Connect @ the Library," 2016).

While the increase in discussion of veteran and military issues suggests that librarians have become open to the idea of treating veterans and service members as a unique patron population, many librarians may not be quite sure where to begin.

This book can help. The authors are librarians as well as Army veterans. Kristen served in the Army as a linguist and paratrooper during the first Gulf War, earning a Meritorious Service Medal by the end of her four-year service. Sarah served in the Army as an Arabic linguist from 2002 to 2007, including a year-long deployment to Iraq. They also have ongoing experience with immediate family members and close friends serving in Iraq and Afghanistan or coping with the transition from military to civilian life. And both authors currently work at libraries that provide programming and services to assist veterans and service members from all branches of the military.

As librarians and veterans with personal and professional experience on this topic, the authors are uniquely positioned to help librarians understand some of the most crucial aspects of military and veteran culture. They are likewise qualified to discuss the unique information-seeking challenges and opportunities of those who have served and to make suggestions for how libraries can become friendlier and more welcoming for veterans, service members, and their communities.

Scope

Although this book attempts to explain the most fundamental aspects of the veteran and military communities and to answer some of the most common questions asked about veteran and military-affiliated patrons, it is impossible to include every potentially relevant aspect of military life in one resource guide. The veteran and military communities constitute an enormous group with a number of disparate subgroups who have their own unique characteristics and needs, including veterans, service members, military spouses, children of military personnel, and even the parents and extended family members of military personnel. Although all of these groups have needs or interests related to the military experience, this book primarily focuses on the needs of the veterans and service members themselves. Much of this information can be relevant to veterans' and service members' families, both immediate and extended, because family members often play a role in seeking information on behalf of their loved ones. Some sections of the book also include information about the needs of military and veteran family members, such as a segment about the children of military personnel in the school libraries section of chapter 5.

Readers should be aware that information about specific veteran and military-related benefits and resources can change rapidly. For example, legislation and associated policy changes can significantly impact the details of U.S. Department of Veterans Affairs (VA) benefit eligibility from one year to another. Although this book is intended to answer many librarians' questions, it is also intended to help librarians know where they can look for answers when information changes, old resources disappear, or new resources develop.

How to Read This Book

This book is intended to be a starting point, a desktop guide, to provide librarians with an increased awareness of the veteran and military communities. It will provide a brief overview of the most important things to know in terms of answering questions at a reference desk, developing new programs and partnerships, and enhancing a collection for those who are serving or have served in the military, as well as for those who care about them. Regardless of whether a library is big or small, rural or urban, academic, public, or special, its patron population will include veterans, service members, and the family members and friends of veterans and service members. Every library can benefit from employees who are knowledgeable about resources that are helpful for veterans, service members, and their families.

The first two chapters of the book are intended to provide a general introduction appropriate for all librarians, regardless of the library setting. Chapter 1 answers such questions as the following: What is a veteran? How many veterans and service members are there? What are some of the unique groups within the veteran and military communities? Chapter 2 goes a little bit deeper by addressing the following questions: How should you address someone in uniform? What might offend someone when asking them about their service? Who are the advocates and agencies in the community waiting to hear from librarians, hoping they are willing and ready to be a part of the community that they too serve? These first two chapters are intended to discuss the basics and to provide all librarians with essential background about veteran and military communities.

Subsequent chapters offer suggestions for librarians in public, academic, and other library settings to help them better understand which members of the veteran and military communities may be using their library and steps they can take to begin or improve services and programs for veterans and service members. These services and programs include such efforts as collection management, readers' advisory, targeted outreach, and instruction. They also include relationship building with strategic partners and with the veterans and service members themselves to ensure that they feel welcome and supported by their library. The goal for each chapter is to help readers identify resources where they can follow up for more information, recognize who to ask, and learn where to start or restart efforts to connect with veteran and military communities. Chapter 3 provides information and suggestions specifically aimed at public libraries, while chapter 4 focuses on academic libraries and how they can support student veterans and service members. Finally, chapter 5 provides resources and information for school, health sciences, military, law, and prison libraries.

Throughout this guide, the authors provide insights based on their personal experiences serving in the military, becoming veterans, and connecting with benefits needed for themselves and their family members. These personal insights are meant to help familiarize readers with some of the potential challenges and pitfalls that veterans and service members may face in their everyday lives. Although these personal experiences are intended to provide context for the suggestions and recommendations in each chapter, it is important to remember that needs, challenges, and strengths can vary widely from one era to another and from one veteran or service member to another. One veteran's experience is not necessarily indicative of what all veterans experience.

This book is also intended to provide support and advice from one librarian to another. It is designed to help public librarians who are trying to create a Veterans Day display, school librarians who are struggling to support students with a deployed parent, and librarians who are thinking of developing targeted outreach to veterans and service members in their communities. Although the authors use the term *librarian* throughout the book, it is also intended to provide support to library school students and library staff members, administrators, and volunteers who represent key contributors and engaged advocates of any library community.

Finally, this book is intended to encourage librarians to apply the skills they already have, both in building relationships with patrons and strategic partners and at finding the best resources and points of contact to assist patrons. In addition to helping librarians avoid assumptions or pitfalls, the book aims to provide librarians with a better understanding of the scope and diversity of veterans' experiences so they can help ensure that members of the veteran and military communities throughout the country are made to feel welcome in any library setting. And as a result, librarians can enjoy the rewarding experience of connecting with this unique set of individuals who have the potential to become an integral part of any library's community.

References

American Library Association. (2015). Diversity research grant: 2015 winner(s). Retrieved from http://www.ala.org/awardsgrants/diversity-research-grant

Blansett, J. & Blansett, C. (2012). *Invisible wounds, invisible warriors: How can libraries meet the needs of these students?* Poster session presented at the annual meeting of the American Library Association, Anaheim, CA.

Fawley, N. & Krysak, N. (2013). Serving those who serve: Outreach and instruction for student cadets and veterans. In Mueller, D. (Ed.) *Imagine, innovate, inspire: The proceedings of the ACRL 2013 conference* (pp. 525–531). Chicago, IL: Association of College and Research Libraries.

Institute of Museum and Library Services. (2016). *Fiscal year 2017 appropriations request to the United States Congress: Creating a nation of learners*. Washington, D.C.: Institute of Museum and Library Services. Retrieved from https://www.imls.gov/sites/default/files/publications/documents/fy17cj_0.pdf

LeMire, S. (2015). Beyond service: New outreach strategies to reach student veterans. In *Creating Sustainable Community: The Proceedings of the ACRL 2015 Conference* (pp. 66–71). Chicago, IL: Association of College and Research Libraries.

Merrill, J. W. (1944). Checklist of public library activities in demobilization and readjustment. *ALA Bulletin, 38*(3), 109–111.

Mills, C. P., Paladino, E. B., & Klentzin, J. C. (2015). Student veterans and the academic library. *Reference Services Review, 43*(2), 262–279. doi:10.1108/RSR-10-2014-0049

Roy, L., Mulvihill, K., Rickard, F., Taft, J., & Olney, C. (2016). *Services to those who serve: Library programs for veterans and active duty military families.* Presentation at the annual meeting of the Public Library Association, Denver, CO.

Taft, J. & Olney, C. (2014). Library services for the "new normal" of military families. *Public Libraries, 53*(6), 28–33.

Tinoco, E. & Hoppenfeld, J. (2015). *Boots on the ground: Making academic libraries work for veterans.* Presentation at the annual meeting of the American Library Association, San Francisco, CA.

Veterans Connect @ the Library. (2016). Retrieved from http://calibrariesforveterans.org.

War Ink. (2014). Retrieved from http://www.warink.org

1

Who Are Veterans and Military Service Members?

To serve veterans and service members effectively, librarians need to develop an understanding of these populations. This chapter is intended to help all librarians learn the basics: Who, exactly, do people mean when they're talking about veterans and service members? How large are the veteran and military populations? How can librarians find information about the size of the veteran and military populations in their areas? Who are some of the unique groups within the veteran and military populations? What are some of the things that librarians should know about veterans and service members? What are some of the unique strengths they bring to the table and the challenges they face? And, finally, what does the future look like for those working with veteran and military populations? These questions and more will be addressed over the course of this chapter.

The first step toward understanding veteran and military populations is to define the terms *veteran* and *service member*. The definition of a service member is simple: service members are individuals who are currently serving in a branch of the U.S. Uniformed Services. The Uniformed Services includes the five branches of the Armed Forces (Army, Navy, Air Force, Marine Corps, and Coast Guard) as well as the Commissioned Corps of the National Oceanic and Atmospheric Administration (NOAA) and the Commissioned Corps of the Public Health Service (U.S. Department of Veterans Affairs, 2016a). Service members can serve on active duty, which means that the military is their full-time occupation, or as a Reservist. Reservists are members of the National Guard or the reserve component of one of the other branches of the Armed Forces (e.g., Army Reserve, Air Force Reserve). Reservists' service is often characterized by the standard "one weekend a month and two weeks a year" described by recruiters, but in recent years, Reservists have frequently been called to active duty in response to stateside national disasters (National Guard) as well as for combat deployments (both National Guard and Reserves). Regardless of whether an individual is on active duty or is a Reservist, they are a military service member.*

---

* In this book, the authors have chosen to use *they* as a singular, gender-neutral pronoun in order to be inclusive of all veterans' and service members' gender identities.

In contrast to service members, who have a current U.S. military contract, veterans are those who have served in the military in the past. Although many people only think of veterans as those who served in the Armed Forces, just as with service members, a veteran is someone who served in one of the seven branches of the Uniformed Services. However, there are several factors that determine whether someone is considered a veteran, which can lead to a number of questions. For example, does the term *veteran* only refer to people who served during a time of war or do people who served in peacetime also count? What about people who served in the National Guard or Reserves and were never called up on active duty? Does the type of discharge matter (e.g., honorable, general, other than honorable)? What if the person served in the U.S. military but isn't a U.S. citizen? The answers to these types of questions are not always consistent from one organization to another. The U.S. government also doesn't provide a single definition. For example, when applying for a federal job, the U.S. Department of Labor defines a veteran as someone who served in the Armed Forces during specified times of conflict, at least when it comes to veterans' preference for employment (Veterans' Preference, 2015). However, the U.S. Department of Veterans Affairs (VA) has a different set of criteria:

> Eligibility for most VA benefits is based upon discharge from active military service under other than dishonorable conditions. Active military service means full-time service, other than active duty for training, as a member of the Army, Navy, Air Force, Marine Corps, Coast Guard, or as a commissioned officer of the Public Health Service, Environmental Science Services Administration or National Oceanic and Atmospheric Administration, or its predecessor, the Coast and Geodetic Survey. (U.S. Department of Veterans Affairs, 2016b)

Although the VA's definition of a veteran is broader than the Department of Labor's, it still excludes some members of the veteran and military communities. The VA's definition of a veteran does not include those who are currently serving in the military, those who were in the National Guard or Reserves but were never activated, or those who received a dishonorable discharge. Nevertheless, librarians should avoid using definitions of a veteran or service member that exclude anyone who has served in a branch of the Uniformed Services. This practice ensures that library support and services for veterans reach even those on the periphery of the veteran community, who may be those most in need of support. Therefore, for the purposes of this book, the term *veteran* will be used in the most inclusive way possible. In most library settings, a veteran can be defined as follows: a veteran is an individual who served in the U.S. Uniformed Services, on active duty or in the National Guard or Reserves, for any period of time, regardless of combat service, deployment, or type of discharge.

Although the term *veteran* is being used in this book in a broad and inclusive manner, librarians should be aware that there are many more exclusive definitions that may prevent library patrons from identifying themselves as veterans despite their history of military service. For example, because individuals typically must have completed their military service to be eligible for VA benefits, those currently serving in the military might not believe themselves included when an event is marketed to veterans. Some veterans may consider themselves to be "former military," rather than veterans, because they consider only people who served for 20 years, thus earning a veteran's pension and "military retiree" status, to be veterans. Other veterans may not think of themselves as veterans because they never served overseas or in combat. As a result, not all veterans realize that they can call themselves a veteran. When librarians reach out to veterans and service members, special effort may be necessary to ensure that groups such as those on active duty or serving in a reserve component or those who feel that their service was not distinguished enough to be thought of as a veteran feel included and welcomed.

Many of the organizations that collaborate with libraries may also have narrower definitions of veterans, and they may ask a library to comply with their parameters when creating new programs or services. Nevertheless, librarians should avoid taking a limiting view of veterans. Similarly, librarians should not place themselves in the position of verifying veteran or service member status as a condition of receiving services or support. If a partnering organization is concerned about asserting limits, librarians can be creative about how they market collaborations with that partner to ensure maximum inclusivity. One way to do this is to use broad wording in promotional documents; for example, "The benefits offered by this organization are based on criteria the organization uses to improve its focus on specific populations. Please note that the library welcomes all visitors who have served in the U.S. military. If you or the veteran you care about does not meet the criteria used by this organization, please visit our reference desk to learn about alternatives."

The mission of a library is to provide equal access to information for all visitors. This means that libraries function as one of the few places where those on the fringe of the veteran community, such as veterans who were dishonorably discharged, can seek information about resources. By offering support to all those who have served or are still serving, librarians can build trust with the veteran and military communities and position themselves to better understand and support their information needs.

Veterans and Service Members by the Numbers: Methodology

Nearly every community in the United States includes members of the veteran and military communities. Statistics from the VA, the U.S. Census Bureau, and other organizations can help librarians understand how large the veteran and military communities are, as well as where these groups are clustered, in order to get a better understanding of how the library can begin to develop services and programming to meet their needs. Although statistics about the veteran and military communities are readily available, staying abreast of the most recent information may be challenging. To locate the most recent statistics, librarians need to know where to look. National, state, and local statistics about veterans and service members can all be useful tools for librarians to gain insights into the size of the veteran and military populations in their area. Librarians can also use this information to start a dialogue in their community or library about the need for new programs and services to support service members and veterans.

Finding up-to-date statistics about the current number of U.S. military service members is fairly straightforward, as the Department of Defense (DoD) publishes monthly reports on the manpower strength of each of its branches. Some of these reports also include Coast Guard data for a complete count of members of the Armed Forces. Librarians can visit the Defense Manpower Data Center to track the number of service members serving on active duty and in the Reserves at any given time (Defense Manpower Data Center, 2016). Information about the size of the NOAA Commissioned Officer Corps and the Commissioned Corps of the U.S. Public Health Service can be found by visiting their respective websites (NOAA Corps, 2016; Commissioned Corps of the U.S. Public Health Service, 2015).

Data on military veterans is not as easily accessible because the definition of a veteran is complex and veterans are often not tracked unless they are receiving veterans' benefits. However, there are a number of good estimates available. One of the most reliable sources of information on veterans is the Census Bureau, whose website is familiar to many librarians. Effectively searching for information about veterans may require visiting the site periodically to check for new data. Strategies for accessing information about veterans can change from year to year as the website's organization changes. For example, the "veterans" section of the Census Bureau website tracks any new publications about veterans in an attempt to compile information about the many aspects of veterans in one place (United States Census Bureau, 2016). Although this is an excellent resource for librarians, it may also be advisable to do a simple search for "veterans" on the Census Bureau website to see whether there are any hidden gems that may not be available on the veterans section of the website. Librarians should also explore the Census Bureau's American Factfinder site to retrieve community-level data about veterans (United States Census Bureau, n.d.). Another important source of veteran-related data is the National Center for Veterans Analysis and Statistics (NCVAS), administered by the VA (U.S. Department of Veterans Affairs, 2016c). NCVAS provides detailed information based on data gathered by the VA from veterans who are registered for benefits or seeking sources of support.

However, librarians should also recognize that statistics about veterans and service members can vary, depending on the organization that collected the data and its organizational goals. In addition to these official sources of information, there are a number of private organizations that publish statistics and information about veterans and service members. Several organizations, such as the Institute for Veteran and Military Families, RAND Corporation, and Blue Star Families, publish independent survey results and research findings with additional data. Most nonprofit organizations that advocate for veterans also publish annual reports with information about the veterans they serve, not just the veterans who form their membership. Additionally, some metropolitan areas are home to military installations, DoD contractors, and advisory groups that conduct their own research (e.g., Chamber of Commerce Hawaii, 2016; San Diego Military Advisory Council, 2016).

Finally, librarians may find that the most helpful source of information is not a published source at all, but a Vet Center in their community. Many communities have a Vet Center, where veterans are invited to visit on a walk-in basis to meet with other veterans, representatives of the VA, and counselors. These Vet Centers are staffed by people who interact with local veterans each day and are knowledgeable about the questions asked most often and the types of resources they seek. In addition, librarians can contact a county veterans service officer (CVSO) or a veterans service representative (VSR) who may already be knowledgeable about the demographics of veterans and service members in the local area. These CVSOs and VSRs can help librarians prioritize and determine how much research to seek about veterans and service members in the area to achieve the library's goals.

In all of these cases, the goals and priorities of the organization gathering the data should be considered when interpreting the data. For example, some homeless veterans may not have been reached by the Census Bureau. Veterans who have had negative experiences in the military or with the VA may not register with the VA or participate in their surveys. Just as librarians consider the people who do not visit the library when conducting a community analysis, they should take into account veterans who do not want to be counted when gathering demographic data. Moreover, no matter how many statistics are gathered, librarians will benefit from learning about the veteran and military communities from the veterans, service members, and family members who visit their library.

Veterans and Service Members by the Numbers: Current Picture

The reported number of veterans and service members in the United States can vary somewhat depending on the source used. For example, the Census Bureau's reported number of veterans may differ slightly from the VA's projected numbers. There is also natural fluctuation in these numbers, so a source from a year ago can have numbers that differ from more recent reports. However, these fluctuations and natural discrepancies should not diminish the value of examining national-level data, as the value in this data lies in contextualizing the size and scope of the overall veteran and military populations.

According to recent VA and DoD estimates, 1.34 million individuals serve in the active-duty military, 800,000 serve in the Reserves, and 21.4 million veterans are living throughout the county (Defense Manpower Data Center, 2016; U.S. Department of Veterans Affairs. National Center for Veterans Analysis and Statistics, 2014). There are an additional 6,500 members of the Public Health Service Commissioned Corps and 320 in the NOAA Commissioned Officer Corps (Commissioned Corps of the U.S. Public Health Service, 2015; NOAA Corps, 2016). This means that the veteran and military populations make up a significant portion of the U.S. population. According to recent estimates, approximately 7.3 percent of Americans have served in the military (Chalabi, 2015).

Librarians can also delve further into the data to get a more comprehensive picture of the veteran and military communities. For example, within the veteran population, the number of Post-9/11 veterans is expected to increase significantly over the next few decades, from about 4.3 million veterans to 6 million (U.S. Department of Veterans Affairs. National Center for Veterans Analysis and Statistics, 2014). This recent generation of veterans and service members differs in significant ways from previous generations. For example, multiple sources report that veterans of recent conflicts overseas survived injuries that would have killed a service member in previous conflicts (e.g., Goldberg, 2010; Eastridge et al., 2012; Gawande, 2004). This increase in survival rates among service members with severe injuries has resulted in an unprecedented increase in the need for physical and psychological long-term care (Holder, 2016). Additionally, there is an increased need to provide for caregivers, to modify homes so that they are accessible to someone with a disability, and for resources to find flexible employment for those with chronic conditions. Caregivers and spouses who provide assistance to someone with a disability or chronic illness as a result of their military service are now a priority among some advocacy groups (Bradbard et al., 2014).

When considering the size and scope of the veteran and military communities, librarians should also consider that service members and veterans may have spouses, children, parents, siblings, or other loved ones affected by their military service. Up to 2 million American children have a parent who has been on active duty and deployed at least once, and many may have parents who have been deployed by the U.S. military multiple times (Clever & Segal, 2013; Baiocchi, 2013). Furthermore, it is estimated that for every military service member who is killed in combat, at least 10 people are affected by that loss (Tragedy Assistance Program for Survivors, 2016). As a result, most communities in the United States include someone affected by the recent wars in Iraq and Afghanistan. Even a community without veterans or service members would likely include residents who are the parents, siblings, spouses, children, survivors, friends, or caregivers of veterans or service members. Therefore, when thinking about whether the library should develop services or programming aimed at the military and veteran communities, librarians should be aware that it is very likely that the number of people who may be interested in those services or programs will far exceed the number of veterans and service members in the United States.

Veterans and Service Members of Different Eras

Among the 21.4 million veterans in the United States, there are veterans from many different eras of conflict. There are 7 million living veterans who served during the Vietnam War era, 7.4 million living veterans from the Gulf War era, 1.6 million living veterans from the Korean War era, and 700,000 living veterans from World War II. Librarians should note that some veterans may have served in multiple conflicts, so they may be represented more than once in these statistics. Additionally, there are 5.2 million veterans who served in the military during peacetime (U.S. Department of Veterans Affairs National Center for Veterans Analysis and Statistics, 2014). These statistics reveal the significant age diversity of the veteran population; a veteran may have lived and fought in World War II or be barely old enough to vote.

Librarians should not assume that all veterans and service members have had similar experiences or that it will be easy for all veterans to relate to one another. Although many veterans find that they feel some level of solidarity with one another and that they can derive support from veterans of any era, other veterans feel most comfortable connecting with veterans from the same era. For example, the mistreatment of Vietnam War veterans in the 1960s and 1970s, though largely recognized by the American populace as a grave error in later years, resulted in cultural differences between Vietnam veterans and veterans of later conflicts. Vietnam veterans may sometimes struggle to empathize with the challenges faced by veterans of the wars in Iraq and Afghanistan because Vietnam veterans faced the added challenges of the draft and an unsupportive civilian population (Sanderlin, 2011). Indeed, NBC News once published an article about "cultural fault lines" among veterans from different generations that suggested that some earlier generations of veterans believed that "the current crop [of veterans] is a tad less tough and lot more needy" (Linsley, 2012). Sometimes veterans of previous conflicts have difficulty relating to the combat experiences of those who fought in Iraq and Afghanistan. After all, the experience of fighting in a foxhole is very different than that of navigating around improvised explosive devices (IEDs). Because of the very different experiences veterans of different eras may have had, they often feel a connection with other veterans of the same era. They may even prefer to connect only with one another (Sanderlin, 2011; Make the Connection, 2016b). Organizations such as the Vietnam Veterans of America work to foster the connections between Vietnam War veterans and to engage them in supporting one another. And newer groups, such as the Iraq and Afghanistan Veterans of America, continue the work of building and maintaining community among veterans from the same era.

Thus, to help veterans connect with other veterans of the same era, librarians may benefit from learning the different eras of conflict through which veterans identify their experiences. These eras of conflict are used by the VA and periodically reviewed by Congress to ensure that all veterans who served in wartime are eligible for an appropriate level of VA benefits, but librarians should take care not to use the eras of conflict or any other VA eligibility criteria to suggest to veterans that any specific benefits are due to them. Discussing eligibility status in terms of specific levels of eligibility is a type of legal counseling reserved for trained and certified representatives of the VA. Nevertheless, these eras of conflict can help librarians understand more about how veterans identify themselves. By understanding the main eras of conflict, librarians can improve efforts to facilitate relationship building with veterans and the organizations that serve them.

In 2012, the Congressional Research Service published a list of officially recognized dates of conflict, although this list may now be considered outdated due to the end of official hostilities in Afghanistan (Torreon, 2012; U.S. Department of Defense. Defense Media Activity, 2014):

- World War II: 1941–1946
- Korean War: 1950–1953
- Vietnam War: 1961–1975
- Lebanon: 1982–1983
- Grenada: 1983
- Persian Gulf: 1990–1991
- Operation Enduring Freedom (OEF) (Afghanistan): 2001–TBD
- Operation Iraqi Freedom (OIF) (Iraq): 2003–2010
- Operation New Dawn: 2010–TBD

Items with an end year of "TBD" refer to periods of conflict where Congress has not yet officially decided on the end year or where the involvement of military forces by the United States have continued to this day (Torreon, 2012).

Congressional Research Service reports can be a good resource for librarians seeking to understand the major conflicts in which veterans may have participated and that they may use as a way to identify their service within the veteran community. However, librarians should bear in mind that many veterans may have served in multiple conflicts or that they may not strongly identify with other veterans of their era for a multitude of reasons. Each veteran is an individual, and although some veterans do feel a sense of connection with other veterans from a particular era of conflict, librarians should not anticipate that all veterans will feel this way.

In addition to understanding veterans of different eras of conflict, understanding the nature of veterans of peacetime eras can improve a library's outreach efforts. There are 5.2 million living veterans who served in the military during peacetime (U.S. Department of Veterans Affairs. National Center for Veterans Analysis and Statistics, 2014). These peacetime veterans may feel left out of many conversations about veterans, which frequently reference the conflict era in which a veteran served. They also may feel differently about their entitlement to benefits and other resources because they are aware that wartime veterans may have made significant sacrifices. Some peacetime veterans may need to be reminded that they made sacrifices of their own. Like wartime veterans, peacetime veterans chose to join the military and accepted that their service could include deployments or combat. Peacetime veterans were simply fortunate that the country was not at war during the time that they served. Furthermore, some peacetime veterans may have participated in deployments, experienced hazards, or made other sacrifices, just like wartime veterans. One example is veterans who were exposed to radiation during military service. The VA has only recently begun to acknowledge that military service members who participated in nuclear tests were indeed exposed to radiation that caused medical issues. These veterans are eligible for programs designed to diagnose and manage the chronic conditions that resulted (U.S. Department of Veterans Affairs. Public Health, 2015).

The service of peacetime veterans may not fall into an era of conflict, but these veterans still made a sacrifice. Some of them delayed finishing college or starting another career until completing their military service. Others made contributions and changes to the way our military operates today. Some of the policies and benefits enjoyed by today's service members are the result of the work of those who served before. For example, many military occupations were opened up to women during the late 1970s and 1980s, after the end of the Vietnam War and during the Cold War (Devilbliss, 1990). Peacetime veterans contributed to the military's strength, and they are a part of U.S. military history and heritage. It is important to recognize the real and inherent sacrifices of peacetime veterans. The United States could not sustain an all-volunteer military force without the contributions and dedication of service members who served in peacetime.

Special Populations

Cohesion is a strong element of the military experience, and veterans and service members are often perceived as a single, unified group. But within this population there are smaller groups who can feel excluded from or disenfranchised within the larger veteran and military communities. Although broad efforts to reach veterans and service members as a whole are valuable and appreciated, it also can be helpful to consider these special populations and whether they feel included in general outreach efforts or would be responsive to a direct form of outreach.

Women Veterans and Service Members

Women are a unique population within the larger veteran and military populations that can be a challenge to reach with general military and veteran outreach efforts. Some women veterans don't consider themselves to be "real" veterans, and they are often invisible within the veteran community. Women do not always match the standard mental image of a veteran or service member, and one of the most common physical markers of the female service member, the military-regulation hair bun, is easily removed in off-hours or after women leave the military. For some women veterans, the act of undoing that bun can feel as though it is also removing all traces of previous military service. Women are often not expected to be veterans or service members, and although the rates of women's service in the military are increasing, women still experience resistance and hostility to their presence in the military, in war zones, and in the veteran community.

Within the veteran and military population, women remain a minority group. Women veterans make up approximately 10 percent of the overall veteran population and over 16 percent of those currently serving. Although their numbers are steadily increasing, the number of female veterans and service members are still overwhelmed by the number of male veterans and service members (U.S. Department of Veterans Affairs. Health Care, 2015a; U.S. Department of Defense, 2015a). Because women remain a substantial minority, women veterans and service members are often misidentified as military or veteran spouses. Moreover, when women are correctly identified as veterans or service members, it is still assumed that they did not serve within combat arms units (e.g., infantry). Thus, some still think of women veterans' and service members' service as less valuable than that of male veterans and service members, who are often assumed to have greater combat experience simply by virtue of their sex.

Women have served in the U.S. military in an unofficial capacity since the American Revolution and have been serving in an official capacity for over 100 years (U.S. Department of Defense, 2015b). Women were first officially integrated into the military in 1901 with the establishment of the Army Nurse Corps, and as of 2016, all military occupations are now open to women (Pellerin, 2015). During the Iraq War (Operation Iraqi Freedom, or OIF) and the Afghanistan War (Operation Enduring Freedom, or OEF), women Soldiers, Sailors, Airmen, and Marines have served in a variety of stressful and dangerous situations, and over 1,000 female service members have been wounded and over 160 killed (Kamarck, 2015). Since the secretary of defense lifted the ban on women in combat in January 2013 and opened all military roles to women in 2016, women have taken on new roles in U.S. combat missions (Roulo, 2013; Pellerin, 2015). However, many civilians are unaware of the extent to which female service members have been exposed to combat, and the traditional image of a veteran or service member remains consistently male.

Pervasive assumptions that veterans and service members are male, even in institutions purporting to serve women veterans and service members equally, create an unwelcoming environment for women. Women veterans are less likely than their male counterparts to take advantage of veterans' benefits, such as VA health care (U.S. Department of Veterans

Affairs National Center for Veterans Analysis and Statistics, 2015b). In an attempt to improve services for women veterans, the VA mounted a "Culture Change Campaign," complete with posters reminding VA employees to "Please don't call me mister" (U.S. Department of Veterans Affairs. Health Care, 2015b). As women veterans, the authors of this book can attest to feeling excluded, mostly inadvertently, from veteran services and programming on many occasions. The problem goes beyond how women feel, however. Women veterans and service members also have needs distinct from their male counterparts.

Women veterans and service members face a unique set of pressures and challenges. Research has shown that, although women in the military are less likely to experience combat, they have similar rates of post-traumatic stress disorder (PTSD) (U.S. Department of Veterans Affairs. National Center for PTSD, 2016). In fact, almost 20 percent of OIF and OEF women veterans have been diagnosed with PTSD (Williamson, 2009). One reason for this is that women are more likely to experience military sexual trauma (MST), defined as sexual harassment or sexual assault that occurs while an individual is serving in the military. According to the VA, women service members are 20 times more likely to experience MST than their male counterparts (U.S. Department of Veterans Affairs. Mental Health, 2015; U.S. Department of Veterans Affairs. Mental Health, 2016).

MST is profoundly damaging for service members, causing them to feel betrayed by the perpetrator and often by the military as well (Aktepy, 2010). MST is not only a painful betrayal of trust but also an ongoing challenge to survivors, who often must live and work with the person who assaulted them while coping with their experience. Indeed, the survivors of MST are often forced to trust their lives to a perpetrator of a previous act while in a combat zone or in high-stress environments. Research suggests that less than 15 percent of survivors officially file a report, and more than half of those who do face social or professional retaliation for reporting (Morral, Gore, & Schell, 2016). MST survivors can therefore be on the receiving end of two betrayals: the betrayal of trust in the fellow service member who perpetrated the MST, and then the betrayal by military leadership and others who failed to support the survivors.

Research has demonstrated that trauma associated with betrayal, especially institutional betrayal, is particularly challenging for survivors (Smith & Freyd, 2013). MST survivors can have a difficult relationship with their fellow veterans and with the military organization because their trust has been undermined. Because many women veterans and service members have either experienced MST or have fellow service members who have experienced MST, some women feel uncomfortable about participating in standard veteran or military-oriented events, where they would be returning to an environment in which they would once again be outnumbered by male veterans or service members.

Women veterans also face logistical issues in taking advantage of services and programming for veterans and service members. Women veterans are more likely than their civilian counterparts to have children while in their 20s and early 30s, and they are also more likely to be divorced than their civilian counterparts or male veterans (U.S. Department of Veterans Affairs. National Center for Veterans Analysis and Statistics, 2011; U.S. Department of Veterans Affairs. National Center for Veterans Analysis and Statistics, 2015b). This leaves many women veterans in the position of caring for dependents, often as single mothers, and makes programming that requires women veterans to find childcare very challenging.

Kristen frequently works with military families at a public library near a military housing neighborhood in San Diego. One of the greatest challenges shared by military parents who visit the library, particularly those who belong to a support group that meets at the library once a month, is finding childcare during a meeting. It became necessary for the library manager to explain that it is against library policy for younger children to be left unattended and that the library is not permitted to provide childcare in an official capacity. At first, the group arranged for some parents to be designated chaperones who supervised the children in the children's area of the library while the other parents met in another room. However, it was still difficult for the parents to coordinate who would miss the meeting to chaperone the children, and in some cases, the chaperones felt outnumbered by the children. Eventually, the manager worked with the support group leader to schedule their meetings in a larger space. The larger room was divided in half, with tables furnished with craft supplies on one side of the room. A volunteer performer or crafts instructor would supervise activities among the children on one side of the room, while the military parents met on the other side. The children were within sight of all of the parents, yet they were kept entertained so as not to distract the parents too frequently. This arrangement has continued to be successful.

Women veterans and service members can feel marginalized from the larger veteran and military communities because of their sex, which marks them as noncombat troops, and because many are survivors of MST or other military-related stressors. However, women veterans, like their male counterparts, benefit from connecting with other veterans and service members who understand their lingo and their experiences. Nevertheless, engaging women veterans and service members can be challenging. They may not respond to general veteran and military outreach efforts, either because they have experienced barriers to inclusion within the larger veteran and military communities, because they anticipate being marginalized, or because they face real logistical issues that make attending veteran and military events challenging. Although women veterans and service members can be a difficult group to engage, they are an important element of the veteran and military communities and have a unique perspective to share with one another and with the larger community.

LGBT Veterans and Service Members

LGBT veterans are another group that can feel distant or excluded from the general veteran and military communities. Most librarians are probably familiar with "Don't Ask, Don't Tell," the 1993 Department of Defense directive that prohibited potential service members from being forced to disclose their sexual orientation when joining the military. This policy pushed lesbian, gay, and bisexual service members into the closet and threatened them with loss of their jobs if they disclosed their sexual orientation. In some cases, service members felt threatened not only about losing their jobs but about losing their chosen careers. Indeed, over 13,000 men and women were discharged from the military under Don't Ask, Don't Tell (DADT) (Gates, 2010). The military's restrictions on gay service members, in fact, date back much further, with a policy formalized in 1982 that declared that "homosexuality is incompatible with military service," leading to an average of 1,500 individuals discharged annually in the 1980s (United States General Accounting Office, 1992). Similarly, transgender individuals were barred from serving openly until this policy was overturned in 2016 (Cronk, 2016). Despite this ban, evidence suggests that transgender people have been overrepresented in the military (Gates & Herman, 2014).

DADT and other policies that restricted the service of sexual minorities and transgender individuals have had a long-term effect on LGBT veterans and service members. LGBT veterans who were discharged under DADT and the ban on transgender service members may feel as though they have been rejected from the military for being who they are rather than because of their actions. This rejection can lead to feelings of alienation from the military community. LGBT service members who were forced to hide part of their identity for years to pursue their career of choice were also affected by the long-term effects of alienation and fear of being reported. And LGBT service members serving openly after the repeal of DADT and the ban on transgender service members can feel the burden of DADT's history and lingering hostility to sexual minorities in the veteran and military communities. Furthermore, LGBT veterans and service members may feel that their relationships, political affiliations, and even identity are incongruous with the traditionally conservative military community. This long history of formalized discrimination against LGBT service members has left many, including those who were not discharged, with a tenuous relationship with the veteran community as a whole and with many organizations that serve veterans.

For example, although LGBT veterans are entitled to care at VA facilities, research indicates that these veterans experience barriers to care related to their gender or sexual identity (Sherman et al., 2014). And transgender veterans may experience difficulty correcting their discharge paperwork (DD-214) to reflect a name change, but they also may face discrimination when using a DD-214 with their former name (National Center for Transgender Equality, 2015). These barriers can prevent LGBT veterans and service members from feeling fully included in the general veteran population. Because of these barriers, because LGBT veterans may not affiliate themselves with traditional veterans' organizations, and because LGBT individuals still face barriers in the civilian world, LGBT veterans should be treated as a unique veteran population that needs and deserves particular attention.

Veterans with Disabilities

Veterans with disabilities are not a marginalized population in the same manner as women and LGBT veterans and service members. The service of veterans with disabilities, or "wounded warriors," is generally held in high esteem by other veterans and the general public. However, veterans with disabilities often cope with physical and mental challenges that can limit their access to services and resources. These issues may create barriers that are not readily apparent and yet separate or marginalize veterans with disabilities from the rest of the veteran and military communities.

The number of veterans with disabilities is dramatic, and it continues to increase. As of 2013, over 17 percent of all veterans have a service-connected disability, totaling nearly 4 million individuals (U.S. Department of Veterans Affairs. Veterans Benefits Administration, 2015;

U.S. Department of Veterans Affairs, 2014). The numbers are even more dramatic for veterans of recent conflicts. Thirty percent of Post-9/11 veterans have a service-connected disability, and these Gulf War–era veterans with disabilities have an average of six disabilities per person, compared to 4.5 disabilities per person for the overall disabled veteran population (U.S. Department of Veterans Affairs. National Center for Veterans Analysis and Statistics, 2015a; U.S. Department of Veterans Affairs. Veterans Benefits Administration, 2015). The most common service-connected disabilities are tinnitus, hearing loss, and post-traumatic stress disorder (PTSD) (U.S. Department of Veterans Affairs. Veterans Benefits Administration, 2015). Many service-connected disabilities may not be directly related to combat; for example, hearing loss can be associated with many military occupations, including everyone from helicopter pilots to linguists. These, as well as many other types of service-connected disabilities, are invisible but impact veterans' ability to access libraries and other services in very tangible ways.

When Kristen recently visited the local VA offices to get a tune-up on her hearing aid, she spoke with the representative of a veterans service organization (VSO) that had offices in the building. He reminded her that veterans may have a service-connected disability that civilians might not automatically assume could be service-connected. For example, if a service member has a genetic condition and is exposed to an environment that exacerbates the condition before it has been diagnosed, or if they are asked to wait to seek medical care and the delay worsens the condition, it could still be considered a service-connected issue by the VA even though it is a genetic condition.

Similarly, veterans who repeatedly experience a health issue may have their condition regarded by the military and the VA to be a chronic health issue. Some chronic health issues, such as arthritis, are often considered service-connected issues and may be included in a disability claim, depending on the circumstances. This is not to say that everyone in the military who has ever had a health problem qualifies for disability status. Many veterans are unaware, however, that some health issues, minor or seemingly unrelated to their military service, are taken into account by the VA. During Kristen's visit, the representative reminded her that many VSOs highly encourage veterans to avoid going it alone when seeking a disability claim.

Veterans with disabilities may have difficulty accessing libraries for a number of reasons. Transportation can be a challenge for some veterans, as well as mobility within the physical space of the library. Veterans with and without disabilities may dislike visiting the library if it is a noisy, bustling place. Some veterans, especially those recently returned from a combat zone or those with PTSD, may feel more comfortable in spaces where people are unlikely to approach them from behind and prefer to sit with their backs to a wall where they can view building and room entrances. These veterans may have difficulty feeling comfortable in the open-concept spaces embraced by many libraries.

To accommodate some of the needs of veterans with disabilities, librarians can develop solutions to make the libraries more welcoming for those uncomfortable in crowded spaces, such as designating and highlighting quiet areas and making seating available against walls. They can also work to provide support to patrons outside the library. Librarians can improve online resources for veterans or partner with organizations supporting veterans with disabilities to bring services and materials to veterans' homes. Most importantly, as libraries make these changes, promoting the availability of these services so that veterans with disabilities can use them is essential. Creative solutions for veterans with disabilities can do much to support this marginalized group and can also support nonveterans who may share similar needs.

Veterans from Traditionally Underrepresented Groups

Veterans from traditionally underrepresented groups have a long history of service in the U.S. military. Indeed, military service has long been a way for marginalized groups, including women, LGBT people, and people from traditionally underrepresented groups, to stake a claim for the full rights and privileges of U.S. citizenship. Military service has also been long perceived as a way for those from underprivileged backgrounds to gain social mobility. These and many other reasons may explain why service members from traditionally underrepresented groups make up such a significant portion of the veteran and military communities. Non-White service members make up approximately 31 percent of the military, and veterans from minority backgrounds now comprise 22 percent of the overall veteran population (U.S. Department of Defense, 2015a; U.S. Department of Veterans Affairs. National Center for Veterans Analysis and Statistics, 2016).

Although veterans from traditionally underrepresented groups have served honorably in the U.S. military since the Revolutionary War, they have also experienced a long history of discriminatory treatment with regard to their military service and veterans' benefits. For example, Black Civil War veterans were discriminated against when filing claims for veterans' pensions (Shaffer, 2000). And although World War II veterans are widely known to have benefited significantly from the GI Bill, research suggests that these benefits did not apply equally to all veterans:

> The availability of benefits to black veterans had a substantial and positive impact on the educational attainment of those likely to have access to colleges and universities outside the South. Unfortunately, for those more likely to be limited to the South in their collegiate choices, the GI Bill exacerbated rather than narrowed the economic and educational differences between blacks and whites. (Turner and Bound, 2003, p. 172)

Practical, if not prescribed, barriers prevented Black veterans from fully capitalizing on the GI Bill, a benefit that provided tremendous opportunities for their White counterparts. Jim Crow laws limited Black veterans' access to higher education, as "black men in the South faced explicitly segregated colleges and much more limited opportunities within historically black institutions" (Turner & Bound, 2003, p. 145). These veterans served their countries honorably, but because of their racial or ethnic background, they suffered discriminatory treatment and were barred from the full advantages of the benefits they had earned through their service.

Veterans from other traditionally underrepresented groups have also faced discriminatory treatment in the military and as veterans. For example, during World War II, Japanese American citizens were sent to internment camps and then drafted to serve in segregated military units that were promoted as "a precious opportunity to prove the loyalty and patriotism of all Japanese Americans" (Muller, 2003, p. 1). A study of Native American veterans from several eras of conflict revealed that many "reported that their military experience had included racial/ethnic discrimination, such as name-calling or being passed over for promotions" (Harada, Villa, Reifel, & Bayhylle, 2005, p. 783). And research indicates that "Black and Hispanic Vietnam-era veterans experienced racial discrimination and greater exposure to combat-related trauma than their White counterparts, which contributed to significantly greater rates and severity of post-deployment mental health disorders" (Muralidharan, Austern, Hack, & Vogt, 2016, p. 273). Veterans from traditionally underrepresented groups have also faced unequal treatment during and after recent conflicts, as racial barriers persist for Gulf War–era veterans. For example, studies show that although White female service members are more likely to report sexual harassment, Black female service members report sexual coercion at higher rates than their White counterparts (Buchanan, Settles, & Woods, 2008). And researchers studying veterans of Iraq and Afghanistan observe that "ethnoracial minority veterans reported greater perceived threat in the warzone and more family-related concerns and stressors during deployment than White veterans of the same gender" (Muralidharan, Austern, Hack, & Vogt, 2016, p. 273).

Although discrimination against service members and veterans from traditionally underrepresented groups persists, the VA and the military continue to make strides, both toward more equitable treatment and toward correcting wrongs from the past. For example, during President Obama's administration, 19 veterans whose awards were blocked due to racial or other prejudices received the military's highest recognition, the Medal of Honor (Wilson, 2014). However, there is still progress to be made. For example, Black veterans remain less likely to pursue higher education using the Post-9/11 GI Bill benefits for which they are eligible (Ottley, 2014). And service members from traditionally underrepresented groups continue to experience discrimination and disparity in treatment; in 2014, the DoD faced controversy not only for banning hairstyles popular with Black female service members but also for using offensive terminology when describing those hairstyles in military regulations (Joachim, 2014).

Librarians can play a role in supporting veterans and service members from traditionally underrepresented groups by helping them gain access to the benefits they earned by virtue of their service. Many eligible veterans from traditionally underrepresented groups have not used their VA benefits, in part because they faced discrimination during their time in the military or as veterans. Other veterans from traditionally underrepresented groups who were previously denied benefits due to their racial or ethnic background have never appealed the ruling, perhaps because they are unaware that such an appeal is possible or are reluctant to interact with the VA because of their experiences. These patrons may benefit from referrals to the VA's Center for Minority Veterans, which has Minority Veterans Program Coordinators in each state to help connect veterans to the benefits for which they may be eligible (U.S. Department of Veterans Affairs. Center for Minority Veterans, 2016). Veterans from traditionally underrepresented groups who are in need of support but who are reluctant to work with the VA may be receptive to a referral to a program specifically intended to support their needs.

Librarians should also consider veterans from traditionally underrepresented groups when developing and marketing programming and services for veterans. To identify the needs and strengths of the veterans from traditionally underrepresented groups in the local community, librarians can reach out to organizations that specifically serve veterans from traditionally underrepresented groups. VSOs such as the National Association for Black Veterans, the National American Indian Veterans, the National Association of Black Military Women, and the Hispanic War Veterans of America may have concrete ideas for library programming or services, and they may also be willing to collaborate with the library to develop programming.

Other Marginalized Populations

In addition to the populations mentioned above, there are a number of other groups that may feel marginalized within the overall veteran and military communities. Groups that do not easily fit within the stereotypical profile of a military service member or military veteran may experience barriers to participation in library events marketed to veterans and service members. They may anticipate receiving microaggressions, such as being asked to defend or document their military service. They may even anticipate open hostility or harassing treatment, based on their experiences in the military. Religious minorities such as Muslims, for example, have reported being "harassed or reprimanded" in the military due to their religious beliefs (Constable, 2014). The military is overwhelmingly composed of service members who self-identify as belonging to a Christian denomination (Defense Manpower Data Center, 2012). The small number of service members from other faiths means that they can be particularly vulnerable to harassment and discrimination. For example, a Sikh Army officer was forced to sue the Army to obtain a religious accommodation to wear a beard and turban in uniform (Philipps, 2016). Religious expression, coercion, and discrimination are ongoing issues in the military, as some service members feel coerced to participate in religious services while others feel that their ability to express their religious faith is being stifled (Lakin, 2010; Carroll, 2014). This ongoing conflict encompasses not only those from minority religious groups but also atheists and those who claim no religious affiliation.

Similarly, veterans and service members who are not U.S. citizens may feel marginalized within the veteran and military communities. Many civilians are surprised to learn that not all members of the U.S. military are citizens, although military service is a common way for noncitizens to expedite the naturalization process (U.S. Citizenship and Immigration Services, 2015). The U.S. military actively recruits noncitizens, who may have unique skills, such as language fluency, that native-born service members lack (McIntosh & Sayala, 2011).

Even when these minority populations feel welcome and included by their peers, they may be marginalized by the institutions that serve the veteran and military communities or by the civilian population. Librarians should take care when developing programs, services, and collections for veterans and service members to consider the full scope of the veteran and military communities, including those from marginalized groups. Librarians may have to make targeted efforts to ensure that veterans from minority and other marginalized groups are included in library outreach and programming, but these efforts are important and ultimately worthwhile, as their presence is vital to a complete representation of the diversity of the veteran and military communities.

Intersectionality and the Veteran and Military Communities

For many veterans and service members, their military service becomes an integral part of their identity. Years or even decades after their service, their veteran status remains a core part of who they are. However, there are other aspects of veterans' and service members' identities that are equally fundamental. Fobazi Ettarh astutely reminds librarians that "spheres of identity intersect in a variety of different ways. The experiences of a white queer patron (or librarian) will be very different from those of a black queer one" (Ettarh, 2014, para. 2). Similarly, a White woman veteran experienced the military not only as a woman but also as a White person; her experience may differ in significant ways from the experiences of a Black woman veteran. When considering the veteran and military communities, librarians should remember that any individual veteran or service member will have multiple identities that influence their experience and that these identities may intersect in ways that make them particularly vulnerable to exclusion. To effectively reach the veteran and military communities, librarians should consider whether they are consulting veterans and service members from a variety of backgrounds and experiences. They should make a deliberate effort to include members of the marginalized populations within the veteran and military communities. And they should take care to reflect whether a library event, program, or service will reach even those veterans and service members who feel excluded from full participation within the veteran and military communities because of their identities.

Understanding Veterans and Service Members

Although each veteran and service member is a unique individual with their own strengths, challenges, and preferences, it can sometimes be helpful to understand characteristics of the veteran and service member that are common but by no means ubiquitous. In this section, the authors will provide some insights based on their military service and experiences as military family members. These insights are based on the authors' perceptions and are intended to provide librarians with some starting points for understanding where veterans and service members may be coming from. However, librarians should take care not to stereotype veterans and service members. They should refrain from making assumptions that a patron may behave in a particular way or have particular needs due to their military service.

By understanding some common characteristics and behaviors of veterans and service members, librarians may be able to approach an interaction with a veteran or military-affiliated patron with additional empathy or sensitivity to difficult issues and make that interaction more successful. The following is a list of common characteristics and behaviors of veterans and service members based on the authors' experiences as veterans and as librarians:

- Some veterans love to talk about their experiences in the military. Some veterans who enjoy talking about their experiences may live in isolation and have few opportunities to share their stories. Because isolation can make depression worse (Dunn et al., 2004), librarians should realize that occasionally listening to a veteran's stories can help that veteran feel less isolated and therefore less depressed. It may also add to the librarian's understanding of some members of the library community. Librarians who find that there are several veterans at the library with the same interest in sharing stories may be able to explore ways to facilitate those conversations.

- On the other hand, some veterans are reluctant to acknowledge that they ever served in the military because they had a negative experience in the military or have been treated poorly as a result of their military service. Librarians should not press acknowledged or suspected veterans to discuss their military service. Instead, librarians can build a relationship with veterans by asking questions about topics that are not sensitive for them. Where appropriate, librarians may also consider inviting patrons to check out library programs provided for veterans.

- Some veterans may have had a negative experience with the VA in the past and maintain negative feelings toward the VA as a result. Those veterans may be unaware of policy or service changes by the VA in recent years. However, the librarian's job is not to push a patron to return to the VA. Instead, librarians should focus on connecting veterans with resources that work for them, not just VA resources. If a veteran who has strong negative feelings about the VA seeks resources or indicates that they might be interested in seeking help again, it may be helpful for librarians to be aware of alternative resources in addition to the VA. For example, librarians can keep contact information on hand for the local VSOs that specialize in providing services for veterans who have had difficulty receiving benefits.

- Some veterans may have very deep feelings about countries whose people fought for the opposing side when they were in the service. This may cause conflicts between veterans and other library patrons. Depending on the circumstances, if other patrons are not disrupted by a veteran's behavior, librarians can be flexible about handling the issue and seek help with how to address the situation from local VSOs.

- Some veterans may experience increasing isolation as they grow older. Their military buddies may have passed away, leaving them without the military support structure on which they had relied. These veterans may not have been interested in getting to know younger veterans in the past, but their isolation may make them more open to trying something new. The library can play a role as a safe place for veterans and service members from different generations to connect with one another.

- If the United States is still at war with another country, even technically, veterans may be surprisingly agitated about current events regarding that situation. Veterans who have suffered injuries or who have had friends killed or wounded in the war may be particularly sensitive to perceptions of lost ground or questions about the war's purpose or value. Many veterans avoid reading news stories about places where they have been deployed in an attempt to avoid feelings of anxiety, anger, or frustration. For example, an Iraq War veteran may experience negative feelings at news reports of ongoing conflict in a town that they fought to secure during a deployment. If the library hosts events that focus on conflicts with other countries, librarians should bear in mind that some veterans may resist revisiting experiences that relate to current events.

- Some veterans will feel very hostile toward celebrities who may have been outspoken against the Vietnam War. Even an informal conversation about "Hanoi Jane" could possibly trigger an outburst that disrupts other patrons. Librarians who are developing programming for veterans should consider consulting with such VSOs as Vietnam Veterans of America to ensure that they are cognizant of potentially sensitive issues or topics like Hanoi Jane that could arise during the course of a program.

- Although the era between the Vietnam War and the first Persian Gulf War is considered by most to be an era of peacetime, veterans who served during this era experienced major shifts in military management and work culture. For example, women became prevalent in all branches of the military, but incorporating women challenged both military leaders and unit members, who had to adjust to a new culture. Military training also changed during this era as many older tactics labeled as brutal and outdated were replaced. Veterans from this era may not have served in a war but may have been deployed to places where they were injured during combat experiences. Librarians should take care not to overlook peacetime veterans when developing programming. These veterans may have a lot of stories to share about the changes in the military and the changes in tactics used to manage a low-intensity conflict.

- Some veterans were taught to never complain, so librarians may find that veterans, especially those from earlier conflicts, may still be reluctant to admit that they suffer from an injury received during military service. These veterans may be less likely to openly ask for needed accommodations. In contrast, veterans of recent conflicts have often been encouraged to report an injury immediately and may be more comfortable requesting accommodations to better access library services and resources.

- Veterans of recent conflicts may feel compelled to downplay their combat service in deference to the sacrifices of veterans of previous conflicts. This behavior is often both a measure of respect for earlier generations of veterans and an acknowledgment of the significant changes in warfare from one conflict to another. Librarians who are interested in programming such a panel of combat veterans should be aware that veterans of recent conflicts may have some feelings of awkwardness or discomfort in sharing the stage with veterans of earlier conflicts due to their instinctive deference to the combat experiences of World War II, Vietnam War, and Korean War veterans.

- Many Post-9/11 veterans have served in multiple deployments to Iraq or Afghanistan, even those in military branches that would not have been likely to deploy or engage in ground combat in the past. Both the Navy and the Air Force were more involved in ground operations than in the past, and the National Guard was used in unprecedented strategic maneuvers after 9/11 to minimize the impact of multiple deployments on active-duty military service members. Veterans and service members served alongside members of different branches in an unprecedented manner, and although there can be some teasing and lighthearted rivalry between veterans and service members of different branches, they generally appreciate and respect one another's contributions. Librarians should take care to be inclusive of veterans and service members from all branches of service and of active duty as well as Reservists.

- Post-9/11 veterans have borne and are still bearing a heavy load from the wars in Iraq and Afghanistan. A 2013 RAND Corporation study reported that approximately 73 percent of Army active-duty service members had deployed at least once. It also noted that "most of these soldiers were working on their second, third, or fourth year of cumulative deployed duty" (Baiocchi, 2013, p. 2). Veterans of the wars in Iraq and Afghanistan may have survived injuries that would have killed service members in previous conflicts, yet their survival resulted in chronic medical and psychological conditions that the VA and the medical profession have yet to adequately understand or treat (Kotwal et al., 2016). Post-9/11 veterans have a significantly higher risk of suicide (Kang et al., 2015). Also, the increase in the number of veterans after 9/11 in addition to the increase in elderly veterans seeking medical care means that the VA and other organizations that have traditionally assisted veterans are sometimes overwhelmed. Like Vietnam War veterans, many Post-9/11 veterans now seek strength in numbers by creating or joining such veterans service organizations as the Iraq and Afghanistan Veterans of America. Librarians should be aware that some members of this most recent generation of combat veterans may still be in some turmoil as they continue to adapt to life after combat, transition to civilian careers, and cope with the loss of their battle buddies.

- Although veterans and service members in general are a fairly cohesive group that honors and appreciates one another's sacrifices, there can be some undercurrents of tension within the veteran and military communities. One source of tension can be the limited resources of the VA and other organizations serving veterans. As more and more Post-9/11 service members leave the military and become eligible for VA benefits and services, the VA has become increasingly overwhelmed. Veterans of earlier conflicts can perceive such changes as increasing wait times at VA hospitals as a shifting focus from the earlier generations of veterans to the new Post-9/11 veterans. Some veterans display a sense of competition over limited resources and also over the attention of the American populace. Some of these earlier veterans served during a time when military service did not receive the respect that it has in recent years, and feeling a shift in attention toward a new group of veterans can be challenging for them. By including veterans of all eras and remembering the sacrifices of earlier eras, librarians can help ensure that veteran and military-oriented programming is successful with many types of veterans in their area.

These insights are not a comprehensive list of veteran and service member traits and behaviors, nor are they representative of all veterans and service members. Librarians interested in working with the veteran and military communities should seek more information from veterans in their local communities and from the variety of additional resources available to those interested in learning about the military and veteran experience. One free resource that librarians may find helpful is Make the Connection, a website hosted by the VA that is dedicated to archiving testimonials by veterans, their family members, and caregivers. Make the Connection provides an extensive database of videos that anyone can watch. Civilians may view Make the Connection videos to better understand the experiences of veterans and service members and to learn about available resources, while veterans and service members may watch the videos to validate their feelings in coping with the challenges of their military experiences. Each interview recorded on Make the Connection is divided into excerpts and indexed according to the era of conflict and topic. As a result, videos from veterans from a particular era are easily discoverable. The testimonials are a very powerful tool for learning about the variety of experiences veterans may have during and after their military service ("Make the Connection," 2016a).

Challenges for Transitioning Service Members and Veterans

Transition, the period when service members are in the process of leaving the military and adjusting to civilian life as a veteran, is a time that can be particularly challenging for the veteran and military communities. Some of the challenges related to transition can also extend to those who are still serving, such as members of the National Guard and Reserves who straddle the line between veteran and service member. To alleviate the challenges faced by transitioning service members, the DoD and each branch of the military provide training that includes information about applying for VA benefits, translating military experience into a civilian résumé, and the like (U.S. Department of Defense. Transition Assistance Program, n.d.). However, some veterans find that transition training is insufficient to help them bridge the cultural divide between the military world and the civilian community.

As a veteran and as a librarian in San Diego, a very military-heavy community, Kristen has seen a number of examples of cultural differences between service members, veterans, and civilians. Some common cultural differences include the following:

- Assertive behavior that is praised in the military may seem like bullying or excessive ambitiousness in some civilian workplaces.

- Veterans and service members are taught to pay close attention to hierarchy in the military and are often reluctant to be seen as questioning authority in the civilian workplace.

- Veterans are taught to be resilient and to solve their own problems and can be reluctant to admit that they need help with new challenges faced in the civilian community.

- When veterans or service members attempt to build rapport with a nonmilitary coworker for the first time, they may accidentally use military jargon or share too much about their experiences in the military, making it difficult for civilian colleagues to relate to them.

- Many service members regard their fellow service members with loyalty and trust that civilians reserve only for family members; civilian workplace relationships can be surprisingly shallow in comparison. Veterans who are used to regarding their battle buddies as family can sometimes feel isolated when they join the civilian workforce.

- During the already challenging period of transition, some veterans no longer have access to the social circles that provided them with moral support in difficult times. When not on the job, military service members often socialize with each other at the installation or at military-oriented pubs or restaurants. After leaving the military, veterans can feel cut off from this social outlet because they cannot easily return to the same installation or they may have relocated.

- The civilian work ethic is different from the military work ethic. Service members are often heavily invested in their jobs, which makes sense because lives can depend on their ability to do their jobs well. Veterans may be frustrated to find that their commitment to work may be considered an overinvestment, while a civilian coworker's more limited investment in the job is seen as normal.

- Sometimes civilians are fearful of being disrespectful toward a veteran or service member and therefore avoid talking to them or asking them about their experiences. However, veterans and service members may perceive this avoidance as prejudice against those who have served in the military.

- Some civilians make assumptions about veterans' and service members' political beliefs and therefore avoid or feel awkward talking about some topics in front of them.

In addition to facing the cultural contrasts between military life and civilian life, veterans must also manage several challenging experiences immediately after leaving the military. Most transitioning service members must settle on a place to live, find a job, complete paperwork with the VA and the military to finalize military records and registration, and ensure that any changes in location are handled with regard to vehicle registration, voting records, and their driver's license. Transitioning service members who have a spouse or children may also have to support their spouse's job search as well as find schools and childcare for children. Additionally, transitioning service members must find new doctors, dentists, and other professionals. These relationships are already well established for civilian adults who remain in the same city where they grew up, but because service members are assigned by the military to specific practitioners, transitioning service members may be doing these tasks for the very first time as an adult. And because military service often requires service members to relocate to a different part of the country than their extended family, they often must face these transition challenges without much support from family members. Building new support networks may be difficult for transitioning service members.

Veterans' benefits do not provide for these transitional challenges. Most veterans' benefits are long-term resources for veterans who eventually want to return to college or buy a home. Any transitioning service member who seeks specific VA benefits must "hurry up and wait" by providing paperwork as quickly as possible but then waiting patiently for VA paperwork to be processed. In the meantime, transitioning service members will have to find resources outside of the VA to help them stay afloat. This challenge can be particularly difficult for service members who are leaving the military because of a disability.

In addition to the challenges of the initial transition from the military to civilian life, veterans and service members may also face other challenges later in life. Some veterans may find that health concerns related to their service, such as hearing loss, do not fully manifest until years or even decades after they separate from the military. Other service members deny having any medical or psychological problems while in the military, particularly because military culture encourages service members to avoid complaining, or "suck it up," when they experience discomfort. It sometimes takes several years for a veteran to admit that they might actually have a medical problem or need psychological help. In some cases, the veteran is forced by a spouse or friend to acknowledge the need for help. In fact, in many cases, the person asking for help in seeking information about veterans' benefits is not the veteran, but a friend or spouse who is trying to persuade the veteran to seek help.

Librarians can play an important role in supporting service members transitioning out of the military. Librarians can provide services and programs to support job-seeking service members and military spouses, such as résumé review services and other employment support. They can work with the VA and local VSOs to provide effective referrals for newly separated veterans who may be interested in filing for any veterans' benefits for which they may be eligible. And they can provide a safe space for transitioning service members and their families who are adjusting to civilian life and may need a place to make new friends, learn about the local area, and find a friendly ear.

Veterans' and Service Members' Needs on the Rise

Although recent VA and DoD estimates indicate that there are 1.34 million individuals serving in the active-duty military, 800,000 in the Reserves, and 21.4 million veterans nationwide, the number of veterans in the United States is projected to decrease over the next few decades (Defense Manpower Data Center, 2016; U.S. Department of Veterans Affairs. National Center for Veterans Analysis and Statistics, 2014). However, history indicates that the challenges veterans and service members face as a result of their military experience do not always diminish over time; veterans will continue to require support from veterans' organizations and from the community for decades after they serve (U.S. Department of Veterans Affairs. National Center for Veterans Analysis and Statistics, 2014). In 2016, veterans' organizations are serving veterans from peacetime periods as well as multiple conflicts, ranging from World War II to the Post-9/11 wars in Iraq and Afghanistan. Even as veterans' organizations have responded to the needs of Post-9/11 veterans, those veterans from earlier conflicts have continued to need support and services.

Although veterans from multiple conflicts will continue to require services, the needs of Post-9/11 veterans and service members loom large on the horizon of organizations that serve the veteran community. The vast majority of veterans are able to reintegrate into the civilian community, either on their own or with the help of veterans' organizations. However, a small but significant number of veterans will continue to struggle. Gulf War–era veterans, which include Post-9/11 veterans, have a higher number of disabilities per veteran and more severe disabilities per veteran, which, for some, can act as a substantial barrier to reintegration (Bass & Golding, 2014). These veterans also share many of the same disparities that affected previous generations; for example, they have higher risk of suicide than the general population (Kang et al., 2015). For some veterans, their service-related challenges do not necessarily diminish over time. For example, veterans have a higher risk of homelessness, even years after their service ended (Perl, 2015). And a recent longitudinal study of Vietnam War veterans indicates that PTSD symptoms persist over 40 years after the end of the Vietnam War (Marmar et al., 2015). This suggests that Gulf War–era veterans and service members, a group of over 7 million individuals, will continue to face challenges and require support from veterans' organizations and the larger community for years to come (U.S. Department of Veterans Affairs. National Center for Veterans Analysis and Statistics, 2014).

Even those veterans who seem to integrate seamlessly back into the civilian community need the support of their communities. "Supporting the Troops" means recognizing military service while it is being rendered, but also after, when sacrifices are often forgotten by all but those who offered them. Veterans bear the scars of their service, both physical and psychological, throughout their lives and deserve the continued support of their communities even after the wars in which they fought have been relegated to the history books.

References

Aktepy, S. L. (2010). *A rhetoric of betrayal: Military sexual trauma and the reported experiences of Operation Enduring Freedom and Operation Iraqi Freedom women veterans* (Unpublished master's thesis). Indiana University-Purdue University Indianapolis (IUPUI), Indianapolis, IN.

Baiocchi, D. (2013). *Measuring Army deployments to Iraq and Afghanistan*. Santa Monica, CA: RAND Corporation. Retrieved from http://www.rand.org/content/dam/rand/pubs/research_reports/RR100/RR145/RAND_RR145.pdf

Bass, E. & Golding, H. (2014). *Veterans' disability compensation: Trends and policy options* (CBO Publication No. 4617). Washington, D.C.: Congressional Budget Office. Retrieved from https://www.cbo.gov/publication/45615

Bradbard, D. A., Maury, R. V., Kimball, M., Wright, J. C. M., LoRe', C. E., Levingston, K., ... White, A. M. (2014). *Military family lifestyle survey*. Falls Church, VA: Blue Star Families. Retrieved from https://bluestarfam.org/survey

Buchanan, N. T., Settles, I. H., & Woods, K. C. (2008). Comparing sexual harassment subtypes among black and white women by military rank: Double jeopardy, the Jezebel, and the cult of true womanhood. *Psychology of Women Quarterly, 32*(4), 347–361. doi:10.1111/j.1471-6402.2008.00450.x

Carroll, C. (2014, December 28). Rivals in military religious freedom dispute say rule is unclear. Retrieved from http://www.stripes.com/news/rivals-in-military-religious-freedom-dispute-say-rule-is-unclear-1.321384

Chalabi, M. (2015, March 19). What percentage of Americans have served in the military? [Blog post]. Retrieved from http://fivethirtyeight.com/datalab/what-percentage-of-americans-have-served-in-the-military

Chamber of Commerce Hawaii. (2016). Hawaii military affairs council (MAC). Retrieved from http://www.cochawaii.org/military-affairs-council

Clever, M. & Segal, D. R. (2013). *Future of Children, 23*(2), 13–39.

Commissioned Corps of the U.S. Public Health Service. (2015). Overview: FAQs. Retrieved from http://www.usphs.gov/questionsanswers/overview.aspx

Constable, P. (2014, January 22). Pentagon clarifies rules on beards, turbans for Muslim and Sikh service members. *Washington Post*. Retrieved from https://www.washingtonpost.com/local/pentagon-clarifies-rules-on-beards-turbans-for-muslim-and-sikh-service-members/2014/01/22/13b1fc22-83a9-11e3-9dd4-e7278db80d86_story.html

Cronk, T. M. (2016, June 30). Transgender service members can now serve openly, Carter announces. Retrieved from http://www.defense.gov/News-Article-View /Article/822235/transgender-service-members-can-now-serve-openly-carter -announces

Defense Manpower Data Center. (2012). Religion of active duty personnel by service (no Coast Guard). Retrieved from http://www.dod.mil/pubs/foi/Reading_Room /Statistical_Data/14-F-0928_ADMP_Religion_Sep-30-12.xlsx

Defense Manpower Data Center. (2016). DoD personnel, workforce reports & publications. Retrieved from https://www.dmdc.osd.mil/appj/dwp/dwp_reports.jsp

Devilbliss, M.C. (1990). *Women and military service: A history, analysis, and overview of key issues*. Maxwell Air Force Base, AL: Air University Press. Retrieved from http://www.dtic.mil/dtic/tr/fulltext/u2/a229958.pdf

Dunn, N. J., Yanasak, E., Schillaci, J., Simotas, S., Rehm, L. P., Souchek, J., ... Hamilton, J. D. (2004). Personality disorders in veterans with posttraumatic stress disorder and depression. *Journal of Traumatic Stress, 17*(1), 75–82. doi:10.1023/B:JOTS.0000014680.54051.50

Eastridge, B. J., Mabry, R. L., Seguin, P., Cantrell, J., Tops, T., Uribe, P. ... Blackbourne, L. H. (2012). Death on the battlefield (2001–2011): Implications for the future of combat casualty care. *Journal of Trauma and Acute Care Surgery, 73*(6), S431–S437. doi:10.1097/TA.0b013e3182755dcc

Ettarh, F. (2014). Making a new table: Intersectional librarianship. *In the Library with the Lead Pipe*. Retrieved from http://www.inthelibrarywiththeleadpipe.org /2014/making-a-new-table-intersectional-librarianship-3

Gates, G. J. (2010). *Discharges under the Don't Ask, Don't Tell policy: Women and racial / ethnic minorities*. Los Angeles, CA: Williams Institute. Retrieved from http:// williamsinstitute.law.ucla.edu/wp-content/uploads/Gates-Discharges2009-Military -Sept-2010.pdf

Gates, G. J. & Herman, J. L. (2014). *Transgender military service in the United States*. Los Angeles, CA: Williams Institute. Retrieved from http://williamsinstitute.law.ucla .edu/wp-content/uploads/Transgender-Military-Service-May-2014.pdf

Gawande, A. (2004). Casualties of war—military care for the wounded from Iraq and Afghanistan. *New England Journal of Medicine, 351*(24), 2471–2475. doi:10.1056/NEJMp048317

Goldberg, M. S. (2010). Death and injury rates of US military personnel in Iraq. *Military Medicine, 175*(4), 220–226. doi:10.7205/MILMED-D-09-00130

Harada, N. D., Villa, V. M., Reifel, N., & Bayhylle, R. (2005). Exploring veteran identity and health services use among Native American veterans. *Military Medicine, 170*(9), 782–786. doi:10.7205/MILMED.170.9.782

Holder, K. A. (2016). The disability of veterans. Retrieved from https://www.census.gov /content/dam/Census/library/working-papers/2016/demo/Holder-2016-01.pdf

Joachim, D. S. (2014, August 14). Military to ease hairstyle rules after outcry from black recruits. *New York Times*. Retrieved from http://www.nytimes.com/2014 /08/15/us/military-hairstyle-rules-dreadlocks-cornrows.html

Kamarck, K. N. (2015, December 12). *Women in combat: Issues for Congress* (CRS Report No. R42075). Washington, D.C.: Congressional Research Service. Retrieved from http://www.fas.org/sgp/crs/natsec/R42075.pdf

Kang, H. K., Bullman, T. A., Smolenski, D. J., Skopp, N. A., Gahm, G. A., & Reger, M. A. (2015). Suicide risk among 1.3 million veterans who were on active duty during the Iraq and Afghanistan wars. *Annals of Epidemiology, 25*(2), 96–100. doi:10.1016/j.annepidem.2014.11.020

Kotwal, R. S., Howard, J. T., Orman, J. A., Tarpey, B. W., Bailey, J. A., Champion, H. R., ... Gross, K. R. (2016). The effect of a golden hour policy on the morbidity and mortality of combat casualties. *JAMA Surgery, 151*(1), 15–24. doi:10.1001 /jamasurg.2015.3104

Lakin, J. (2010). Atheists in foxholes: Examining the current state of religious freedom in the United States military. *First Amendment Law Review, 9*(3), 713–748.

Linsley, B. (2012, November 24). Older vets to Post-9/11 vets: 'We had it harder.' Did they? Retrieved from http://usnews.nbcnews.com/_news/2012/11/24/15392392 -older-vets-to-post-911-vets-we-had-it-harder-did-they?lite

Make the Connection. (2016a). Retrieved from http://maketheconnection.net

Make the Connection. (2016b). Treatment and hope after Vietnam [video recording]. Retrieved from http://maketheconnection.net/stories/453

Marmar, C. R., Schlenger, W., Henn-Haase, C., Qian, M., Purchia, E., Li, M., ... Kulka, R.A. (2015). Course of posttraumatic stress disorder 40 years after the Vietnam War: Findings from the National Vietnam Veterans Longitudinal Study. *JAMA Psychiatry, 72*(9), 875–881. doi:10.1001/jamapsychiatry.2015.0803

McIntosh, M. F. & Sayala, S. (2011). *Non-citizens in the enlisted U.S. military.* Arlington, VA: CNA Analysis & Solutions. Retrieved from https://www.cna.org/CNA_files/PDF/D0026449.A1.pdf

Morral, A. R., Gore, K. L., & Schell, T. L. (Eds.) (2016). *Sexual assault and sexual harassment in the U.S. military: Volume 2. Estimates for Department of Defense service members from the 2014 RAND military workplace study.* Santa Monica, CA: RAND Corporation. Retrieved from http://www.rand.org/pubs/research_reports/RR870z2-1.html

Muller, E. L. (2003). *Free to die for their country: The story of the Japanese American draft resisters in World War II.* Chicago: University of Chicago Press.

Muralidharan, A., Austern, D., Hack, S., & Vogt, D. (2016). Deployment experiences, social support, and mental health: Comparison of black, white, and Hispanic U.S. veterans deployed to Afghanistan and Iraq. *Journal of Traumatic Stress, 29*(3), 273–278. doi:10.1002/jts.22104

National Center for Transgender Equality. (2015). Know your rights: Military records. Retrieved from http://www.transequality.org/know-your-rights/military-records

NOAA Corps. (2016). About. Retrieved from http://www.omao.noaa.gov/learn/noaa-corps/about

Ottley, A. H. (2014). Empty promise: Black American veterans and the new GI Bill. *New Directions for Adult and Continuing Education, 2014*(144), 79–88. doi:10.1002/ace.20116

Pellerin, C. (2015, December 3). Carter opens all military occupations, positions to women. Retrieved from http://www.defense.gov/News-Article-View/Article/632536/carter-opens-all-military-occupations-positions-to-women

Perl, L. (2015). *Veterans and homelessness* (CRS Report No. RL34024). Washington, D.C.: Congressional Research Service. Retrieved from http://fas.org/sgp/crs/misc/RL34024.pdf

Philipps, D. (2016, April 1). Sikh captain says keeping beard and turban lets him serve U.S. and faith. *New York Times.* Retrieved from http://www.nytimes.com/2016/04/02/us/sikh-army-captain-simratpal-singh.html

Roulo, C. (2013, January 24). Defense department expands women's combat role. Retrieved from http://archive.defense.gov/news/newsarticle.aspx?id=119098

Sanderlin, R. (2011, November 3). Getting beyond 'who had it worse' [Blog post]. Retrieved from http://atwar.blogs.nytimes.com/2011/11/03/getting-beyond-who-had-it-worse

San Diego Military Advisory Council. (2016). What is SDMAC? Retrieved from http://sdmac.org/History.htm

Shaffer, D. R. (2000). "I do not suppose that Uncle Sam looks at the skin": African Americans and the Civil War pension system, 1865–1934. *Civil War History, 46*(2), 132–147. doi:10.1353/cwh.2000.0049

Sherman, M. D., Kauth, M. R., Ridener, L., Shipherd, J. C., Bratkovich, K., & Beaulieu, G. (2014). An empirical investigation of challenges and recommendations for welcoming sexual and gender minority veterans into VA care. *Professional Psychology: Research and Practice, 45*(6), 433–442. doi:10.1037/a0034826

Smith, C. P. & Freyd, J. J. (2013). Dangerous safe havens: Institutional betrayal exacerbates sexual trauma. *Journal of Traumatic Stress, 26*(1), 119–124. doi:10.1002/jts.21778

Torreon, B. S. (2012). *U.S. periods of war and dates of recent conflicts* (CRS Report No. RS21405). Washington, D.C.: Congressional Research Service. Retrieved from http://fpc.state.gov/documents/organization/202883.pdf

Tragedy Assistance Program for Survivors. (2016). TAPS Fact Sheet & Statistics on Families of the Fallen. Retrieved from http://www.taps.org/uploadedFiles /TAPS/RESOURCES/Documents/FactSheet.pdf

Turner, S. & Bound, J. (2003). Closing the gap or widening the divide: The effects of the GI Bill and World War II on the educational outcomes of black Americans. *Journal of Economic History, 63*(1), 145–177. doi:10.1017/S0022050703001761

United States Census Bureau. (n.d.). American FactFinder. Retrieved from http:// factfinder.census.gov/faces/nav/jsf/pages/index.xhtml

United States Census Bureau. (2016). Veterans. Retrieved from http://www.census .gov/topics/population/veterans.html

United States General Accounting Office. (1992). *Defense force management: DOD's policy on homosexuality* (GAO/NSIAD-92-98). Washington, D.C.: General Accounting Office. Retrieved from http://www.gao.gov/assets/160/151963.pdf

U.S. Citizenship and Immigration Services. (2015). Naturalization through military service: Fact sheet. Retrieved from https://www.uscis.gov/news/fact-sheets /naturalization-through-military-service-fact-sheet

U.S. Department of Defense. (2015a). *2014 demographics profile of the military community*. Washington, D.C.: Office of the Deputy Under Secretary of Defense. Retrieved from http://download.militaryonesource.mil/12038/MOS/Reports/2014 -Demographics-Report.pdf

U.S. Department of Defense. (2015b). National women's history month. Retrieved from http://archive.defense.gov/home/features/2015/0315_womens-history

U.S. Department of Defense. Defense Media Activity. (2014, December 28). Obama, Hagel mark end of Operation Enduring Freedom. Retrieved from http://www .defense.gov/News-Article-View/Article/603860/obama-hagel-mark-end-of -operation-enduring-freedom

U.S. Department of Defense. Transition Assistance Program. (n.d.). Welcome to DoD TAP. Retrieved from https://www.dodtap.mil

U.S. Department of Veterans Affairs. (2014). VETPOP 2014: Living veterans by period of service, gender, 2013–2043. Retrieved from http://www.va.gov/vetdata /docs/Demographics/New_Vetpop_Model/2L_VetPop2014.xlsx

U.S. Department of Veterans Affairs. (2016a). I am an active duty servicemember. Retrieved from http://www.va.gov/opa/persona/active_duty.asp

U.S. Department of Veterans Affairs. (2016b). I am a veteran. Retrieved from http:// www.va.gov/opa/PERSONA/index.asp

U.S. Department of Veterans Affairs. (2016c). National center for veterans analysis and statistics. Retrieved from http://www.va.gov/vetdata

U.S. Department of Veterans Affairs. Center for Minority Veterans. (2016). Minority veterans program coordinators (MVPC). Retrieved from http://www.va.gov /centerforminorityveterans/Minority_Veterans_Programs_Coordinators _MVPC.asp

U.S. Department of Veterans Affairs. Health Care. (2015a). Women veterans health care. Retrieved from http://www.womenshealth.va.gov/WOMENSHEALTH /latestinformation/facts.asp

U.S. Department of Veterans Affairs. Health Care. (2015b). Women veterans health care: Culture change campaign. Retrieved from http://www.womenshealth.va .gov/WOMENSHEALTH/culture_change.asp

U.S. Department of Veterans Affairs. Mental Health. (2015). Military sexual trauma general factsheet. Retrieved from http://www.mentalhealth.va.gov/docs/mst _general_factsheet.pdf

U.S. Department of Veterans Affairs. Mental Health. (2016). Military sexual trauma. Retrieved from http://www.mentalhealth.va.gov/msthome.asp

U.S. Department of Veterans Affairs. National Center for PTSD. (2016). Traumatic stress in female veterans. Retrieved from http://www.ptsd.va.gov/professional /trauma/war/traumatic_stress_in_female_veterans.asp

U.S. Department of Veterans Affairs. National Center for Veterans Analysis and Statistics (2011). *America's women veterans: Military service history and VA benefit utilization statistics*. Washington, D.C.: U.S. Department of Veterans

Affairs. Retrieved from http://www.va.gov/vetdata/docs/specialreports/final _womens_report_3_2_12_v_7.pdf

U.S. Department of Veterans Affairs. National Center for Veterans Analysis and Statistics. (2014). Projected veteran population: 2013 to 2043. Retrieved from http://www.va.gov/vetdata/docs/quickfacts/population_slideshow.pdf

U.S. Department of Veterans Affairs. National Center for Veterans Analysis and Statistics. (2015a). Profile of Post-9/11 veterans: 2013. Retrieved from http://www.va .gov/vetdata/docs/SpecialReports/Post_911_Veterans_Profile_2013.pdf

U.S. Department of Veterans Affairs. National Center for Veterans Analysis and Statistics. (2015b). Profile of women veterans: 2013. Retrieved from http://www.va .gov/vetdata/docs/SpecialReports/Women_Veterans_2013.pdf

U.S. Department of Veterans Affairs. National Center for Veterans Analysis and Statistics. (2016). 2014 minority veterans report. Washington, D.C.: U.S. Department of Veterans Affairs. Retrieved from http://www.va.gov/vetdata/docs/Special Reports/Minority_Veterans_2014.

U.S. Department of Veterans Affairs. Public Health (2015). Radiation. Washington, D.C.: U.S. Department of Veterans Affairs. Retrieved from http://www.publichealth .va.gov/exposures/radiation/index.asp

U.S. Department of Veterans Affairs. Veterans Benefits Administration. (2015). *VBA annual benefits report fiscal year 2014 - compensation*. Washington, D.C.: U.S. Department of Veterans Affairs. Retrieved from http://www.benefits.va .gov/REPORTS/abr/ABR-Compensation-FY14-10202015.pdf

Veterans' Preference, 5 U.S.C. § 2108 (2012).

Williamson, R. B. (2009). *VA health care: Preliminary findings on VA's provision of health care services to women veterans*. Washington, D.C.: United States Government Accountability Office. Retrieved from http://www.gao.gov/products /GAO-09-884T

Wilson, S. (2014, February 21). Obama to award Medal of Honor to two dozen veterans, including 19 discrimination victims. *Washington Post*. Retrieved from https:// www.washingtonpost.com/politics/obama-to-ward-medal-of-honor-to-19 -soldiers-who-were-overlooked-because-of-their-ethnicity/2014/02/21/209594e8 -9b10-11e3-975d-107dfef7b668_story.html

2

What All Librarians Should Know about the Veteran and Military Communities

Librarians in any type of library, including public, academic, school, and special libraries, may encounter patrons who are members of the veteran and military communities. Although the interactions librarians have with veteran and military-affiliated patrons may vary widely depending on the type of library, all librarians can benefit by understanding some of the general characteristics and challenges of military service as well as the most essential resources available to members of these communities. This chapter will focus on these foundational characteristics and resources to provide common ground for all librarians who are interested in serving the veteran and military communities. Subsequent chapters will then provide targeted information for each type of library, including public libraries (chapter 3), academic libraries (chapter 4), and school, health sciences, law, military, and prison libraries (chapter 5).

To serve the veteran and military communities effectively, it is important to understand the richness and complexity of these communities. Although this chapter will explore some of the common characteristics, challenges, and strengths of veterans and service members, it is important to remember that each veteran and service member is an individual. Though they sometimes share similar characteristics, veterans and service members may resist stereotypical representations.

Not long ago, Sarah attended an event honoring local women veterans. The event attracted a number of women veterans from multiple generations and was a wonderful opportunity to experience a feeling of community with other women veterans. However, she found one well-intended gesture by the organizers to be a little discouraging: the organizers decided to hand out pink camouflage baseball caps to all of the women veterans at the event. This is an example of what not to do when attempting any kind of outreach with the veteran or military communities. Although it is quite possible that some women veterans would appreciate pink ball caps, others may feel that this kind of memorabilia is demeaning. The contributions and sacrifices made by women veterans should not be reduced to adding pink to some camouflage.

Although veteran and military-affiliated patrons do constitute a unique patron group that deserves special attention, librarians must be careful to not make assumptions about the wants, needs, and expectations of veteran and service member patrons. This chapter will provide some general precepts for working with veteran and military-affiliated patrons: How should librarians approach these patrons? What should librarians know to avoid inadvertently offending a war veteran? What are the cultural competency issues related to veterans and service members? And what kinds of challenges and opportunities do all libraries have in common when serving the veteran and military communities? This chapter will provide librarians with answers to these essential questions (and more).

This chapter is organized into four main sections. The first section is intended to help librarians understand some of the basic characteristics about veteran and military culture. Next are provided common resources for referrals, including elements such as crisis hotlines, organizations that serve veterans, and organizations that serve military service members and their families. The third section discusses strategies and suggestions for librarians interested in developing partnerships with veteran and military service organizations, a strategy that can help librarians better develop targeted services for veteran and military-affiliated patrons and extend their reach. Finally, the chapter will discuss examples of common veteran and service member information needs and provide suggestions for a few essentials to include in nearly any library collection.

Veteran and Military Culture

To work effectively with their patrons, who belong to myriad diverse communities, it is imperative that librarians understand and respect the unique characteristics of these communities. Many librarians participate in cultural competence training to identify and practice new strategies for working with patrons from other communities. Veterans, service members, and their families constitute their own unique patron group, with its own cultural norms and distinctive needs and challenges, and librarians who work with the veteran and military communities can better serve those patrons by seeking a deeper understanding of veteran and military culture and norms. It is not necessary for librarians to know every aspect of veteran and military culture, but librarians should make an effort to prepare themselves to assist veterans and military-affiliated individuals who are seeking information or services when they visit a library. This section will cover the basics: the essential information that all librarians should learn to ensure that those from military and veteran communities are understood.

Frequently Asked Questions about Working with Veteran and Military Patrons

Because veterans, service members, and their families can be found in virtually any community around the United States, most librarians have at least some experience working with veteran and military populations. But in the authors' experience, librarians often have some questions about best practices for working with veterans and service members. These best practices can vary based on the kind of library, the type of veterans and service members that visit the library, and the individual veteran or service member's preferences and information needs. However, this section is intended to provide answers to some of the most fundamental questions that are asked by librarians across types of library and military populations.

What do librarians need to know about working with veterans and service members? For the most part, effectively working with veterans and service members requires many of the same skills that librarians use in their jobs on a daily basis. Librarians strive to ensure that libraries are welcoming and safe places and to offer the best possible customer service to library visitors, and these same skills can be applied to providing the best services and spaces to veteran and military patrons as well. Librarians already work to build rapport with patrons from all walks of life, and these skills can also be used to build rapport with veteran and military patrons. The questions librarians would normally ask when making an effort to get to know patrons better are the same questions they can ask of someone from the military or veteran communities.

What should librarians know when answering veteran or military-related reference questions? The same skills librarians use every day during reference transactions can be applied when veterans or service members approach the reference desk. The most essential elements of a successful reference transaction with veterans and service members are listening carefully, using empathy, and remaining open-minded—the same elements employed when assisting other patrons with a reference question.

What should librarians avoid doing when working with veterans and service members? Many librarians ask whether there are questions they should not ask or things they should avoid doing when working with veterans and service members. Because each veteran and service member is unique, the first rule of thumb for librarians is to avoid treating all veterans and service members alike. This means that librarians should avoid making assumptions about their experiences, lifestyles, or political views. They should also take care not to use marketing or outreach techniques that rely on stereotypical views of the military and veteran communities. For example, librarians should recognize that there may be significant differences between the experiences of different generations and eras of veterans and differences between the experiences of wartime and peacetime veterans. Library programming can and should include and even embrace this myriad of experiences, but take care to recognize and acknowledge that each experience is unique.

Another mistake for librarians to avoid is discouraging veterans and service members from receiving services. This discouragement can take the form of a perceived lack of welcome or prematurely turning someone away. Wherever possible, librarians should avoid the word "no" when working with veterans and military-affiliated patrons, especially when these patrons are seeking help in accessing veterans' benefits. Some veterans may be seeking assistance for the first time after having spent decades refusing to ask for help, and if they receive a "no" too early, they may never seek that help again. Librarians can instead strive to connect veterans and their families with organizations that specifically work with veterans and may be in a better position to explore all of the options with a veteran before giving them a final answer. Librarians who are still learning the local landscape of veterans' organizations should feel comfortable explaining that they are still developing their expertise related to veterans' issues but are committed to figuring out these resources together. For many veterans, librarians who simply demonstrate that they care and are not giving up can go a long way toward preventing veterans from getting up and walking away.

What is the right way address someone in military uniform? Sometimes civilians aren't quite sure how to talk to someone wearing a military uniform. Some librarians may wonder whether they are supposed to adhere to military protocol when addressing service members. Although a service member must pay attention to other service members' rank and military branch to address them correctly, these expectations do not apply to civilians. For example, although officers in the military are addressed as Sir or Ma'am, they do not expect civilians to recognize their officer rank and address them accordingly. Furthermore, if a civilian attempts to use a military form of address and makes a mistake, the service member should not be offended, as civilians are not expected to know all of the ins and outs of military protocol. Librarians who do decide to try to address a service member with military protocol should be prepared to not take it personally if the service member corrects them. Although service members are unlikely to be offended by such an error, they are often proud of their rank and want to share the opportunity to use the correct one.

How should librarians treat someone in uniform? Some librarians may be a little uncomfortable with someone wearing a military uniform in the library; perhaps they find it intimidating or just a little unusual for the environment. Librarians should feel confident that the best way to address someone in military uniform is exactly the same way they would address anyone else. This means that, just as with other patrons, librarians should make no assumptions about patrons in uniform, remain respectful, and assist them with their goals in coming to the library. They are probably there for the same reasons anyone else comes to the library.

Some librarians may have a military background or friends or family members who serve in the military; therefore, they may have some knowledge about how to properly wear the uniform. Even librarians with some military knowledge should try to avoid correcting a service member's appearance. Although these types of corrections may be well-intentioned, they can make service members feel conspicuous and uncomfortable. For example, sometimes people will bump into a service member as they dash from the car to the building and try to be helpful by reminding a service member that they have to wear their cover, or military headgear, when wearing their uniform outdoors. But that service member may just be rushing in to pick up a book on hold before heading home after a long day and may find it frustrating or annoying to have people making such a minor correction during off-hours, when they are just trying to get their errands done. By refraining from making minor corrections and treating the service member just like any other patron, librarians can reinforce the image of the library as a welcoming place and a space where the service member can be treated as an individual, not as a representative of the military.

If a librarian learns that someone is a veteran, what should they call them? Librarians shouldn't worry about using a particular form of address with veterans. Unlike service members, veterans are now civilians;

in most cases, there is no specific form of address to use. Some military retirees may prefer being addressed according to their rank at retirement; for example, a retired sergeant major may prefer being addressed as "Sergeant Major." Civilians are not expected to know a veteran's preferred form of address, nor will they be expected to use that form of address unless asked to do so. Just as with all patrons, if someone asks to be addressed in a specific way, it is the best practice to address them in the preferred manner. If in doubt, librarians can always ask what the person prefers to be called.

Should librarians thank a person for serving in the military?
Thanking veterans and service members for their military service has become very common. However, these expressions of thanks, frequently offered in perfunctory fashion, can be problematic both for those expressing gratitude and for those receiving it. On the side of those expressing thanks, there are people who have strong political beliefs about how the U.S. military is currently being used, and they do not want to feel like they are saying that they are thankful that people are sacrificing so much for the wrong reasons. Others may just feel nervous about thanking someone because they are afraid that it will seem fake. And this is a valid concern, as many veterans can tell whether someone means it when they express thanks for their service! On the side of veterans and service members, they can feel awkward receiving expressions of gratitude from a complete stranger. They may feel that their service was not deserving of thanks, especially if they are new to the military and have not yet even completed their initial training. Others may find the thanks of a civilian uncomfortable because they feel that their sacrifices were made on behalf of their fellow service members, rather than on behalf of the civilian population (Richtel, 2015).

Although thanking a veteran or service member can be problematic for some people, many do feel strongly that it is the right thing to do. Librarians who feel called to thank veterans and service members should feel comfortable doing so. Most veterans and service members are accustomed to receiving expressions of thanks and understand that these thanks are offered with positive intentions. However, librarians may also want to think about whether there are alternate ways of expressing their gratitude that may be more meaningful to the veteran or service member as well as to the librarians themselves. For example, instead of simply thanking someone for their service, librarians could ask questions about it. Questions such as "What branch of the military were you in?" "When did you serve?" and "What kind of work did you do in the military?" allow librarians to show veterans and service members that they are interested in and value their service, and they have the added benefit of allowing librarians to build rapport.

Kristen finds that, for her, engaging in a conversation with veterans and service members is much easier than simply thanking them. She doesn't have to worry about awkwardness, and she feels like she's being her genuine self by showing her curiosity and getting to know a library visitor as someone who once served in the military. She prefers to show her gratitude through friendliness and helpfulness toward veteran and military-affiliated patrons. She also gives back through her personal efforts working with organizations, making donations, honoring people who served with a moment of silence, and participating in events where people commemorate the sacrifices that veterans and their families have made.

Should librarians ask for proof of military service? Many organizations that serve veterans and service members require some sort of proof of military service, such as a current military ID card or a DD-214, which is a copy of the military discharge papers. It makes sense for most of these organizations to require proof, especially if they are providing benefits or services that are of monetary value. The concept of *stolen valor*, which is when someone claims military experience or awards that they did not earn, is important in veteran and military circles. For this reason, even when organizations are not providing services or benefits of monetary value, they often ask for proof of military service to prevent problems with impostors in their organizations.

However, libraries have a mission that is distinctly different from other organizations that serve veterans and the military. Libraries offer equal access to information to all patrons, regardless of their background or military experience. Unlike social services agencies and veterans service organizations (VSOs), the library is in the business of keeping people informed, referring people to the right places, and providing a space where people can connect with one another. Asking for a military ID or a DD-214 can create a barrier for those already on the periphery of the veteran community, such as veterans with less than honorable discharges, veterans who do not consider their service worthwhile or distinguished, or veterans who are homeless. Also, some veterans can be very sensitive to being asked for proof of service, especially if they do not fit the standard profile of a veteran.

Although most organizations are well-intentioned when they ask veterans to provide proof of service, this requirement is not always equally applied, which can lead some veterans to feel that their service is perceived as less important. For example, Sarah remembers attending a college baseball game advertised as free for veterans and service members. She and her husband, also a veteran, arrived at the game, approached the gate, and identified themselves as veterans. The person at the gate gave her husband a ticket, no questions asked. However, he required that Sarah provide proof of her service before giving her a ticket. Although this event was intended to honor veterans and service members, the unequal requirement for documentation meant that Sarah left the event feeling as though her service was not recognized in the same way as her husband's.

This type of discrimination is not uncommon and can be very frustrating for veterans because it sends the message that only veterans of a stereotypical appearance are preferred or welcome. Instead of asking for proof of military service and thus potentially turning away veterans who do not carry a DD-214 around or who might feel that they are only being asked for proof because they do not fit a profile, librarians should evaluate the potential harm of including an individual who is not really a service member or veteran in a library program, service, or policy. In many cases, the harm may be negligible. For example, if one or two people who claim to be veterans were to attend a library-sponsored writing workshop for veterans, there would likely be little real harm to the library, the program, or the other participants. However, unnecessary barriers to participation in the form of a requirement to provide proof of their military service may have a direct impact on the number of veterans and service members who attend the workshop. A higher level of scrutiny may be appropriate if the library were to sponsor a scholarship or other program with a financial benefit attached or for programs that publicly honor or reward veterans and service members for their service.

Although librarians should, whenever possible, avoid erecting barriers by requiring proof of service, they should also be aware that many potential partner organizations do ask veterans and service members to provide an ID card or DD-214. When libraries develop partnerships with the VA, a military library, a VSO, or another organization that requires documentation for eligibility, librarians should strive to keep programs and services conducted within the library as open as possible. For example, an information session in the library should remain open to the public, which would allow not only veterans and service members without identification to attend, but also friends, family members, and other interested patrons. Or a book club cosponsored by a VSO could target veterans and service members but also include other interested parties as well. By keeping programs and services open to all veterans and service members, not just to those who can provide identification, librarians can remain constant to the mission of libraries to serve the public, which also can help ensure that library services reach even marginalized groups of veterans. For these reasons, librarians are encouraged to err on the side of inclusiveness when developing policies, programs, and services related to the veteran and military communities and to leave verification of veteran and service member status to the agencies and organizations that offer tangible services and financial benefits to these communities.

Myths and Misconceptions about Veterans and Service Members

There are many common myths and misconceptions about veterans and service members that inadvertently affect how veterans and service members are treated in the library. This section will unpack some of them and explain why they may not be applicable to all veterans and service members. The general rule of thumb is to remember that, like everyone else, veterans and service members are individuals. There is no blanket statement that applies to all members of the veteran and military communities, and it is important to respect veterans' and service members' individual needs, even when trying to serve them as a group.

Most veterans have PTSD. Post-traumatic stress disorder, or PTSD, is one of the most common service-connected disabilities of veterans, only ranking behind tinnitus and hearing loss (U.S. Department of Veterans Affairs. Veterans Benefits Administration, 2015). Although any individual can have PTSD, studies show that combat veterans are at a higher risk of PTSD, with approximately 11–20 percent of Iraq War and Afghanistan War veterans and up to 30 percent of Vietnam War veterans suffering from PTSD at some point in their lifetimes (U.S. Department of Veterans Affairs. National Center for PTSD, 2016a). These numbers are significant and confirm the importance of designing veteran programming that is considerate of individuals with PTSD. They also mean that the majority of veterans, including combat veterans, do not have PTSD. Maintaining sensitivity toward individuals with PTSD is helpful and appreciated, but assuming that all veterans have PTSD is not.

Veterans with PTSD are dangerous and likely to become violent.
The majority of veterans do not have PTSD, and the majority of veterans
with PTSD are not and have never been violent. To quote the National Center for PTSD, "Although PTSD is associated with an increased risk of violence, the majority of Veterans and non-Veterans with PTSD have never
engaged in violence" (U.S. Department of Veterans Affairs. National Center
for PTSD, 2016b). Libraries should be inclusive of individuals with PTSD,
including veterans, but not be afraid of them. Just as librarians should avoid
asking any veteran or service member questions that that can bring up bad
memories, when working with patrons with PTSD, they should focus the
conversation on neutral topics that are unlikely to cause stress for the veteran. If librarians encounter a veteran patron with PTSD who is in crisis,
the crisis hotlines identified in the following section can be good resources
for referrals.

*All veterans and service members want to talk about their
service/No veterans and service members want to talk about their
service.* Just like everyone else, veterans and service members are unique
individuals with their own needs and preferences. One area in which veterans and service members can vary widely is in their willingness to talk
about their service. Some veterans and service members are very comfortable talking about their service, or at least some aspects of it. Then again,
librarians may know a veteran for years and never realize that they served
because it is never mentioned. It is important to understand that either
preference is valid and to avoid defining veterans according to their willingness to talk about their military service. There are many reasons why
veterans and service members may not want to talk about their service. For
example, it could bring up difficult or painful memories, or elements of their
service could be classified. It is a common belief that veterans and service
members who have experienced combat are unlikely to talk about it, while
those who never served on the front lines are more than happy to talk about
their service. However, reality is much more complicated. Some veterans
and service members who have never deployed may not mention or talk
about their service because they have no combat experience and therefore
they do not consider their service worth mentioning. Some veterans and
service members who experienced close-range combat may be happy to talk
about their experiences. Moreover, veterans and service members who are
uncomfortable talking about combat may be more comfortable talking about
the mundane details of life in the military and life in a war zone, such as the
ever-appetizing MREs (Meals Ready-to-Eat). Librarians should let veterans
and service members define their comfort level when talking about their
service. Even if a veteran or service member brings up their service, it can
be helpful for librarians to express interest but also to confirm that the individual is comfortable sharing more about their military service experiences
before asking questions.

All veterans and service members are heroes. The people of the
United States learned one major lesson from the war in Vietnam—that
regardless of any person's feelings about a military conflict, the troops
deserve support. Determined to make up for the terrible treatment Vietnam
War veterans faced upon returning home, many people have provided veterans and members of the military with extraordinary support. Many service
members have experienced the kindness of being applauded on airplanes,
greeted by gauntlets of cheering civilians in airports, and having meals paid
for by kind strangers. As veterans, this kindness continues, especially on
Veterans Day, when well wishes and free meals for veterans and service

members abound. These wonderful gestures are often accompanied by the sentiment that all veterans and service members are heroes. Although the actions of veterans and service members may seem heroic, many simply feel that they were just doing their jobs and looking out for their battle buddies. Veterans and service members can squirm a bit when receiving accolades that feel unmerited. Indeed, even Medal of Honor recipients express a sentiment of unworthiness despite the extreme heroism of their actions (Ferdinando, 2014). Although veterans and service members appreciate sentiments of support, be careful not to overdo it and inadvertently make a veteran or service member feel uncomfortable or unworthy of praise.

All veterans are broken. Many veterans do bear scars, physical or psychological, from their service. However, many other veterans leave the military with nothing more than fond memories and perhaps an enhanced vocabulary. Regardless of which group a veteran falls into, they are unlikely to want to be treated as broken, damaged, or somehow lesser than anyone else. In the military, service members are trained to be strong and resilient in both mind and body. In a world in which a service member's life can literally depend on the strength of their comrades, no service member wants to be perceived as the weak link or as someone who cannot be trusted to back up their battle buddies. This mentality can carry over into civilian life, as veterans resist having their military experience perceived as a problem or point of vulnerability. Veterans see their service as an asset and evidence of their strength. For veterans with a disability, military culture honors its wounded warriors, who are seen as survivors. Veterans bear their wounds as a sign of strength and the challenges that they have faced and overcome. Even when veterans need accommodations or additional services, they may resist asking for help if they perceive it as acknowledging a weakness. Libraries should avoid inadvertently implying that veterans are broken or needy by framing services for veterans as a resource offered to support those who have served, rather than helping those in need.

All veterans and service members are conservative. Military service members and veterans are more likely to identify as Republicans than their civilian counterparts (Newport, 2009; Craighill, 2014). One reason for this is that veterans and service members can feel that not just their livelihood but also their lives can hang in the political balance. Some veterans and service members feel that Republicans are stronger supporters of the military, which can influence their voting choices. But surveys show that only about a third of veterans identify themselves as Republicans; the rest identify themselves as Independents or Democrats (Newport, 2009). Indeed, in a recent poll, nearly half of service members identified themselves as Independents (Craighill, 2014). Although veterans and service members do tend to lean toward the conservative mind-set, it is important not to make assumptions about an individual's political leanings, affiliation, or ideology.

Veterans and service members wanted to go to war. It can be easy to assume that service members joined the military to go to war. This assumption is often accompanied by an attempt to diminish their sacrifices in combat by declaring that these sacrifices were made voluntarily. This assumption makes a lot of sense on the surface. After all, the draft hasn't been implemented since 1973, so service members volunteered to be there, right? They must have known that there was a chance that they could be deployed, so why did they join if they did not want to go to war? The answers to these questions seem obvious to civilians (and even some service members), but in reality, many veterans and service members may not have fully known what they were getting into. People join the military for many reasons. Some join because they want to fight, but others join to get money to go to college or to make a better life for themselves or their children. Some join the military in an effort to seek structure or a way of life that offers them an opportunity to learn new skills and find pride in their knowledge, maturity, and reliability. Some sign up for noncombat roles in the military and are not savvy enough to understand that the lines between combat and noncombat roles are blurrier than they were in the past. And still others join the military not realizing that they aren't suited for military life.

However, once service members have signed on the dotted line, they belong to the military until Uncle Sam decides to release them. This leaves many service members in the position of having to carry out contracts, deploy to war zones, and even serve past their contract end dates despite being ill-suited to military life. However, even veterans and service members who find that the military is not a good fit for them do not expect sympathy for having to carry out their commitments. Even if service members feel that they did not quite understand what they signed up for or regret their choice to join the military, they recognize the need to fulfill their obligations, both contractual and to their fellow service members, whose lives can depend on them. And once their service has been completed, veterans are proud of their contributions and their persistence through difficult circumstances. It can be an oversimplification, therefore, to assume that in a volunteer military, all service members and veterans wanted to go to war or even understood that they were likely to go to war. And it is a disservice both to service members and veterans who joined to go to war, and to those who did not, to ascribe a different level of valor to those who knew what they were getting into. Service in the military involves sacrifice, regardless of why or how someone joined.

Veterans and service members are pro-war. The idea that many veterans and service members, especially of recent conflicts, do not agree with the political decision to go to war can be surprising for some civilians. Veterans and service members are often expected to be pro-war. They are often depicted as being ready and willing to get back in the fight, whether in reality or vicariously through the next generation of service members. Veterans' and service members' opinions about going to war will vary from individual to individual and from war to war. But many veterans and service members are unlikely to endorse going to war at the drop of a hat. Many veterans and service members have been to war, and they know firsthand the challenges and sacrifices that come from combat. They have also had an up-close view of the impact of war on the civilian population. In recent conflicts, many U.S. civilians have not had to cope with the impact of war on their day-to-day lives. There were no victory gardens, no war bonds, and no Rosie the Riveters during the wars in Iraq and Afghanistan. Instead, the military community has borne the brunt of the wars' burdens alone, with some individual service members deploying as many as half a dozen times or more over the course of the wars. Because veterans and service members have borne this burden, they understand the sacrifice involved when a country chooses to go to war and are not likely to forget the effects that new conflicts will have on the military community.

It is easy to tell who is a veteran. Some veterans bear physical markers of their service. They may wear baseball caps emblazoned with the name of a war in which they served. They may have tattoos indicating their old military units or wear wristbands commemorating lost battle buddies. They may keep a bit of camouflage; for example, some veterans keep their old camouflage assault packs to use as backpacks when they go back to school.

Male veterans may keep the traditional high-and-tight haircut. But not everyone who wears camouflage or has a buzz cut is a military veteran. And many veterans do not wear their service on their sleeves, literally or meta-phorically. Many veterans are invisible, either because they do not choose to wear physical markers of their service or because they do not fit many people's mental profile of what a veteran looks like, which is usually a white male. Although many veterans do fit this profile, the veteran population is becoming increasingly diverse. More and more, the U.S. military is includ-ing women, people of color, and individuals without U.S. citizenship (Lee & Beckhusen, 2012). Librarians should not assume that an individual is, or is not, a veteran based on their appearance or accent. Such assumptions can be hurtful and force veterans who may already feel marginalized into the position of having to claim or defend their status, while others are granted their status by default.

All veterans and service members served in combat. Some civil-ians assume that because someone serves or served in the military, espe-cially during a time of war, that they are a combat veteran. Most veterans and service members from the Post-9/11 era have served in a combat zone, but a significant minority have never deployed (Baiocchi, 2013). Veterans and service members who have deployed are often proud of their service and the sacrifices they have made, but librarians should take care not to inad-vertently make noncombat veterans feel excluded by focusing too heavily on veterans and service members with combat experience. Military personnel are generally not given a choice about deployment, so whether an individual has served in combat is often the luck of the draw. What is important is that all veterans and service members have been at risk of being sent into com-bat, whether voluntarily or through the draft.

Additionally, not all veterans and service members who have served in a combat zone served in a combat role. The military deploys cooks, doctors, photographers, translators, and many other individuals in support roles, in addition to the combat arms service members (infantry, tankers, etc.). These individuals are, by definition, combat veterans because they have served in a combat zone, although their experiences tend to be very different from those of an infantryman who spent most days on patrol. Although veterans and service members sometimes subdivide themselves into combat arms and noncombat arms or combat veterans and noncombat veterans, librar-ians should strive to include all types of veterans and service members and not privilege one type of service over another. The level of danger and sacri-fice experienced by an individual veteran is not necessarily defined by their military occupation or even by the amount of time spent in a combat zone.

Common Resources for Referrals

In order to build or improve library services for veterans, librarians should not only build their foundational knowledge of the veteran and mili-tary communities, but they should also identify local, state, and national resources to whom veterans and service member patrons in need of services or resources can be referred.

There are a wide variety of organizations and resources dedicated to the needs of veterans and service members. However, the number of resources available can lead to real problems of information overload for veterans and service members who are in need of support, especially for those seeking resources for the first time or in times of a crisis. Veteran and military-related resources can be found at the local, state, and national levels as well as through many nonprofit organizations, and the availability of certain resources and benefits may vary from one state or region to another. Furthermore, eligibility for veteran or military-related resources can depend on a number of factors, from type of military discharge to VA disability rating to financial need. Because of this complexity, veterans and service members may need librarians' assistance to find ways to access the resources they need.

Librarians who are helping veterans and service members identify resources should bear in mind that it is the role of the librarian to find organizations to whom the veteran or service member can be referred, and it is the role of the veteran or military-related organization to make a determination of eligibility. When there is any doubt of a veteran's or service member's eligibility for a particular benefit or service, librarians should always err on the side of making the referral.

Librarians can play a significant role in helping veterans and service members unravel the complex network of resources to find potential sources of support. This section will identify different types of resources that librarians of all types should be familiar with in order to provide support to veteran and military-affiliated patrons. Subsequent chapters will explore additional resources that are more applicable to a specific type of library, but the four categories of support all librarians should know include the following:

- crisis hotlines
- veterans' organizations
- military organizations
- other government and nonprofit resources

These are general resources to which any veteran or service member, young or old, in school or out of school, may need referrals. The list of resources included in this chapter is not intended to be comprehensive, and inclusion does not constitute an endorsement of any individual resource or service.

Crisis Hotlines

For veterans and service members in crisis, the most efficient way of referring them to care is via a crisis hotline. There are a number of targeted crisis hotlines, as well as a general hotline. This is not intended to be an exhaustive list of resources, and librarians are encouraged to seek out additional resources that may be available in the local area. Librarians who have a veteran or service member patron in crisis and who can safely do so should refer the individual in crisis to one of the crisis resources available.

If a veteran or service member is in crisis in the library, librarians should remember to take their own and their patrons' safety into account as well. Librarians who believe that they, the individual, or their patrons are in danger, and who can safely do so, should contact the authorities immediately. If possible, relay to the 911 operator that the individual is a military veteran or service member.

The following are common veteran and military crisis hotlines:

- For veterans and service members in crisis

Veterans/Military Crisis Line
1-800-273-TALK (1-800-273-8255) and press 1, send a text message
to 838255, or chat online at www.VeteransCrisisLine.net/chat
For more information: http://www.mentalhealth.va.gov/
suicide_prevention

- For veterans who are homeless or at risk of homelessness
National Call Center for Homeless Veterans
1-877-4AID VET (1-877-424-3838)
For more information: http://www.va.gov/homeless/
nationalcallcenter.asp

- For women veterans
Women Veterans Call Center
1-855-VA-WOMEN (1-855-829-6636)
For more information: http://www.womenshealth.va.gov/
WOMENSHEALTH/ProgramOverview/wvcc.asp

- For combat veterans
Vet Center Combat Call Center
1-877-WAR-VETS (1-877-927-8387)
For more information: http://www.vetcenter.va.gov/media/Call-
Center-PSA.asp

- For service members and their family members
Military OneSource
1-800-342-9647 or chat online at https://livechat.
militaryonesourceeap.org/chat
For more information: http://www.militaryonesource.mil

- For caregivers
VA Caregiver Support Line
1-855-260-3274
For more information: http://www.caregiver.va.gov

Veterans' Organizations

Patrons who are veterans, meaning that they have already separated
from the military, have a number of resources available to them. This section will include some of the organizations and services commonly sought
by veterans.

U.S. Department of Veterans Affairs (VA). The VA, as it is more
commonly known, is the most common resource to which librarians can refer
veterans. Some veterans may be reluctant to seek out VA resources because
they do not believe that they will be eligible for services or due to poor previous experiences. However, the VA is the largest provider of services for
veterans, so it is an important referral to make, even if a veteran is not sure
whether they are eligible for benefits.

Although it has the most comprehensive suite of services and benefits
for veterans, the VA is also notoriously difficult to navigate. Just looking
through the VA website and discovering all of the different programs can
be overwhelming, but figuring out how to access a program can require
another level of persistence. A referral to the VA in general may not be as
helpful as it is intended to be, but a referral to a specific VA program or
service along with the relevant contact information is more likely to be
beneficial.

As a recently separated veteran, Sarah needed to gain access to health care. Her husband had received a card in the mail from a VA social worker notifying him that he was eligible for VA health care services because he had deployed to Afghanistan within the last five years. As Sarah had deployed to Iraq during that same time period, she decided to investigate her eligibility for VA health care. However, she found it nearly impossible to find a contact number for the women's health clinic at her local VA. Although the clinic had a website describing its suite of services, there was no information on how to schedule an appointment, and Sarah eventually had to resort to contacting her husband's VA social worker to figure out how to make an appointment.

To refer veterans appropriately, librarians should be aware of some common VA resources. This is not intended to be a comprehensive list. Librarians may wish to explore VA benefits and services more extensively if they receive questions about veterans' services not included below.

- *National Resource Directory* (https://www.ebenefits.va.gov/ebenefits/ nrd). This site is a joint effort between the VA and the Department of Defense (DoD) to aggregate information about resources and services for veterans, service members, and caregivers. It also connects to the application portal where veterans and service members can apply to receive federal benefits.

- *VA hospitals and clinics* (http://www.va.gov/directory/guide/division_ flsh.asp?dnum=1). The VA has a complex set of hospitals and clinics organized into 23 separate health care networks based on geographic region. Librarians should familiarize themselves with the VA service network in their region, including the major VA hospitals as well as the smaller outpatient clinics that may be geographically closer.

- *Vet Centers* (http://www.vetcenter.va.gov). The VA has dozens of Vet Centers around the country that provide focused readjustment services for combat veterans. Services include counseling and referrals for additional care.

- *Veterans Choice Program* (http://www.va.gov/opa/choiceact). This program is available to veterans who have been having difficulty accessing VA health care, either because of the unavailability of appointments or travel difficulties. Veterans who have become discouraged with the VA due to these difficulties may be able to receive health care in their own civilian communities through this program.

- *Vocational Rehabilitation* (http://www.benefits.va.gov/VOCREHAB/ index.asp). The Voc Rehab program, as some veterans will colloquially refer to it, provides veterans with service-connected disabilities with education and training to find new jobs or careers. This program can also provide veterans with support to live independently.

- *GI Bill* (http://www.benefits.va.gov/gibill). The VA offers a number of different educational benefits, which are commonly referred to as the GI Bill. Some educational benefits are also available to survivors and dependents. Educational benefits are very complex and are based on the time period in which the veteran served, the length of time served on active duty, service-connected disability ratings, and other factors. Veterans with service-connected disabilities may benefit from talking to a Vet Success on Campus (VSOC) counselor about their educational options (http://www.benefits.va.gov/vocrehab/vsoc.asp). More information about the GI Bill and other education benefits is available in chapter 4.

- *Disability compensation* (http://www.benefits.va.gov/compensation). Veterans who have a disability that is related to their service can file for VA disability compensation. Many veterans leave the service with at least one service-connected disability, and many disabilities are invisible. Indeed, the most common service-connected disabilities are hearing loss and tinnitus (U.S. Department of Veterans Affairs. Veterans Benefits Administration, 2015). Veterans receive compensation based on an official VA disability rating, which can range from 0 percent to 100 percent.

- *Homeless services* (http://www.va.gov/homeless). Veterans make up a significant percentage of the homeless population (National Alliance to End Homelessness, 2015). The VA, in partnership with other organizations, has been working to reduce the number of homeless veterans and provide additional support and services for veterans in crisis. The VA's Community Resource and Referral Centers (CRRCs) are a good resource for veterans who are homeless or at risk of homelessness (http://www.va.gov/HOMELESS/crrc-list.asp).

- *National Cemetery Administration* (http://www.cem.va.gov/CEM/index.asp). Some veterans and their spouses may be eligible for burial in a national cemetery. Family members of deceased veterans may also apply for a burial flag or a Presidential Memorial Certificate in memory of their loved ones.

State Veterans' Affairs Resources. In addition to federal services and benefits for veterans, each state also manages its own suite of benefits and services.

- *State veterans' affairs office* (http://www.va.gov/statedva.htm). Each state has its own veterans' affairs office that works to connect veterans in that state with federal veterans' benefits but also has its own suite of services and benefits. The services and benefits available will vary from state to state, so it is worthwhile for librarians to take a look at their own state's benefits to see what's available. For example, Texas offers the Hazlewood Exemption, a unique education benefit available to veterans from Texas. Common benefits include scholarships, property tax exemptions, employment services, and burial services.

- *County veterans service officer (CVSO).* CVSOs serve as local liaisons between the veteran community and the VA. Because they work at the local level, they are often very familiar not only with national veterans' programs and benefits but also local organizations that work with the veteran and military communities. Librarians should know who the CVSO is for their area and keep their contact information on hand as a good resource for referrals. Librarians can identify their local CVSO by visiting the website of their state veterans' affairs office or by visiting the National Association of County Veterans Service Officers' Find Service Officers page (https://www.nacvso.org/find_service_officers).

- *National Association of State Veterans Homes* (http://www.nasvh.org/index.cfm). The states also run the system of veterans' homes, which provide geriatric and extended care for veterans. A national listing of veterans' homes can be found at the National Association of State Veterans Homes website: http://www.nasvh.org/index.cfm.

Veterans Service Organizations (VSOs). In addition to federal and state organizations, there is also a wide variety of private and nonprofit organizations that provide support and services to veterans and service members. These organizations are often dedicated to supporting veterans from a specific group, such as those who served in a specific conflict (e.g., Vietnam Veterans of America) or veterans with disabilities (e.g., Disabled American Veterans). A list of congressionally chartered VSOs is available on the VA website: http://www.va.gov/vso/VSO-Directory_2013-2014.pdf.

Military Organizations

There are a number of resources available to support those who are currently serving and their family members. These resources are typically divided by military branch, and many are available at the local level, such as a military chaplain assigned to a specific unit. Some common sources of support include the following:

- *Military OneSource* (http://www.militaryonesource.mil). All service members and their families can seek online support through Military OneSource, which serves as a clearinghouse for many types of support, including such services as financial support, legal support, and counseling.

- *American Red Cross* (http://www.redcross.org/find-help/military-families). The Red Cross plays a key role in military family crises, including providing communication services when a family member needs to contact a deployed service member in an emergency. The Red Cross also connects service members with the emergency financial assistance organization affiliated with their military branch (e.g., Army Emergency Relief, Navy-Marine Corps Relief Society).

- *Servicemembers Civil Relief Act* (SCRA) (https://www.law.cornell.edu/uscode/html/uscode50a/usc_sup_05_50_10_sq9.html). The Servicemembers Civil Relief Act, or SCRA, provides some financial relief to active-duty servicemembers. For example, it caps interest on debt incurred by servicemembers prior to their service. It also provides some protection against evictions (Servicemembers Civil Relief Act, 1940). For more information about legal information resources for veterans or servicemembers, see chapter 5.

- *Nutrition assistance* (http://www.fns.usda.gov/get-involved/military-and-veteran-families). Some service members, primarily those in the enlisted ranks, and their families are eligible for the Supplemental Nutrition Assistance Program (SNAP), more commonly known as food stamps, as well as the Special Supplemental Nutrition Program for Women, Infants, and Children (WIC) and other programs. The

U.S. Department of Agriculture maintains a website on food assistance programs for which service members may be eligible (United States Department of Agriculture. Food and Nutrition Service, 2016).

Other Government and Nonprofit Resources

In addition to official governmental resources, there are a number of organizations and services available for veterans and service members at the national, regional, and local levels. Librarians should familiarize themselves with the resources available in their local areas, but some common resources include the following:

- *Disability compensation resources.* Some VSOs, such as the Disabled American Veterans (DAV), provide support for veterans who are trying to obtain compensation for a service-connected disability. Some veterans have their disability compensation applications rejected by the VA and give up any hope of receiving any disability compensation. Organizations such as the DAV, Veterans of Foreign Wars (VFW), and American Legion help veterans prepare their disability compensation application packets and appeal the VA's decisions on disability ratings.

- *Legal support.* Although the VA does not provide legal services, a number of VA facilities provide space for legal aid organizations who provide pro bono legal services for veterans (http://www.va.gov/ogc/legalservices.asp). The American Bar Association also provides a list of pro bono services for veterans. More information about providing support for veterans with legal issues is included in chapter 5.

- *Veterans history.* Veterans hold a tremendous piece of U.S. collective memory, and saving their recollections and stories for the benefit of future generations is of increasing interest to many veterans and their families. The Library of Congress' Veterans History Project (https://www.loc.gov/vets) is one place librarians can refer veterans if they are interested in sharing their experiences with future generations. There are also a large number of smaller veterans' oral history projects, and librarians should see if there are any ongoing projects in their area in which veterans can participate.

Building Relationships with Veterans' and Military Organizations

There are significant benefits to libraries partnering with veterans' and military organizations, including federal organizations such as the VA, state organizations, and VSOs. Such partnerships can help librarians better understand the types of services and resources available for their veteran patrons, and therefore help librarians make more effective patron referrals. They can also lead to referrals from the organization to the local library as a potential resource for veterans, service members, and their families and caregivers and bring new patrons into the library. These types of advantages are familiar to librarians, who are often accustomed to outreach and building community partnerships. However, librarians who have experience fostering relationships with external organizations understand that for a partnership to work in the long term, it must benefit both partners.

Unfortunately, the advantages of a library partnership are not always readily apparent to veterans' organizations.

Some military and veterans' organizations can find partnering with libraries counterintuitive, or they can struggle to understand the value that a partnership with a library can add to their organization. A major reason for this is because the organization's staff may not have an accurate understanding of libraries' diverse programs and services. As many librarians know, people often think of libraries in terms of warehouses for books. If they are not library users themselves, they may not know that libraries even have programs or displays. Beyond a lack of familiarity with basic library services, many people are unaware that some libraries play an active role in connecting patrons with community resources. For example, some libraries provide space for social service organizations or even hire social workers as library employees (Hines, 2015; Nemec-Loise, 2014; Zettervall, 2015). Because the veterans' organization's staff members are not likely to have a well-developed sense of the scope of the library's services and programs, they may not understand what the library may be able to do to support their mission. They may assume that there is little overlap between what they do and what the library does and therefore be reluctant to develop a partnership with the library.

Even if an organization does express interest in partnering with the library, if their staff members do not understand all of the potential ways in which the library can work with them, the partnership may develop in a shallow or one-sided manner. For example, they may be willing to give the library some military or veteran-related brochures to keep at the reference desk and place some library brochures in their facility. This type of surface-level partnership can be a low-risk way to try out the partnership and examine the level of commitment involved on both sides before committing any significant resources. A low-intensity partnership can be indicative of an organization that is willing to work with the library but is not aware of the richer collaborations that might be possible.

Such a partnership can also be indicative of an organization that is unsure about whether the library is truly committed to supporting the veteran and military communities. Service members, veterans, and veterans' organizations of recent years have been grateful to receive a lot of support from the general public. This support takes a lot of different forms, from handshakes and yellow "Support Our Troops" car magnets to scholarships and houses built for veterans with disabilities. It is not always easy for an organization to determine whether a general offer of support is meant to be sharing a verbal sentiment or whether it is a more tangible offer. A shallow or one-sided partnership can be a good start to building a relationship, but to develop a richer collaboration, the library will likely have to work to expand the organization's knowledge of library services and capabilities and also of the library's commitment to supporting the veteran and military communities.

To develop a collaborative partnership with a military or veterans' organization, it is crucial to convince the organization that the library can act not just as a partner but as a force multiplier. The military uses the term *force multiplier* to refer to a technique, tool, or tactic that multiplies the effectiveness of a unit, enabling a small group to do the work of a much larger unit. Force multipliers are more than just a tool; they are a pivotal element that can extend resources far beyond their original capacity. Libraries can play this role in helping to extend the outreach capability of military and veterans' organizations, allowing them to reach service members, veterans, and caregivers who are in need of support but unaware of or disillusioned with military and veterans' organizations.

Libraries are perfectly suited to serve as force multipliers for military and veterans' organizations because they are already positioned within their communities as a third space and as a neutral point of information access. Indeed, many librarians are already fielding questions from service members, veterans, and their communities about how to access military records and veterans' benefits. Librarians can enhance the efficacy of their existing veteran and military services by seeking out partnerships with veterans' and military organizations to better understand available resources and make more accurate and even targeted referrals. But military and veterans' organizations can also benefit significantly by harnessing the existing resources of libraries to help ensure that service members and veterans in need are being connected to the benefits and services available to them.

To serve not just as a partner but as a force multiplier, librarians must work to familiarize military and veterans' organizations with the extensive services and programs offered at the library, but they must also go a step further to bring to the organization concrete ideas for what the partnership could look like. A general offer to partner is a lovely gesture, but it requires the partnering organization to understand all of the different ways the library could partner with them, and it also requires the organization to do the heavy lifting of developing ideas for collaborative projects. This can be a significant barrier for any organization, let alone a military or veterans' organization that may well be overwhelmed and understaffed. By identifying a few concrete ways that the library might be able to support the military or veterans' organization's mission, the librarian may be able to remove that initial barrier to collaboration and lay the foundation for a long-term collaborative partnership.

As a new librarian and as a veteran herself, Sarah was very interested in exploring how the university library could better meet the needs of student veterans. Her first stop was to visit the campus veteran center to talk about the needs and challenges of student veterans and to brainstorm ways the library could better support veterans on her campus. She shared a few ideas for potential partnerships and programs with the center's director, which were met with interest and approval, and they agreed on a few different avenues for programming and services that the library and the veteran center would begin exploring together. Before she left, the veteran center director mentioned that others from the library had stopped by in the past to offer support, but because they did not bring any ideas for what that support would look like, no partnership had developed. The veteran center was very willing to collaborate, but they were busy establishing their organization and did not have the time or resources to explore all of the different services the library could offer or identify potential areas for collaboration. By coming prepared with a few ideas, Sarah was able to overcome this barrier and set the library on a course for regular collaboration with the campus veteran center.

Like this campus veteran center, other military and veterans' organizations also are likely to be willing to develop partnerships with the library. By showing interest in the organization's goals and challenges and bringing a few ideas to the table, a librarian can make the initial steps of developing a full partnership simpler and easier. And through the process of collaborating on these initial projects or programs, the partnering organization will get a better sense of the library's capacity and capabilities and will be in a better position to propose new collaborations in the future.

Common Information Needs of Veterans and Service Members

Veterans and service members are likely to have many of the same information needs as their civilian peers. Librarians should take care not to make assumptions about a veteran's or service member's information needs; just because a patron is in uniform doesn't mean that their information need will necessarily be military related. They might not be searching for a copy of *The Art of War* or *Jane's Encyclopedia of Military Weapons*. In fact, most people in the military or who have served in the military are interested in the same things that any library has to offer. They may need a library card, want to check out a movie, need access to a computer, or just want to hang out and read the daily newspaper. They may need picture books for their children, exam prep books before going back to school, or scholarly databases for a research project.

Although the information needs of veterans and service members are just as complex as any other patron's, there are some common information needs of veterans and service members for which librarians should be prepared to provide support. Subsequent chapters will include additional information needs that are more likely to be encountered in a specific type of library.

Military records. When transitioning out of the military, service members are often taught that the most important document they will ever receive will be their Department of Defense Form 214, or DD-214. The DD-214 is the government form number for the military's official discharge paperwork, the "Certificate of Release or Discharge from Active Duty." The DD-214 is required for a veteran to register with the VA, to sign up for various VSOs, or to request consideration for veterans' preference when applying for a job.

Service members are frequently given a brief lecture about the DD-214 while they are processing out of the military. This lecture often presents a worst-case scenario about what would happen if they lose all copies of their DD-214. Service members are told that if they lose their DD-214, it is almost impossible to obtain new copies. The lecture often includes the story of a fire in the building where the National Archives was storing some military records; as a result of this fire, many military records were lost forever. Thousands of veterans who lost their military records after their initial release were never able to replace them. Veterans are also often told that it can take months or even years to acquire a copy of their military records once they are sent to the National Archives. Veterans are even warned that military installations might misfile the records or send them to the wrong location. As a result, many veterans simply do not even try to request copies of their records if they lose the copies given to them when they first get out. In fact, many veterans may be reluctant to participate in an event or attend a program just because they have misplaced their military records.

Kristen once met a young veteran who had recently been diagnosed with a serious illness and was seeking health care from the county health services office instead of the VA. He did not make an attempt to obtain VA health care for the simple reason that he had lost his DD-214. This veteran was very young when he left the Navy, and he had lost his records while moving, never imagining that he might need them again. He had only been out of the military for a year when he was diagnosed with his health condition, but he did not believe it would be possible to get another copy of his DD-214 to prove his eligibility for VA health care services. Because requesting a copy of his military records was perceived as an insurmountable task, this young veteran did not even try to access the health care services he needed.

The National Archives takes the management of military records very seriously. They even issued a YouTube video showing how easy it is to request and receive a copy of one's military records (U.S. National Archives and Records Administration, 2010). Veterans can access the military records request form on the National Archives website and mail or fax in their signed request (U.S. National Archives and Records Administration, n.d.). Although a fax machine is the quickest way for veterans to submit their request for military records, access to a fax machine is a significant barrier for some veterans. To reduce this barrier, California libraries funded by the IMLS/LSTA Veterans Connect @ the Library grant are provided assistance in acquiring a dedicated fax machine and phone line for the sole purpose of assisting veterans with requesting military records by fax. Librarians should consider whether their libraries could provide similar support by giving any veteran who wishes to order copies of their military records access to a fax machine.

Medical information. It is commonly understood that veterans and service members may experience health-related difficulties as a result of their service; after all, this is why the VA provides disability compensation to eligible veterans. However, some librarians and even veterans are surprised to learn that veterans can experience new health-related challenges related to their service years and even decades after their service ended. Sometimes veterans are completely unaware that they were exposed to environmental hazards that can lead to health problems later in life. For example, a veteran who served in Iraq was probably well aware that there were inherent health risks, such as the risk of injury as a result of an improvised explosive device (IED), related to service in a combat zone. However, that veteran may not have realized that they were also at risk of health problems resulting from environmental exposure and other hazards. Many Iraq War veterans have reported health issues resulting from their exposure to burn pits, which were a common waste management method used during the war in Iraq. Open burn pits were used to dispose of all manners of waste, ranging from rubber tires to medical waste, with fuel as an accelerant. Some service members were exposed to the resulting smoke and other airborne pollutants from burn pits for the length of their deployment and returned to the United States to find that they had difficulty breathing (Risen, 2010).

The VA is still studying the issue of burn pits and other environmental exposures from the wars in Iraq and Afghanistan, so although veterans can register their health concerns related to burn pits with the VA, they may also want to do some investigating on their own to discover what research-ers are finding about the patterns of environmental exposures in veterans of the wars in Iraq and Afghanistan (U.S. Department of Veterans Affairs. Public Health, 2016). Librarians can support veterans who suffer from health concerns as a result of burn pits or other health hazards by helping them access such resources as PubMed to find the most recent research on military-related health exposures. More information about common veteran health-related questions can be found in the health sciences libraries section of chapter 5.

Accessing benefits. When service members transition from the mili-tary, they are provided with information about filing for any veterans' benefits for which they may be eligible. Sometimes service members are advised to begin the process of filing for veterans' benefits, such as dis-ability compensation, even before they have completed their separation from the military. However, many veterans do not seek out benefits until months, years, or even decades after they separate from the military. These benefits can range from disability compensation to educational benefits to homeless services. Librarians may receive requests from veterans to help them figure out how to submit paperwork for VA benefits, or they may ask for help identifying resources, such as a CVSO or VSR who may be able to help them with their paperwork. Librarians may also receive requests, especially from family members, for help in finding geriatric care or burial services for veterans. In many cases, veterans and their family members will have a problem they are trying to solve and not realize that there may be a resource available to help. Librarians should be aware of the most common services and programs offered by the VA and local VSOs, but they should also be prepared to refer questions about eligibility for such services and programs to a CVSO or VSR qualified to make a determination about such eligibility.

In addition to these common information needs that may be encoun-tered in many types of libraries, there are also information needs that are commonly encountered in specific types of libraries. For example, public librarians are likely to encounter veterans and service members who are seeking employment, law librarians are likely to encounter veterans and service members in need of information about legal issues, and academic librarians are likely to encounter veterans and service members seeking information about the GI Bill or scholarships for veteran and military-affil-iated students. These types of questions will be discussed in further detail in chapters 3, 4, and 5.

Collection Essentials

Librarians can support veterans and service members not only by responding to their common information needs at the reference desk but also by building collections that can provide veteran and military-affiliated patrons with the opportunity to find answers to their own information needs. Although a comprehensive list of resources is beyond the scope of this book, the following list provides some examples of the types of books and online materials that librarians may wish to consider including in their collections. Collection development suggestions that are more specific to certain types of libraries are also included in subsequent chapters; the suggestions included here are those that are likely to be useful to librarians in many types of libraries. These specific materials are intended to serve as examples, and their inclusion should not be construed as a recommendation.

Military required reading. Some branches of the military have reading lists that their service members are encouraged to read (Odierno, 2014; Chief of Naval Operations Professional Reading Program, n.d.). Depending on a service member's branch or rank, these reading lists may even be required. Librarians whose libraries are near a major military installation may want to collaborate with the installation's military librarians to identify required reading resources and ensure that they are available in the library. Librarians who are able to supply some or all of the books from these required reading lists may also want to make an effort to make service members aware that these materials are available. Examples include the following:

> Bouvard, M. G. (2012). *The invisible wounds of war: Coming home from Iraq and Afghanistan.* Amherst, NY: Prometheus Books.

> Cutler, T. J. (2005). *A sailor's history of the U.S. Navy.* Annapolis, MD: Naval Institute Press.

> Grossman, D. (1995). *On killing: The psychological cost of learning to kill in war and society.* Boston, MA: Little, Brown.

Handbooks for veterans. Some members of the military receive a handbook when they separate from the military. There are several kinds, though the most informative and reliable type of handbook is the federal government publication that is updated and issued each year by the Department of Veterans Affairs. Each state may also publish a handbook for veterans that summarizes the most commonly used federal benefits and also outlines unique benefits that are available just for veterans in that state. Although these state handbooks may be a helpful resource, librarians should be aware that not all states update their handbooks annually. Therefore, librarians should ensure that their libraries keep both handbooks readily available in print and bookmarked for easy access online. They should also ensure that patrons are aware that the federal handbook will be patrons' best source of information about federal VA benefits, but that state handbooks will be the best guide for patrons who want to learn about state tuition waivers, Department of Motor Vehicles (DMV) policies, and other resources unique to that particular state. Examples include the following:

> Florida (2016). *Florida veterans' benefits guide 2016.* Tallahassee: Florida Department of Veterans Affairs.

> Missouri (2015). *2015–2016 Missouri benefits & resource guide for veterans & military.* Jefferson City: Missouri Veterans Commission.

> United States Department of Veterans Affairs (2016). *Federal benefits for veterans and dependents.* Washington, D.C.: U.S. Department of Veterans Affairs

In addition to handbooks published by state and federal VA offices, many guides to veterans' benefits are written and published commercially. Because these guides are not created by the same organizations that administer benefits, they may or may not have the most up-to-date information about veterans' benefits. Commercial guides may also not be vetted or approved by veteran advocacy groups, so librarians should take care to research these guides to verify their quality before adding them to the library collection. However, because these guides are designed to make the process of navigating information about veteran resources easier, some veterans and service members may find them to be helpful tools. Examples include the following:

Armstrong, R. E., & Rizzuti, T. P. (2001). *Veteran's benefits: A guide to state programs*. Westport, CT: Greenwood Press.

Budahn, P. J. (2011). *Veteran's guide to benefits*. Mechanicsburg, PA: Stackpole Books.

Roche, J. D. (2006). *The veteran's survival guide: How to file and collect on VA claims*. Washington, D.C.: Potomac Books.

Handbooks for families of service members. Although libraries located near a military installation may be the most likely to have large numbers of military-affiliated patrons, all librarians are likely to encounter not only service members, but military spouses, military children, and other family members of service members. Military family members may be interested in what they can do to help their children get started with a military career, how to cope with a loved one's deployment, or where they might be able to meet up with other military family members experiencing similar circumstances. Librarians may want to provide access to handbooks and other resources specifically aimed at military family members, including military spouses and children as well as parents, siblings, and other loved ones of service members. Additional collection recommendations for military family members are located in the school libraries section of chapter 5. Examples include the following:

Leyva, M. (2009). *Married to the military: A survival guide for military wives, girlfriends, and women in uniform*. New York: Simon & Schuster.

Maxwell, M. C. B. (2007). *Surviving military separation: A 365-day activity guide for the families of deployed personnel*. New York: Savas Beatie.

Pavlicin, K. M. (2003). *Surviving deployment: A guide for military families*. St. Paul, MN: Elva Resa Pub.

Background information about deployments. Service members who are preparing for a deployment may be interested in seeking out civilian sources of information about the country or region to which they will be deployed. Military family members may also seek background information about their loved one's deployment area to better understand what their loved one may be experiencing. Librarians can include in their collections books and other resources that explore the culture, history, and politics of countries where service members may be deployed. Examples include the following:

Cha, V. D. (2012). *The impossible state: North Korea, past and future*. New York: Ecco.

Packer, G. (2005). *The assassins' gate: America in Iraq*. New York: Farrar, Straus and Giroux.

Rashid, A. (2000). *Taliban: Militant Islam, oil, and fundamentalism in Central Asia*. New Haven, CT: Yale University Press.

Although veterans, service members, and their families may be interested in books and other resources specifically aimed at the veteran and military communities, librarians should not forget that they are also likely to enjoy the same types of resources as their civilian patrons. Librarians should make these veteran and military-oriented resources available to their veteran and military-affiliated patrons, but, as always, they should take care to treat them as individuals whose information needs and interests may have little or nothing to do with their military service.

References

Baiocchi, D. (2013). *Measuring Army deployments to Iraq and Afghanistan*. Santa Monica, CA: RAND Corporation. Retrieved from http://www.rand.org/content/dam/rand/pubs/research_reports/RR100/RR145/RAND_RR145.pdf

Chief of Naval Operations Professional Reading Program. (n.d.). Navy reading: The Chief of Naval Operations professional reading program. Retrieved from http://navyreading.dodlive.mil

Craighill, P. M. (2014, April 1). Iraq and Afghan vets are conservative. But, they're not all Republicans. *Washington Post*. Retrieved from https://www.washingtonpost.com/news/the-fix/wp/2014/04/01/iraq-and-afghan-vets-are-conservative-but-theyre-not-all-republicans

Ferdinando, L. (2014, November 16). Medal of Honor recipient says he's 'no hero' during defense forum. Retrieved from http://www.defense.gov/News-Article-View/Article/603662/medal-of-honor-recipient-says-hes-no-hero-during-defense-forum

Hines, S. S. (2015). *Connecting individuals with social services: The library's role*. Paper presented at the IFLA RISS Satellite Meeting, University of Botswana, Gaborone. Retrieved from http://www.ifla.org/files/assets/reference-and-information-services/publications/512-hines-en.pdf

Lee, J.-H. & Beckhusen, J. B. (2012). *Veterans' racial and ethnic composition and place of birth: 2011*. American Community Survey Briefs. Washington, D.C.: United States Census Bureau. Retrieved from https://www.census.gov/prod/2012pubs/acsbr11-22.pdf

National Alliance to End Homelessness. (2015, April 22). Fact sheet: Veteran homelessness. Retrieved from http://www.endhomelessness.org/library/entry/fact-sheet-veteran-homelessness

Nemec-Loise, J. (2014, September 23). A little extra help: Why public libraries need social workers. *Public Libraries Online*. Retrieved from http://publiclibrariesonline.org/2014/09/a-little-extra-help-why-public-libraries-need-social-workers

Newport, F. (2009, May 25). Military veterans of all ages tend to be more Republican. Retrieved from http://www.gallup.com/poll/118684/military-veterans-ages-tend-republican.aspx

Odierno, R. T. (2014). *The U.S. Army chief of staff's professional reading list*. Fort McNair, D.C.: U.S. Army Center of Military History. Retrieved from http://www.history.army.mil/html/books/105/105-1-1/CMH_Pub_105-5-1_2014.pdf

Richtel, M. (2015, February 21). Please don't thank me for my service. *New York Times*. Retrieved from http://www.nytimes.com/2015/02/22/sunday-review/please-dont-thank-me-for-my-service.html

Risen, J. (2010, August 6). Veterans sound alarm over burn-pit exposure. *New York Times*. Retrieved from http://www.nytimes.com/2010/08/07/us/07burn.html

Servicemembers Civil Relief Act, 50 U.S.C. App. §§501-597b (1940).

United States Department of Agriculture. Food and Nutrition Service. (2016). Get involved: Military and veteran families. Retrieved from http://www.fns.usda.gov/get-involved/military-and-veteran-families

U.S. Department of Veterans Affairs. National Center for PTSD. (2016a). How common is PTSD? Retrieved from http://www.ptsd.va.gov/public/PTSD-overview/basics/how-common-is-ptsd.asp

U.S. Department of Veterans Affairs. National Center for PTSD. (2016b). Research findings on PTSD and violence. Retrieved from http://www.ptsd.va.gov/professional /co-occurring/research_on_ptsd_and_violence.asp

U.S. Department of Veterans Affairs. Public Health. (2016). VA's airborne hazards and open burn pit registry. Retrieved from http://www.publichealth.va.gov /exposures/burnpits/registry.asp

U.S. Department of Veterans Affairs. Rehabilitation and Prosthetic Services (2015). Hearing aids. Retrieved from http://www.prosthetics.va.gov/psas/Hearing_Aids.asp

U.S. Department of Veterans Affairs. Vet Center Program. (2016). Eligibility. Retrieved from http://www.vetcenter.va.gov/eligibility.asp

U.S. Department of Veterans Affairs. Veterans Benefits Administration. (2015). *VBA annual benefits report fiscal year 2014 - compensation*. Washington, D.C.: U.S. Department of Veterans Affairs. Retrieved from http://www.benefits.va.gov /REPORTS/abr/ABR-Compensation-FY14-10202015.pdf

U.S. National Archives and Records Administration. (n.d.). Veterans' service records. Retrieved from https://www.archives.gov/veterans

U.S. National Archives and Records Administration. (2010). America's veterans and the National Archives [Video file]. Retrieved from https://www.youtube.com /watch?v=_p5HMLR5tEg

Zettervall, S. (2015). Whole person librarianship. *Public Libraries, 54*(2), 12–13.

3

Public Libraries and the Veteran and Military Communities

Libraries are at their very best when they are building connections with the people in the community they serve while offering innovative programs, resources, and space. Public libraries, as institutions that celebrate curiosity, freedom of speech, and equal access to information, hold a central place in the community. They offer their visitors voter registration applications, tax forms, eldercare directories, college catalogs, local event calendars, and even access to the yellow pages. Patrons can expect to find posters and brochures about local water treatment efforts, announcements about neighborhood street closures, and information sessions by community organizations. Many public libraries post signs on the front door that signal to the community that the building is a designated "cool zone" during heat waves and a "safe place" for runaway teens. City, county, and state government agencies collaborate with the public library to keep the community updated on new initiatives. Social services agencies, schools, and health agencies can collaborate with the public library to offer seminars that meet the interests and needs of people who live in the area. Serving veteran and military communities is yet another part of what public libraries do to stay connected with their communities.

This chapter is intended to provide public librarians with information to help them better connect with and serve members of the community with current or previous military experience. Although many of the topics covered in the chapter, such as outreach, will not be entirely new to librarians, the focus will be on how these topics specifically apply to working with the veteran and military communities.

The first two chapters of this book offered recommendations to help librarians from all types of libraries improve their knowledge about the veteran and military communities and the organizations that serve them. The recommendations in this chapter aim to help public librarians assume a role as coordinators and facilitators in the veteran and military communities. The chapter will begin by sharing some suggestions about how public librarians can use outreach to build connections between the library and the veteran and military communities. The next section provides key contacts for all public librarians to know and then provides some tips to guide a librarian's approach to outreach to veteran and military service organizations. After that, this chapter will give some library programming ideas and suggestions collected from public libraries around the country. Then the chapter will answer some of the common questions public librarians ask about serving the veteran and military communities, including some common dos and don'ts. The chapter will conclude with some rules of thumb that librarians should bear in mind when developing their collections of veteran and military-related materials.

Building Connections with Outreach

The unique needs of veterans, military personnel, and military families can sometimes require knowledge beyond the basics of librarianship. Even librarians with years of firsthand experience working with those who are serving or have served in the military sometimes express the need to learn more about outreach to the veteran and military communities. Fortunately, public library employees are accustomed to participating in an ongoing cycle of learning. Most library employees are used to updating their knowledge about emerging technologies, literacy skills, and the latest approaches to remaining relevant in a community. Adding to a librarian's awareness of military culture and the needs of veteran and military communities is merely one part of this process. Gaining aptitude in the cultural competencies of working with veteran and military communities will prepare librarians to better reach the veteran and military-affiliated patrons in their neighborhoods.

Successful work with veterans and military personnel in a public library is grounded in the librarian's ability to build relationships within the community. How public librarians build these relationships has changed since the recession nearly 10 years ago. The financial hardship experienced by many local governments in the United States resulted in budget cuts that threatened to render some public libraries extinct. This forced librarians, advocacy groups, and consultants to reassess how the library connects with the community. Librarians learned, or in some cases relearned, the importance of communicating their relevancy to community stakeholders. Efforts by such library futurists and consultants as Joan Frye Williams and George Needham led to a new paradigm in thinking about the strategic planning process, with outreach at the cornerstone of how libraries reinvent themselves.

Williams and Needham taught workshops and webinars through Infopeople, an IMLS-funded organization that specializes in educating and inspiring public librarians. They also regularly consulted with public libraries throughout the country about techniques to quickly realign the strategic goals of public libraries to correspond to the goals of the people in their communities (Williams & Needham, 2010). One technique highlighted by Williams and Needham was the "strategic reality check," in which public library managers were encouraged to increase their focus on community outreach and to spend time actively listening to what community leaders had to say. Williams and Needham taught public librarians to use this extended outreach method to connect with organizations and leaders throughout the community. In doing so, public library managers could identify the community's vision of the future and align the public library's goals and mission with this vision. This approach has achieved many successes in the public library community. Siskiyou County local officials, for example, reported that their public library was saved from extinction through the work of Williams and Needham and the use of the strategic reality check (California State Library, 2011).

Public librarians interested in serving veterans and military personnel should consider applying concepts from the strategic reality check to their efforts to reach out to the veteran and military communities. Librarians can reach out to local veteran and military community leaders, including official organizations such as veterans service organizations (VSOs). They can also reach out to individual veterans, service members, military spouses, caregivers, parents of service members, and other loved ones of service members to ensure that the library's efforts match up with the needs of the veteran and military communities. Thus, the starting point for working with veteran and military communities in the public library setting is learning the goals of organizations serving veterans and military personnel. It begins with outreach.

Getting Started: Four Key Resources

Public librarians can begin their outreach effort by identifying and understanding four key resources. These points of reference represent sources of information where librarians can find information quickly and connect with those who are knowledgeable about the needs and interests of veterans and military personnel in any community. Understanding the following resources can also help librarians ensure that any efforts they pursue do not duplicate the efforts of other organizations. By consulting these resources, librarians can ensure that their programs and services are consistent with the needs and interests of the veteran and military communities.

1. *Military librarians.* More widely known in the military community as a type of Morale, Welfare, and Recreation organization (MWR), military libraries, or MWR libraries, are libraries located on military installations. Military libraries offer many of the same programs and services as a public library, and those on major military installations can be as large as a metropolitan library. Librarians located near a military installation may wish to connect with military librarians to explore potential collaborations, but military libraries can also be useful to librarians located nowhere near a military installation. It may seem counterintuitive for public librarians to reach out to a military library located hundreds of miles away, especially if there seem to be no active-duty military service members in the local community. However, military libraries' assets and resources are available to all members of the National Guard and Reserves as well as active-duty military personnel. Military library resources are also available to military dependents, including military spouses and children. Although the physical libraries are most accessible to those living near a military installation, military libraries also provide electronic resources and services for service members stationed anywhere in the world. Because even service members can mistakenly assume that they do not have access to a military library or that a military library might not have the resources that they need, public librarians can play an important role in connecting service members and their families with the military library resources available to them.

In order to be prepared to make effective referrals, public librarians should become familiar with the nearest military library, even if it is located far away. By doing so, public librarians can learn more about military library resources and be better prepared to coordinate future efforts to connect military-affiliated patrons with available resources. One tool that public librarians can use to get started is the Department of Defense (DoD) Directory of Installations website, which provides a directory of military libraries to help librarians locate the nearest one (U.S. Department of Defense, 2016a). Librarians can connect with a military librarian by phoning the nearest military library and explaining their interest in learning how to educate public library employees about military libraries to facilitate future referrals.

Librarians who are not located in close proximity to a military library may want to reach out to a coordinator from one of the branches of the military. The following list provides four major program offices through which military library resources for service members and their families are coordinated and funded:

- Army MWR Libraries
  http://www.armymwr.com/recleisure/libraries
  usarmy.mwr.library@mail.mil

- Navy General Library Program
  http://www.navymwr.org/libraries
  NGLP@navy.mil

- Air Force Library Information Program
  https://www.usafservices.com/AirForceLibraries.aspx
  web.aflis@randolph.af.mil

- Marine Corps Community Services Libraries
  http://library.usmc-mccs.org
  usmclibraries@usmc.mil

Libraries that support Coast Guard facilities are not listed online in a centralized directory. Librarians that have a location near a Coast Guard MWR Library can contact the librarian through the phone directory for that facility.

2. *Military OneSource.* In addition to working one-on-one with a military librarian to learn more about the needs and interests of military service members, public librarians should also be prepared to refer service members and their families to Military OneSource, a DoD website that collects many different resources for service members and their families in one location. Military OneSource provides links to resources for almost all aspects of the military experience. Such resources include advice for a newly married military spouse, tools for families preparing to relocate, an online toolkit for families whose service member is about to be deployed, transition assistance for service members preparing to leave the military, and contact information for those who seek support for a number of issues (U.S. Department of Defense, 2016b). Military OneSource also provides a link to the DoD MWR Digital Library, a collection of online databases and eBooks available to any service member or military family member who qualifies. By becoming familiar with Military OneSource, public librarians can help connect eligible members of the military

community with the resources available to them, even if they are located far from a military installation.

3. *National Association of County Veterans Service Officers.* One of the first steps taken by all California public libraries who participate in Veterans Connect @ the Library, an IMLS-funded grant to assist public libraries with improving their services to veterans, is to contact their county veterans service officer (CVSO) or a liaison of California's Department of Veterans Affairs. The reason for this emphasis on immediate contact with a CVSO is to ensure that public librarians can quickly learn about the highest priorities of the organizations that serve veterans in their county. CVSOs are responsible not only for monitoring the efforts and resources offered by state and national VA offices, but also for monitoring efforts by other organizations serving veterans in the area. Every public librarian should be aware of how to contact the CVSO. The National Association of County Veterans Service Officers provides a directory of all CVSOs, listed by state (n.d.). CVSOs may sometimes be difficult to reach directly, but they often have staff members who are more than eager to speak to a librarian as well. As public librarians begin outreach efforts, either with other organizations or directly with veterans, attending the meetings of an advisory group coordinated by a CVSO is one way to ensure that library programming is relevant and that partnerships are formed with appropriate and reliable organizations.

4. *Make the Connection.* Make the Connection is a VA website that provides free access to video testimonials from veterans and their family members on a wide variety of topics, including such difficult issues as post-traumatic stress disorder (PTSD), military sexual trauma (MST), and traumatic brain injury (TBI). Librarians can use these testimonials as a resource to increase their knowledge of veteran-related topics and health issues. It is also a valuable website to recommend to any military service member, veteran, or family member who is coping with a challenge or seeking more information about an ongoing situation. This is because Make the Connection's value extends beyond its testimonials. It is part of the larger VA website and includes helpful links to information about popular veteran-related topics, health issues, and other resources (U.S. Department of Veterans Affairs, 2016b).

These four key resources represent only a starting point in a public librarian's search for information about the veteran and military communities. But adding them to a reference binder or a list of online bookmarks gives librarians some readily available resources that they can use to build their own knowledge. They can also use these resources to provide assistance to patrons and colleagues interested in learning more about military culture and the veteran and military communities. Librarians can also coordinate with representatives from the organizations that oversee all four resources to acquire brochures, posters, and business cards that promote these organizations to patrons and other librarians. In fact, offering promotional materials on behalf of the four key contacts above is one low-cost initiative that public librarians can easily and quickly implement to improve the availability of information about resources for veterans and service members.

Tips for Approaching Veteran and Military Organizations

Beyond the four key resources, public librarians will want to become familiar with other veteran and military service organizations, especially those available or popular in the local area. This section provides public librarians with tips for how to improve their outreach efforts with representatives of organizations that work with the veteran and military communities. These tips are applicable to outreach with many other types of organizations as well, but they can be particularly helpful when targeting veteran and military service organizations due to the high volume of solicitations and partnership requests these organizations may receive.

Tip #1: Frame an initial suggested meeting in terms of an informational interview. When beginning outreach efforts with a VSO, librarians should describe their goal for the meeting in terms of wanting to learn about the other organization. The librarian is not asking the VSO to learn about the library but is instead asking to learn about the VSO. This is particularly important when approaching organizations that work with veteran and military communities. They are often bombarded by start-up companies and other organizations looking for an endorsement or an opportunity to make what is essentially a business deal look like it is a nonprofit collaboration to benefit veterans. As a result, many VSOs can be skeptical when receiving an unsolicited request for a meeting. When first speaking to someone at a VSO, therefore, the librarian should emphasize that the purpose of a call or a meeting is to learn about the other organization and that it won't take too much time.

Tip #2: Listen to their needs. During an informational interview with a VSO, as Williams and Needham taught in the strategic reality check, librarians should avoid talking too much about the library. Instead, they should use this valuable outreach opportunity as a chance to learn as much as possible about the other organization. They should take notes and listen for information that might signal an opportunity for the library to assist the other organization in achieving a goal or overcoming an obstacle. They can also ask questions about the VSO as well as about the VSO representative with whom they are meeting. By steering an informational interview toward a global picture of the community, librarians communicate an interest in helping the VSO achieve its goals, either by learning more or by working with the VSO at a later date to address the challenges that are identified.

Although the focus of the informational interview should be on the VSO, some librarians may feel compelled to share some information about the library before the end of the interview. One solution for librarians who want to adhere to the informational interview format but also want an opportunity to share information about the library would be to invite the representative to take a tour of the library at the end of the meeting or at a later date. This type of invitation can remind the VSO representative that the interview's purpose was to learn about the VSO, while also emphasizing that the librarian is interested in talking about the future of the library, the community, and any goals that the library and the VSO have in common.

Tip #3: Prepare. Librarians may find it easier to build rapport if they are prepared with some talking points developed from researching the organization ahead of time. The organization's website or brochures may yield information about its mission, values, and activities that can help librarians identify the organization's goals and priorities ahead of the meeting. Preparation can yield effective results, particularly when librarians have identified possible opportunities for collaboration based on identified common goals between the organization and the library.

Tip #4: Brainstorm to build rapport. Because an organization might not be aware that libraries provide programming, spaces, and services that have little to do with pleasure reading or research, it also helps if librarians are prepared to talk about concrete ideas at the appropriate time. Although the initial meeting should focus on the organization and its goals, during subsequent meetings, librarians can continue to build rapport by brainstorming potential collaborations. Librarians should be prepared to offer an example of previous collaborations with similar organizations to help the representative become more familiar with the types of collaborations that might be possible. For example, a VSO whose goal is to support military families may be intrigued to learn of heavy attendance by military families at library storytime programs. A librarian might use the example of a previous themed storytime event to help persuade the organization to participate or partner with the library to host a military-themed storytime in the future. Acknowledging a successful collaboration with another organization, brainstorming concrete ideas for how the library could help an organization in getting around an obstacle, or agreeing to meet again to discuss any questions the representative may have are some of the ways that librarians can increase rapport and familiarity with the library.

Tip #5: Keep in mind that an organization's goals may not be the same as the library's goals. As librarians learn more about the complex and extensive network of VSOs, they should remember that it is important to thoroughly investigate a VSO's mission, values, and objectives. For example, not all organizations that seek to help the veteran and military communities are nonprofit organizations. It is also important for librarians to research and assess how well the VSO is led. Public libraries should avoid endorsing, or giving the perception that they are endorsing, any individual VSO, especially one whose mission and values may not be in line with the library's mission and values. Choosing a partner for a proposed project should depend on whether a VSO has goals in common with the library and whether the organization has a reputation as a reliable resource, maintains a nonprofit profile, and is a good fit in terms of what the library's community needs are at the moment. If the VSO does not have a nonprofit profile, it may still be possible to collaborate. It is important, however, to communicate clearly about the purpose and objective of any collaboration with every partnering organization. It is essential to ensure that the collaboration remains in line with the library's mission and values. At the same time, most public libraries must comply with policies and procedures created by a parent organization when developing a collaboration or partnership. Librarians need to ensure that their outreach efforts coincide with these policies and procedures, which may limit some types of collaborations or require a memorandum of understanding at the appropriate time.

Types of Organizations Serving Veterans and Military Personnel

Government organizations. Government organizations are the most widely known type of organization serving veterans and military personnel in the local community, but because of the demands on their resources, they can be difficult to reach at times. As was discussed in previous chapters, there are a few primary government organizations of which all librarians should be aware. The most important federal government organization that serves veterans is the U.S. Department of Veterans Affairs, or VA. The most important federal government organization that serves service members is the U.S. Department of Defense, or DoD. Each of these organizations has myriad other organizations and programs that fall under its umbrella. For example, the DoD provides school liaison officers for schools with high populations of military children. It also employs family support centers to provide resources and services to military service members and their families. State and local governments have representatives and initiatives to serve veterans and military personnel as well. Public libraries often serve as a conduit for communicating about or referring residents to many of these organizations, whether or not they offer specific services for veteran and military-affiliated visitors.

Public librarians should be knowledgeable of contact information for referrals and locations when it becomes necessary to give someone directions to another government organization. Many patrons may feel overwhelmed at the task of learning how to locate a government organization, and librarians as information managers and collaborators with some of these service providers are better positioned than most to assist users in accessing government information, learning about resources, and finding where to go so someone can speak in person with the representative of a government agency or organization.

It may be difficult to figure out who to talk to when contacting a VA facility, as each facility is like a corporation with departments and offices dedicated to different responsibilities. A CVSO can help librarians identify the right person to talk to so they can make contact over the phone or via email. However, librarians can also benefit from visiting a VA location. Navigating the physical landscape of a VA facility can provide librarians with real-world experience they can lend when giving patrons directions to the VA or to a specific department or office within the VA. Librarians should be sure to schedule the visit ahead of time to minimize difficulties with parking, security, or other logistical problems and to ensure that someone is available to meet with them. As was mentioned earlier in the chapter, librarians can use the format of the informational interview to ensure that the meeting gets started on the right foot.

---

1. *Local government organizations and social services.* When seeking out potential collaborators among nonprofit organizations in the area, librarians should avoid excluding potential collaborators on the basis that their organization may not focus exclusively on programs or services for the veteran and military communities. In some metropolitan areas, for example, the local government funds an all-in-one call center that provides information about many social services agencies. The call center may be an excellent resource for veterans and service members because it includes representatives from the VA or other organizations, but this may not be well-known

due to a lack of promotion. The public library may be able to distribute promotional materials so area residents are aware that they can learn about social services and veteran resources by calling the same phone number. There can be many other social service organizations in the local area that serve the entire community, including veterans, and librarians should not forget to consider these broader resources when considering collaborations to better support the veteran and military communities.

2. *State department of veterans' affairs.* In addition to federal veterans' benefits and services, states offer their own support for members of the veteran and military communities (U.S. Department of Veterans Affairs, 2016a). These are coordinated by the state's department of veterans' affairs and can vary widely from one state to another. Some states offer such benefits and services as tuition assistance, housing assistance, and even special programs with the DMV. The state department of veterans' affairs also prioritizes the registration of veterans with the VA, as each veteran who registers with the VA increases federal funding for that state's VA system. Public libraries should be knowledgeable of the benefits offered by the state for its veterans.

For-profit organizations. Public librarians interested in supporting the military and veteran communities may also benefit from seeking collaborations with local businesses, nearby franchise locations, and corporations, especially if the corporation has prioritized hiring veterans or military spouses. Each community includes a unique range of these organizations, and choosing the right partner organizations relies heavily on institutional context, priorities, and goals. Therefore, this section will not suggest individual organizations or businesses but will instead suggest types of for-profit organizations that librarians can seek and why.

1. *Local business leaders.* Some local business leaders may have personal experience in the military or have taken the initiative to prioritize charity work and volunteering for the veteran and military communities. Librarians responsible for outreach can identify which businesses are the best match for any events, programs, or other projects planned in support of the veteran and military communities. As part of their normal outreach routine, librarians can ask business owners whether they have experience in the military or family members who have served in the military. If librarians are unsure about which businesses in the community are interested in efforts to work with veteran and military communities, a quick review of the board members of a veteran's museum or similar organization can give librarians some ideas of where to start. Librarians should also remember that although business leaders who have some connection to the military may be more likely to be invested in the veteran and military communities, business leaders who have no military ties can also be important advocates for these communities and collaborators with the library. For example, a local bank might be interested in partnering with the library to sponsor financial literacy workshops targeting military families, or new restaurants in the area that are eager to attract new customers may be happy to donate coupons to a library information fair. Although a local business leader's military

background can be a good starting point for a conversation about a collaboration, there may be many business leaders in the area that would be willing to assist or partner with the library on a new initiative.

2. *Corporations.* In addition to locally owned businesses, major corporations with offices or franchises in the library community may be interested in working with the library on efforts to assist the veteran and military communities. When researching potential partnering corporations with offices in the area, librarians can learn whether board members or executives have served in the military by reading their profiles on their corporations' websites. VSOs may also be able to share with the public library what they know about corporations that are supportive of their efforts. Some corporations, though already contributing to other nonprofit ventures, may still be interested in adding to the diversity of their charitable activities. Even if they are unable to increase their financial contributions to local efforts, their representatives may be willing to serve as advisers to librarians working with veteran and military communities.

Veterans service organizations. In addition to communicating with local business owners and corporate executives, public librarians can also benefit by learning about the many nonprofit organizations already working in the community. Librarians should consider developing relationships with nonprofit organizations that focus on meeting the needs of the veteran and military communities, as well as general nonprofit organizations that specialize in providing resources to the public.

Most nonprofit veterans' organizations that are recognized by Congress and have chapters throughout the country are referred to as certified veterans service organizations (VSOs). Although Congress uses the term *veterans* service organization, some of these organizations focus their efforts on serving the needs of military service members or their families. VSOs are often some of the most efficient and effective organizations helping veteran and military communities today and provide a wide variety of different services for veterans, service members, and their families. For example, some have legal counselors who assist veterans with their appeals for disability claims. Others organize charitable events throughout the year.

Additionally, some VSOs specialize in serving service members and their families. For example, the United Service Organizations (USO) provides services and resources to support the morale of deployed troops in addition to services and supplies for service members while they are traveling. They often have a chapter with office space and a designated space for military service personnel in airports and cities where military personnel must travel to get to a training location (United Service Organizations, 2016). Still other VSOs focus on the needs of other members of the veteran and military communities, such as Blue Star Families, which began by serving the mothers of troops deployed overseas but has now evolved to serve all active-duty military personnel and their families (Blue Star Families, 2016). In addition to the services and programs that VSOs offer, many VSOs are also extremely important as a social outlet for organization members. Examples of VSOs include the Disabled American Veterans (DAV), Paralyzed

Veterans of American (PVA), Veterans of Foreign Wars (VFW), and Vietnam Veterans of America (VVA).

VSOs vary depending on community interests and demographics. Each community will find a different level of interest and support for VSOs with chapters or locations nearby. For example, a library in central California quickly learned that due to a high population of Vietnam veterans living in the area, the most active VSO in the community was Vietnam Veterans of America. Although they had originally planned to collaborate with a different VSO, they adapted their plans after learning that they were more likely to successfully reach veterans in their community by partnering with Vietnam Veterans of America. In contrast, a library in one neighborhood of San Diego County found that Veterans of Foreign Wars and Veteran Villages of America were the most active nearby VSOs.

Librarians can use national databases such as the National Resource Directory to explore and locate many different VSOs. Because there are so many VSOs and their information can change quickly, however, sometimes these resources may not contain the most up-to-date information (Cisco, D., personal communication, April 29, 2016). Thus, librarians may benefit from working closely with a CVSO or a regional liaison for the state department of veterans' affairs to locate and connect with the most active VSOs in their communities.

Libraries can be active collaborators with many different VSOs, working with VSO representatives to identify and develop programming that furthers the goals and missions of both the library and the VSO. For example, it can be challenging for some VSOs to find public meeting space for veteran and military-related support groups. The public library may be able to provide space for such support groups, thus making them more easily accessible for library patrons. As always, librarians can learn through the outreach process about the VSO and identify goals that the library and VSO may have in common.

Although there are many different organizations with which librarians can partner to better support the veteran and military communities, there are some organizations with which librarians may want to avoid collaborating. There are a few strategies that librarians can employ to avoid mistakenly partnering with an organization with a less than stellar record. One important strategy is to coordinate library outreach to the veteran and military communities and the development of any new projects with a CVSO or veterans service representative (VSR). The CVSO is likely to have a good understanding of the landscape of organizations serving veterans, service members, and their families and can assist librarians in learning about any problems that might be found with an organization. A CVSO may be aware, for example, if a VSO has had blemishes on its record in the past. Although CVSOs may not be able to prevent librarians from any potential missteps, working closely with a CVSO should at least guide a librarian in learning what to look for in a reputable VSO. Another helpful strategy is to review websites that monitor the financial reports of nonprofit organizations.

Charity Navigator, for example, provides data about organizations that have a poor reputation in terms of leadership or finances ("Charity Navigator," 2016).

Library Outreach and Programming for Veteran and Military Communities

Connecting with advocates, individuals with insight or personal experience, and organizations that serve veterans and military personnel is essential to understanding the full range of possibilities for public libraries. In addition to recruiting advisers and connecting with the types of organizations described above, public libraries can improve services and resources for everyone in the community by offering a range of events and programs that correspond to their needs. This section offers recommendations on how a public library can begin or improve events and programming that help to communicate to veterans and military personnel, as well as the people who care about them, that the public library welcomes their patronage.

Low-Cost Solutions

If the public library is unable to work with outside organizations to coordinate new programs or services, it is still possible to show an interest in the veteran and military communities by implementing several low-cost solutions.

A website for veteran and military-affiliated patrons. One simple strategy librarians can employ is to develop a simple web page on the library's website. Ideally located in the "services" or "resources" section of a public library website, a web page can list crisis hotlines, the phone number to local VA facilities, locations of VA facilities, and directions to get there via public transit. If the nearest VA facilities provide any transportation assistance, that contact information can also be listed. Other contacts to add could be the nearest military library, a link to Military OneSource, contact information for the CVSO, contact information for the state's department of veterans' affairs, and links to chapters of VSOs that are active in the area. The most important rules in offering a web page for veterans on a public library website is to make sure it is easy to navigate, accessible to all users, and features at least the most basic information about local VA and military resources. The benefit of creating an online guide specific for library patrons with military or veteran experience is that librarians can also use the same web page as a resource when responding to reference questions. As the library's services and programs for veterans and service members grow, this guide can also be a place to feature upcoming events or a place to highlight the library's strategic partners in serving the veteran and military communities.

Many examples of web pages designed for veterans and military families can be found online, particularly in states with higher populations of veterans, such as California, Florida, and Texas. Below are listed some examples of LibGuides that efficiently and effectively gather resources to support their veteran and military-affiliated patrons.

- The New Hanover County Public Library's Support for Veterans LibGuide: http://libguides.nhclibrary.org/supportvets

  This guide is formatted with simplicity in mind and is easy to navigate both for veterans and for military families living in the area. One of the strengths of this LibGuide, as the viewer scrolls down, is multiple tabs of resources created for each branch of service. The LibGuide offers links to representatives of state and federal veterans' affairs offices. The viewer can also find a public service announcement from a VSO as well as a helpful video tutorial about finding military records created by the National Archives.

- Atlantic City Free Public Library's Veterans' Resources LibGuide: http://acfpl.libguides.com/veterans

  This LibGuide offers links to the VA Center for Minority Veterans, local resources, and the Make the Connection website, which features personal video testimonials by veterans for veterans with links to other resources at the VA.

Meeting space for veterans. Another low-cost option is to offer space in the public library where veterans can gather and even meet with representatives of a VSO. Although this type of program does not require a significant outlay of funds, it does require that the library have space that it can allocate, sometimes on a regular basis. The success of this type of program largely depends on the level of interest among veterans who already use the library as well as whether coordination with a local VSO is possible. If the library coordinates the effort with the chapter of a VSO already active in the area, it will have a participant base upon which to build. However, if the library has an interested group of veterans who are already library patrons, they may be able to develop programming, even without a VSO sponsor. For example, some public libraries advertise a monthly "coffee hour" when all veterans in the community can gather in a public space for free coffee and donuts (City of Commerce Public Library, 2011). And the Sedona Public Library hosts a weekly coffee event where trained volunteers meet with veterans to record their stories for the Veterans History Project (Pierson, 2015). This type of event can also be used as a starting point for librarians to learn more about the veterans who take an interest in socializing with one another. Based on what librarians learn from a coffee conversation or a routine meeting scheduled for a local VSO, they can apply that knowledge to create enhanced programs, recruit veterans to become advisers to the library on veteran and military issues, and even gain new collection development ideas from the veterans in attendance.

Library Programs and Services for the Veteran and Military Communities

In addition to the low-cost programs described above, the public library can collaborate with sponsors and VSOs to develop programs and events that will appeal to a larger audience and could be planned on a larger scale. Although each veteran, service member, and family member is a unique individual, libraries can develop programs that are intended to meet common needs within the veteran and military communities. This section provides some common public library services and programs that librarians can consider implementing, although they should work with known veteran and military-affiliated patrons, local VSOs, and other connections developed through outreach efforts to help identify which programs and services would be most useful to the veterans and service members in their local areas.

For many of the recommendations that follow, librarians should plan to find at least one partner. The partnering organization need not sponsor the activity, but it is vital to connect, and stay connected, with organizations already serving veterans or military personnel when planning programs such as these. Without close coordination, the library may unknowingly repeat the efforts of another organization. The library's event may also conflict with an event by another organization. Combining efforts with another organization ensures that the library maximizes the outreach of the event. It also reassures the community that the library is not acting alone, but is matching the event with the articulated needs of the veteran and military communities. It also communicates the idea that the public library is complementing the work of other organizations and not duplicating their efforts. The future of relevant public libraries who are engaged in the interests and needs of community leaders and residents in the neighborhood will depend on successful collaboration with organizations already established in the area.

Although many of the program and event ideas in this section are large scale and may require collaboration with a VSO or other organization, librarians should bear in mind that these are only suggestions. The scale and scope of such a program depends on a variety of factors, including the size of the veteran and military communities in the local area, the resources available in the library, the availability of partnerships, and whether the library is just getting started or has long-standing experience providing library services for veteran and military-affiliated patrons. Librarians should remember to consider their own organizational context and consider ways that a suggested program or event could be scaled up or down or modified to fit the unique needs of their own communities.

Office hours in the public library. Several events and projects throughout the country represent an effort to offer veterans access to the enhanced services that a reference librarian might not always have the time to provide. One effort, begun by public libraries in Chula Vista and Escondido, California, has been to provide meeting rooms for VA representatives to meet with veterans at designated times (Briar, 2011; City of Chula Vista, n.d.). These representatives are not volunteers, librarians, or representatives of a VSO, but certified representatives of the VA. The VA considers the discussion of a veteran's eligibility for specific benefits, based on specific information and using the official eligibility criteria of the VA, to be a legal activity. Librarians are therefore limited in what they can tell a veteran or how extensively they can help a veteran with a specific claim. Only a veterans service representative (VSR), trained for several months by the VA, is qualified and permitted to process a veteran's military records and enter a veteran's data into the VA system where the veteran's benefits eligibility and appropriate level of benefits is decided. In Chula Vista and Escondido, therefore, office space was provided for people who had achieved status as VSRs. Public libraries that can offer meeting space for a VSR or similar representative are in high demand by the veteran community. This is because the public library is often the only place outside of the home where a veteran who has not been registered with the VA would typically go to seek information. It is a natural setting and an ideal venue for VSRs and other organizations to reconnect with veterans.

Office Hours: Veterans Connect @ the Library

California libraries have collaborated with the California State Department of Veterans Affairs (CalVet) to build upon the idea of library office hours and offer an enhanced version called Veterans Connect @ the Library. This program is funded by an IMLS/LSTA grant and provides training, promotional materials, and other resources to public libraries that sign an agreement to offer a suite of services as part of the program. One required service is establishing a meeting room or similar private meeting space in the public library where veterans can meet with CalVet volunteers. The volunteers receive extensive training by CalVet focused on cultural competencies, paperwork processes, and issues important to veterans in California. Once trained, volunteers assist veterans in the public library with the process of registering with the VA in California. They also offer information about specific veterans' benefits. However, because these volunteers are embedded in the library on a long-term basis, they also have the opportunity to build trust with veterans who may be reluctant to ask for help. For example, one volunteer explained how a veteran visited the resource center each week, just to talk. It was only after several weeks of conversations that the veteran asked for help with a résumé (Magente, personal communication, June 9, 2015). Although it took some time for the Veterans Connect @ the Library volunteers to build trust with library patrons, eventually they were able to help veterans in the area find employment opportunities, apply for housing assistance, and register for medical services. Veterans Connect @ the Library provides a website with information that can be used by other states to apply for similar funding so the project's ideas can be duplicated by any library throughout the country ("Veterans Connect @ the Library," 2016).

Although many veterans would be happy to start over with the VA after having had a bad experience previously, many other veterans want nothing to do with the VA because of problems they experienced either with medical care or a disappointing disability compensation claim. In an article featuring "Office Hours" at the Boise Public Library, Bill Roscoe, a Vietnam veteran and president of a local rescue program, explained that many veterans still regard the VA with mistrust after their difficulties in VA hospitals throughout the 1970s (Webb, 2016). To combat this mistrust, a VSR offers office hours every week at the Boise Public Library. This VSR, Bryan Bumgarner, meets with veterans to explain what help is available and that many services that may have not been available in previous decades are available now. In one case, he helped a veteran who was living in his car and paying $400 a month for prescription medication file paperwork to receive free health care from the VA (Webb, 2016).

In addition to VSRs, VSOs throughout the country are also eager to assist veterans with many types of efforts, including filing an appeal for a disability claim, learning about benefits and resources provided by other organizations, and seeking a sense of community by becoming a member of the organization. VSOs, however, often must seek office space in places that are difficult to find, inaccessible by wheelchair, or simply not as centrally located as the public library. Public libraries have an opportunity to extend the outreach potential of both the VA and VSOs that are interested in meeting one-on-one with veterans in a public library setting. The first step toward coordinating this type of project is to learn what space could be used in the library for veterans to participate in confidential meetings. Some libraries have used floor screens, bookshelves, and other types of barriers to create an enclosed space where two people can talk without being overheard. Other libraries already have study rooms or conference rooms that veterans can use. Most organizations that want to offer office hours in the public library also require some desk space where a representative can fill out forms. In some cases, where dedicated space has been set aside on a daily basis, the library can seek grant funding to provide a laptop, access to the Internet, or even a fax machine. In this case, the goal is not to provide an entire office but to provide office hours, usually at the same time each week or month, but only on one day at one time each week or month. The office hours recommendation is particularly helpful in communities where veterans may have difficulty getting to a VA facility by public transit or where a VSO is particularly eager to connect with veterans in the public library.

Financial literacy programs. Financial literacy programs have become popular in many public libraries in recent years, especially during Money Smart Week (American Library Association, 2016). Because the financial situation of military service members has some unique characteristics, including the complications inherent in managing a family budget and bills while a family member is away for military training or deployed, some libraries have developed financial literacy programs aimed directly at the needs of military families. For example, the San Diego Public Library partnered with several other organizations on a grant from the Smart Investing @ Your Library program to develop financial literacy programs and workshops tailored to meet the needs of military families (Smart Investing @ Your Library, n.d.).

Employment search programs. Another program that public libraries may consider developing for veterans, service members, and their families is a workshop on job-hunting resources. Because the military is the first and only job held by many service members, they may be unfamiliar with even the basics of the civilian job hunt. Although the military's programs for transitioning veterans include information about résumé development and job-hunting strategies, the transition period is so stressful and busy that separating service members may not fully absorb this advice. These programs may also include outdated advice, such as suggestions that women veterans should be sure to wear a skirt in an interview to appear professional. For these reasons, newly separated veterans may find themselves ill-equipped to conduct a job search in the civilian world. Public librarians can help veterans, whether they have recently left the military or left decades ago, learn how to present themselves in an interview, craft a résumé that highlights transferable skills they learned in the military and avoids jargon, and develop strategies for finding jobs in a particular field or area. Librarians may find a potential partner for such programs in the state veterans' association, which often has a segment devoted to veteran employment.

Veteran and military writing workshops. Some veterans and service members can find it cathartic to write stories about their military experiences. By converting their experiences to fictional or nonfictional accounts, they share some of the bizarre, humorous, or memorable aspects of military service, and, in some cases, they may be able to begin to make sense of some of the tragedies that they may have encountered. Many public libraries have begun offering writers' groups for veterans and service members to encourage them to share their stories with one another and, in some cases, to add their stories to the written record from which future generations can learn. Some libraries may partner with such organizations as the Veterans Writing Project to get started, while others may rely on locals with writing expertise, especially if they have military experience themselves (Veterans Writing Project, n.d.; Witthaus, 2015).

Spotlight on veterans and service members. Another common way public librarians support veterans and service members is by developing programs that highlight the service and sacrifices of those who serve in the military. For example, the Salt Lake City Public Library frequently offers a panel discussion featuring local veterans and service members in the time period around Veterans Day (Moulton, 2013). Other librarians have also developed innovative strategies to help younger generations understand the service and sacrifices of those who came before them. Librarians at the Amesbury Public Library in Massachusetts created a Call of Duty: Amesbury club for teenagers that engages them in scavenger hunts and strategy games along military themes. This club also invites members of the military and veteran communities to come share their experiences with the teens (Fesko, 2013). By developing programs that recognize veterans and service members, librarians can make it readily apparent to the public that the library is a space where military service is respected. Such programs can also provide the very first opportunity for some veterans to share their experiences publicly without fear of being shamed or harassed for having served in the military.

Veterans History Project. Another way that librarians can recognize and engage veterans is by participating in the Library of Congress' Veterans History Project. This project was created with slightly different guidelines than those used for formal oral history projects. A Veterans History Project, for example, may not require its volunteers to be as schooled in oral history archival techniques as would the principal investigator of a project led by a major university department. Nevertheless, the goals are the same. The Veterans History Project is an effort to acquire as many testimonials from U.S. veterans of all generations as possible before they pass away and their unique observations are lost forever (Library of Congress, 2016a). The interviews and artifacts acquired by the Veterans History Project contribute to the country's archive of data, offering alternatives to the textbook descriptions of military conflict and military experiences learned by students in a classroom setting. Like many oral history projects, the interviews also add to our knowledge of the experiences of people who are sometimes overlooked in creating an official history.

The Library of Congress provides toolkits and guidelines for anyone in the community to interview veterans on an individual basis or through collaboration with another organization (Library of Congress, 2016b). They include essentials, such as how to gain permission from the interviewee and ensuring that the rights of the interviewee are respected in any oral history interview. Other guidelines explain how volunteers and librarians should recruit interviewees, prepare space and equipment in advance, and document the content of the interview so that it can be properly cataloged by the Library of Congress when it is submitted.

The scope of a particular library's involvement with the Veterans History Project can vary widely. Because the people who interview veterans are usually volunteers, the number of interviewers and the time they dedicate to the project can depend on how invested the local community is in preserving the stories of their veterans. The amount of funding a library can dedicate to this project can also vary based on the library's budget, and librarians who seek to host a Veterans History Project in their libraries are encouraged to explore opportunities for grant funding, sponsorships, or other types of support through their own networks.

Public librarians have a wide variety of options when determining how to implement the Veterans History Project in their own libraries. For example, some public libraries may seek merely to provide space for family members in the community to interview veterans and prepare materials for the Veterans History Project. Other libraries may create a different scope, such as focusing on a particular topic or experience. Most projects are led and coordinated by volunteers, and the library merely provides space, guidance, and sometimes equipment. Each library can select a scope, partners, and funding based on the priorities of the library and a partnering organization. The only areas where there is no flexibility is in observing the rights of the interviewee and in using the proper procedures for documenting interviews to submit them and any accompanying artifacts to the Library of Congress.

Book or film clubs. It should come as no surprise to suggest that the public library could host book clubs as an effort to serve veterans and military personnel. The book club can focus less on books, however, and more on the opportunity for the members to socialize and benefit from interacting with one another. Even a film club can be created for veterans and service members who share an interest in various genres of film. Librarians should not assume, however, that veterans and service members will want to read about the war experience or transitioning out of the military. Having experienced war in person, some veterans and service members are reluctant to revisit difficult memories by reading a book on the same topic. Instead, the books or movies selected for this type of social activity should simply encourage social interaction. In some cases, a book or film club can strengthen a sense of community among subgroups of veterans and service members who may have similar interests. In other cases, a book or film club provides all members of a community with a venue to bridge the divide between civilians and the veteran and military communities.

One way to appeal to both the veteran and military communities and civilians is to choose a book about ordinary people who also happen to have military experiences. For example, *Unbroken* by Laura Hillenbrand focuses on the experiences of an individual before and after his military service. Members of a book club discussing *Unbroken* could explore issues related to the civilian-military cultural divide, but it could also focus on other themes in the book, such as aging. Book or film clubs created for veterans or military service members and their families should offer selections that do not focus entirely on the military experience, as the goal of this type of activity is primarily to foster and strengthen the sense of community between those who do and do not have military experience.

Book Club Example 1. Statewide One Book Project: War Comes Home

In 2014, the California Center for the Book, in coordination with Cal Humanities, invited libraries throughout the region to participate in a statewide common reader program related to the military experience. The One Read Program was titled "War Comes Home" and featured *What It's Like to Go to War* by Karl Marlantes (California Humanities, 2016). This program is one example in which the idea for the original program was expanded when several organizations and the grant funders recognized common goals. Although it began as a literacy initiative, an ongoing traveling exhibit and program were added to the project. As a result, the website and exhibit materials not only offered book discussion guidelines but also included recorded interviews with veterans and their families. Cal Humanities facilitated the extensive project in an effort to not only assist communities in starting a discussion about the cultural divide between military and nonmilitary families but also to use its archive of interviews to feature the full diversity of perspectives among veterans who served in the military in different eras.

Many libraries applied for funding from the National Endowment for the Humanities to host the exhibit, an author visit, a book discussion, and materials for the display and promotion of the project. The project highlighted how different generations of veterans experienced war and offered the public an opportunity to review archived materials from the home front of previous U.S. wars. In so doing, the project inspired a wide range of people to become more engaged in community efforts to understand the military-civilian cultural divide. Others responded to the project by recruiting new veterans to share their stories throughout the Library of Congress' Veterans History Project. Cal Humanities interviewed additional veterans throughout the summer of 2014. The exhibit of letters and other materials are still available online, as well as on loan to interested parties, thanks to a partnership with Exhibit Envoy (California Humanities, 2016).

Book Club Example 2. Military Teen Summer Reading Club

During her outreach efforts for the San Diego Public Library, Kristen learned of one successful initiative by the branch library where she worked. The Point Loma/Hervey Branch Library, one of 36 locations of the San Diego Public Library, collaborated with the Navy Fleet & Family Support Center to host a summer reading book club for military teens in 2010. The Navy had recently finished building a major housing area for military families near the Point Loma/Hervey Branch Library. As a result, the library manager saw an opportunity to reach out to coordinators of local organizations that provided assistance to these military families. One result of her outreach efforts was to provide space in the library for a new summer reading club for military teens. Each week, members of the book club met at the library to discuss their reading. The library provided several study rooms after each meeting where the teenagers could, upon request, meet with certified counselors to talk about issues or challenges related to their experiences growing up in a military family.

Since the success of the military teen book club, the Point Loma/ Hervey Branch Library has continued to collaborate with the Fleet & Family Support Center to provide meeting room space for various events as needed. The branch manager has networked with school liaison officers, VSOs, the local veteran advisory group, and the San Diego Military Family Collaborative to stay informed about how the public library can continue to offer services and programs to military families in the area. For example, the library also offers meeting rooms for Family Readiness Groups (FRGs) of various military units. Their members periodically meet in the library while their children participate in library events. Representatives have mentioned that the public library is the only place they have been able to find where their support groups, book clubs, and other committees are able to find adequate space to meet without paying a large deposit or competing with weddings and other events (Ferrer, B., personal communication, November 13, 2015).

Collaborative exhibits and community dialogue. Public libraries are also an ideal venue for offering programs and exhibits that will help a community start a dialogue about the military-civilian cultural divide. Rebekah Sanderlin, an Army wife who has written and spoken about her experiences as a military spouse, once wrote about how her children had never known a world where mommies and daddies did not go to war (All Things Considered, 2009). She and other advocates strive to educate others about the cultural divide between military families and civilian families. Sanderlin suggested, for example, that children in military families think of their world, where the country has been at war since before they were born, differently from how children of civilian families think of their world, where war is usually much farther away (Sanderlin, 2011). Many public libraries have participated in projects to educate both children and adults about these differences in an effort to bridge this cultural divide.

Most communities have war memorials or a veteran museum, and the exhibits they share offer a glimpse into the military world. Public librarians can assist with bridging the cultural divide by starting a collaboration with the caretakers of a museum or memorial. Veteran and military museums and even VSOs may have more artifacts than can be displayed in their exhibit spaces, and they may be willing to lend some of these artifacts to the library as part of a military-themed display. Some libraries already have permanent or annual exhibits to honor local veterans. For example, San Diego's Coronado Public Library features a veteran-oriented exhibit on permanent display. Other public libraries choose to honor war veterans with a memorial at the entrance to the building. In addition to these permanent exhibits, libraries can collaborate with military museums to create temporary exhibits in the library that highlight different topics related to veterans' history. Arranging for military museums or VSOs to lend artifacts for exhibits in the public library can be a starting point for many libraries to build partnerships with other organizations and raise awareness about the veterans in the community and the cultural divide between civilian and military families.

Exhibits Example: War Ink

In one case, a public library found an opportunity to transcend the traditional boundaries of an exhibit to create a multimedia project that is now funded by the National Endowment for the Arts as a national traveling exhibit with an interactive website. War Ink was begun by Chris Brown, now the deputy director of the Santa Clara Public Library, and Jason Deitch, now a professional consultant and advocate for veterans. Brown and Deitch collaborated on several projects as part of Brown's participation in a leadership academy. Their goal was to identify younger veterans in the community and create new programs that corresponded to the interests and needs of veterans of Iraq and Afghanistan. They partnered to implement several ideas for working with veterans in their area south of San Francisco. For example, they recruited veterans from throughout the country to share their stories about how and why they chose to get tattoos. Brown and Deitch arranged for Storycorps to interview the veterans about their military experiences in addition to their experiences leaving the military. They combined the images of veterans' tattoo art with their video testimonials, and the result became War Ink.

Now an interactive website, War Ink also features materials to educate visitors about military culture, the veteran community, and how the public library is able to play a role in supporting the veteran and military communities. The project includes observations by the veterans about their conflicted feelings of honor, disappointment, pride, and hope in having served in the military after 9/11. The project is continuing to evolve as more veterans have offered to share their stories. More information about the exhibit is available online at http://www.warink.org/about.html ("War Ink," 2014).

It might not be readily apparent how an exhibit or museum can personally benefit veterans and service members. With this in mind, Kristen can describe a visit she made to a veteran museum several years ago. At the time, she was experiencing feelings of isolation among non-veteran friends. Current events had triggered some difficult memories from her military service. Serendipitously, she was invited by a relative to accompany him to see an exhibit about women veterans at a museum in town. Upon entering the museum, she immediately recognized artifacts from recent and previous eras of conflict.

Kristen was surprised at the feeling of connectedness she received from examining the clothing items and artifacts that had been part of different service members' experiences in different eras. While she was looking at one item on display, a volunteer approached her to ask if she had served in the military. She was initially surprised at being asked because most friends and coworkers had never thought of her as someone who might have served in the military at one time. Yet this stranger, another veteran, somehow recognized her as someone who was a veteran, too. They spoke, initially with some caution, so as not to distract the other visitors. After a few minutes, however, Kristen felt a tremendous sense of relief to be able to exchange stories with the other veteran. They even had an opportunity to talk about the current events that had triggered difficult memories for her. She learned that this veteran, almost 30 years older than she, had been to some of the same places where she had served. She also learned that he benefited from volunteering at the museum and being able to interact with other veterans.

Eventually, Kristen began to volunteer at a local library, now understanding that the act of volunteering gave her a chance to feel like she had a sense of purpose for the first time since leaving the military. Since that interaction, she realized that she had learned more from other veterans, through word of mouth, about coping with issues after leaving the military and seeking resources than she had ever learned when she initially asked for information after leaving the Army more than 10 years earlier.

Care package events. A powerful way to engage the community in understanding the civilian and military cultural divide is to host events where both civilians and military families can interact with one another. Book clubs, as discussed previously, are one example of an event like this. Another type of event would be the preparation of care packages or letters for deployed troops. Many public libraries have already had success hosting care package events, especially those located near military installations. Folsom Public Library in California and Melrose Park Library in Illinois are two recent examples (Folsom Community Service Day, n.d.; Melrose Park Public Library, 2016).

An important factor in planning a care package event is to collaborate with the right partner, as many organizations offer valuable advice on how to prepare and send care packages so as to not overwhelm the military mail system (Pharr, 2013; United Service Organizations, 2014). Military family support organizations such as Blue Star Families and the USO can be good potential partners for many public libraries. Current library visitors and those who live in the community, however, should be consulted when selecting a partnering organization for this type of activity. In communities with parents of service members, for example, the parents who participate in an event like this may already belong to an organization and may want that organization to participate.

Care Package Event Example: Blue Star Families

Blue Star Families has long had a reputation for organizing care package events, often coordinated with the help of a public library, because many of their members are the spouses or parents of service members deployed overseas. Members of Blue Star Families and similar VSOs often have expertise in how care packages are best assembled and mailed. Libraries may wish to limit their involvement in a care package program to one aspect of the care package assembly, especially if they are uncertain as to how many people will participate the first time such an event is attempted. For example, the library could start off its involvement in care package programs by simply providing a place for people to bring donated items. Librarians should make sure to coordinate a wish list for donated items with their partner organization, however, or many unwanted items may have to be discarded. Depending on the interest level of the people in the community and the availability of space and time for this type of event, librarians might also consider providing space for an external organization to assemble care packages for a designated unit that is deployed.

When considering this type of program, librarians must also make sure that the library's parent organization does not have any regulations that would prohibit soliciting donations on behalf of another organization. Some city and county governments may have strict rules about how a library can raise funds or solicit donations on its own behalf or on behalf of any other organization. That is why it is helpful to know alternative ways to participate, such as offering space to assemble care packages instead of soliciting donated items. Care package events are a great opportunity for the public library to encourage civilian families and military families to socialize in the same setting in an effort to bridge cultural barriers.

USO charity events. Although a care package program for troops overseas is very popular, if the library serves a community where there is an international airport or military installation, the community may also be interested in an event in the public library in support of the United Service Organizations (USO). The USO is most famous for sending Bob Hope and other celebrities overseas to entertain the troops. Many librarians may be unfamiliar, however, with the vital role that the USO plays to assist troops during their travel. For example, many airports have a designated USO space where service members traveling from one location to another can stay while waiting for their next flight. Depending on the space, the USO might provide napping stations, showers, books, DVDs, food, pool tables, or other amenities. The specific amenities of a USO depend in large part on the coordination and funding of the local chapter president. In addition to airport locations, some USO chapters provide similar rest stations within a city where it might be necessary for service members to leave the airport and catch a bus to reach their training location. USO locations in metropolitan areas can provide similar amenities to airport locations, in addition to comfort items such as coupons for a meal, home-cooked meals provided by local residents, and toiletries. As with the care package event, public libraries can work with a USO chapter to coordinate a range of programs to gather donations for deployed troops, assemble care packages, or host events in partnership with the USO leadership.

The Stand Down and other information fairs. *Stand down* is a military command ordering troops to stop fighting and put their weapons in a resting position. This term was used in 1988 at the first of what would become an annual event to assist homeless veterans. The 1988 Stand Down and subsequent Stand Downs have focused on providing veterans with assistance in accessing services from the VA and other organizations (Veterans Village of San Diego, 2016). Examples of services provided during a Stand

Down include assisting veterans with paperwork for a VA disability claim, offering dental care and a haircut, providing several items of new clothing, and hosting numerous booths where veterans can register for additional services or attend other events. The Stand Down allows veterans to reconnect, or connect for the first time, with the VA, VSOs, and the many social services organizations that participate in the event. Today, the federal government offers grants to nonprofit organizations interested in creating a Stand Down in their city (U.S. Department of Labor. Veterans' Employment & Training Service, n.d.). Over the past five years, libraries have increased their efforts to attend, support, or volunteer for Stand Down events throughout the country.

It is important for public librarians to understand the difference between a Stand Down and other types of events. For example, the Stand Down differs from an information fair in some key ways. The Stand Down is a federally funded event that requires certain accommodations in terms of its duration, location, and services. The Stand Down is usually hosted and organized by the VA or a VSO in coordination with the VA. And homeless veterans can have preconceived notions of what to expect when they hear about a Stand Down in any community. In contrast, an information fair can be any type of event hosted by the public library or another organization. It might be just as large as a Stand Down, but it does not necessarily serve only homeless veterans. An information fair can last a few hours or a few days, depending on the scope of the event and its sponsors.

Stand Downs: Successes among Public Libraries

Because the Stand Down event is now so popular, it has become an opportunity for public libraries to offer their help as well. Some libraries simply allow employees to take paid time off to volunteer at a Stand Down event. Other libraries recruit employees to work as representatives of the library, beginning with hosting a booth at the event where veterans can apply for a library card. Other libraries engage in the event with the spirit of guerilla warriors, deploying librarians to volunteer for other organizations while bringing applications for library cards to veterans while they stand in line. Chris Brown and the Contra Costa County Library, for example, have not only succeeded in this proactive approach but have also provided training materials for all public librarians interested in taking the same approach via the Veterans Connect @ the Library website ("Veterans Connect @ the Library," 2016). Specifically, the Contra Costa County Library dispatched volunteers to help veterans register for library cards. Volunteers from the library sought veterans while they were waiting in line at various locations during the Stand Down. The volunteers helped the veterans with paperwork to register for new library cards and then turned in the paperwork to the library's booth to have the applications processed. The volunteers then tracked down the veterans to hand deliver the brand-new library cards, promotional materials about the library, and sometimes free books that were donated for the event (Brown, C., personal communication, October 24, 2013).

Similarly, the San Diego Public Library collaborated with the coordinators of the Stand Down in San Diego to assist Veterans Village in preparing for the event. San Diego's Veterans Village needed to create a more organized system for preparing for a growing number of attendees. They decided to distribute Stand Down paperwork to trained representatives, many of whom were volunteers who worked at various library locations throughout the county. Each set of paperwork was marked with an identification number to track where it originated. Posters listing the San Diego libraries and other organizations where veterans could register to attend the Stand Down were hung at shelters and other locations. Any library listed on the poster was required to have a trained employee available during all business hours to meet with any homeless veterans, confidentially, to assist them in filling out the paperwork. By registering veterans in advance, San Diego's Stand Down could ensure that all supplies, shelters, and other logistics were coordinated to meet the high demand. The San Diego Public Library offered three locations where veterans could register for the Stand Down in advance. Library volunteers and employees also registered to volunteer for the event, both to promote the library and also to assist as needed throughout the Stand Down Weekend in San Diego (Gonzalez, personal communication, June 23, 2016).

These are two examples of libraries thinking not only about the people who are already using the library but also about the people who have not yet used the library. Librarians interested in assisting other veteran groups can participate in a local Stand Down, or they can also work with VSOs and other organizations in the community to organize an information fair. Some nonprofit organizations specialize in advising veterans who are starting small businesses and may be interested in cohosting a small business resource fair for veterans. Many organizations host job or career fairs or seminars and workshops about financial literacy. By hosting some of these events, public libraries can help veterans and military service members connect with new resources, learn more information, and meet organization representatives while appreciating the benefits of socializing with other veterans in the library.

Many of the examples offered in this section have been based on program ideas implemented in California. Although California has one of the largest veteran populations in the country, libraries outside of California are also achieving similar successes. The Maryland Department of Veterans Affairs, for example, has just begun a partnership with public libraries where several programs are underway (Caroline County Public Library, 2016). In Illinois, the Aurora Public Library is promoting the Veterans History Project (Aurora Public Library, 2016). West Florida Public Libraries announced a series of outreach events at various branch locations to offer a review of veterans' benefits provided by the VA and the State of Florida (My Escambia, 2016). The Chapel Hill Public Library, in partnership with the North Carolina Humanities Council and several other states, began a book group to host small monthly meetings among combat veterans (North Carolina Humanities Council, 2016). State librarians throughout the country have also begun to prioritize educating library employees about cultural competencies issues related to veterans and military service members by offering online webinars. The Virginia Library Association, for example, partnered with the State of Virginia Department of Veterans Services to coordinate online educational materials for librarians (Virginia Library Association, 2016).

The outreach success of librarians and libraries across the country demonstrate that, no matter where they live, members of the veteran and military communities may be in need of targeted outreach, services, and programs, and librarians can use the strategies in this chapter as a starting point for developing outreach to the veterans, service members, and family members in their communities.

Dos and Don'ts for Working with Veterans and Military Populations

In addition to providing outreach, programs, and services to the veteran and military communities, public librarians will be working with the members of these communities one-on-one as well. To best serve veteran and military-affiliated patrons, librarians should be familiar with some of the basic dos and don'ts of working with the veteran and military communities. These dos and don'ts are intended to be general rules of thumb to help librarians avoid common pitfalls. Nevertheless, because all veterans and service members are unique, they may not be applicable to all veteran and military-affiliated patrons. Librarians should also be aware that although some of this advice overlaps with the dos and don'ts offered in other chapters, these are some areas that are particularly relevant to public librarians working with veteran and military communities.

Don't: Assume all veterans will be interested in a public library event that is designed for veterans. Some veterans wish to distance themselves from their military experiences. Often, this distance can indicate that the veteran is focusing on a new phase of their life. For example, they may have a new career in a field that suits them in a way that military life may not have. However, many other veterans do derive support and social opportunities through participation in veteran-oriented programming, memberships in VSOs, or visiting a Vet Center.

Do: Be willing to speak up if you are a library employee and a veteran. Some veterans may be visiting the library for the first time, or they may feel uncomfortable in a library environment. Librarians who have military experience of their own may want to share their veteran status with patrons to help establish a sense of common ground with the veteran and military-affiliated patrons and increase their comfort level in the library. Patrons who are veterans may open up to librarians with military experience. They may even ask for assistance with an issue that has plagued them for many years, which can give librarians an opportunity to help them learn about changes in the landscape of VSOs. Librarians who have not served in the military may also wish to share their experiences if they have a family member who has served in the military. Librarians can comment briefly on their sense of pride in a family member's military service, for example, or on how important it is as a librarian to be as helpful as possible to veterans and service members.

Don't: Be afraid to be curious and ask questions when interacting with veterans. It is okay for librarians to be curious and ask questions of a veteran when interacting with them. Librarians should be sure to observe both verbal and nonverbal cues that will indicate whether the person wants to talk more. Someone who is in a hurry or frequently looks or turns away during a conversation, for example, is signaling that they do not want to talk. But someone who seems relaxed and outgoing or someone who has already proudly declared that they have indeed served in the military at one time or another is likely to welcome curiosity from a librarian. Librarians can ask veterans questions about what it was like when they first signed up, where they served, and what makes them proudest about their service.

Don't: Ask a veteran questions that may cause them anxiety or sorrow. For example, never ask a veteran, "What was it like to kill someone?" Never ask a veteran, "What is your worst memory?" Never push an issue if a veteran shows signs of agitation. Librarians who find it difficult to think of a good question should consider which types of questions they themselves would like to answer, regardless of whether or not they have military experience. When in doubt, librarians can even ask veterans what they wish other people would ask!

Do: Be patient with veterans who like to talk. Some veterans may not have many opportunities to talk about their military experiences, and they may turn to the public librarian for a friendly and welcoming ear. Many librarians already know how to redirect a conversation and communicate with someone who wants to keep talking. The solution might be a candid reminder that someone else is in line, followed by, "Talk to you again tomorrow!" However, sometimes a veteran will feel comfortable talking about things that would be better discussed with a professional. If there is an acute issue, librarians should follow library policy for handling patrons in crisis. Crisis contact information for veterans and service members is also located in chapter 2 of this book.

However, for veterans who are not in immediate crisis, librarians should be prepared for a warm handoff to a qualified professional. Instead of referring the veteran to a general phone number, for example, librarians should give the veteran the name of someone who works at the nearest Vet Center. In this way, even though the conversation has to end between the librarian and veteran, the veteran can feel that their willingness to share has led to a positive outcome.

Don't: Make assumptions when someone seems to behave strangely. All patrons, including veterans, may exhibit unusual behavior for a wide variety of reasons. For example, someone who appears to be intoxicated could actually be coping with a mental health condition. Sometimes veterans may come to the library in an attempt to fight depression and the isolation that can make depression worse. However, they may act strangely due to a physical or emotional condition. As always, librarians can gauge how much the person is distracting other library visitors. As long as the individual is not overly disruptive, librarians can respond as they do with all other patrons—by extending a sense of welcome and respect. It helps to learn the names of regular visitors, including veterans who behave strangely, so that it may be easier to respectfully ask them to seek help or leave for the day if their behavior is too distracting to other library visitors.

One of the most challenging aspects of working in the public library is making sure that all visitors feel welcome, even if they have mental health issues. Kristen once observed a library manager handle a tricky situation very well. The manager had learned the names of all of the daily visitors at the library, including some visitors who were homeless and coping with mental health issues. On one afternoon, a visitor was clearly struggling to stay awake. It was possible that she had forgotten to take her medicine or that she might have had to change medication and the side effects were causing problems. Instead of simply reiterating the library's policy prohibiting sleeping in the library, the manager addressed this person by name and took her aside to speak to her quietly. She asked if the patron remembered where she was supposed to go to rest at the nearby shelter. The manager explained that the patron looked tired and that she might want to seek assistance at the shelter where it would be easier for her to rest. The patron was not offended because the manager knew her by name. She left that day and returned the next day after getting some rest.

Not all veterans have mental health issues or are homeless. But most library visitors will be more amenable to a librarian's request if the librarian knows their name. Regardless of the circumstances, however, librarians still must ensure that the public library is a safe place for all visitors. The handling of any situation will depend on many circumstances.

Don't: Take it personally if a veteran seems angry. Some veterans become agitated in situations where their anxiety has been triggered by a noise or the behavior of another library visitor. If a veteran is agitated when talking but otherwise is not disrespectful, remember that it is possible that it has nothing to do with the library or the librarian. It is not possible to anticipate all of the triggers that can cause an episode of anxiety or PTSD. Learning more about some of the common triggers, however, may be a helpful first step toward identifying and reducing sources of anxiety in the library for veterans and service members. For example, librarians may be able to work with library administration in consultation with local VSOs to identify ways that the library space could be arranged to make the library more welcoming to veterans, service members, and other patrons who may suffer from anxiety or PTSD.

Don't: Assume that all veterans and service members are alike. As discussed in previous chapters, veterans and service members come from all walks of life. Efforts to develop programs, services, or a special collection for veterans or military personnel are more successful when librarians consult different library users from different backgrounds. Some veterans, for example, enjoy reading books about military strategy. Other veterans, however, may prefer to read Noam Chomsky. Veterans do not all act alike or feel alike about any current event. Even veterans who have had similar experiences in the same era of conflict may have interpreted those experiences differently, or they may have had different experiences afterward that have continued to shape their identities and beliefs. Veterans and service members deserve to be treated as individuals, just like any other member of an underserved group that is often considered to be a homogenous group.

Don't: Say "no" without being prepared to redirect, refer, or learn more. Public libraries, of course, have a code of conduct where there may be some serious "nos." Setting those aside, just about any question or request that a veteran may ask of a librarian can be handled without saying no. Even in cases where the librarian might not know the answer, it is still possible to find someone who does know the answer or to offer to give the veteran the phone number of an organization that should know the answer. For example, if a librarian does not know which bus to take to get to the nearest VA facility, then the librarian can give the veteran the phone number to that facility so that the veteran can ask someone there. Referring veterans to a source, even if it is the phone number of another organization, is better than saying "no."

This last rule in the public library setting also applies to events that do not yet exist, services that are not yet available, and programs that have not yet been designed. In each of these cases, there is a "no" that may be keeping someone who has been looking for such an event, service, or program from ever finding it. That "no" can be the library's choice not to offer such an event, service, or program, even though the library may be the most logical place to offer it. Because the public library is the one place where community resources, information, and equal access to resources and information are fundamental, the library may in fact be the only place that could develop a particular event, program, or service. Therefore, when a veteran asks whether there is a veteran support group in the library, librarians can turn that "no" into a "yes" by learning whether any Vet Center in the area would be interested in offering a support group in the library. If a veteran asks to use the fax machine to request a copy of military records, although the library's general policy may be to not permit anyone but library employees to use the fax machine, a librarian can turn that "no" into a "yes" by faxing a one-page form to the National Archives on behalf of the veteran. For veterans who have never used the library, librarians attending a Stand Down event to issue new library cards also turn a "no" into a "yes." There is almost always more than one way to answer a question.

In coordination with library managers, there is often more than one way to handle a request for a service or program that doesn't exist, but should. If the event, service, or program matches up with the public library's vision, librarians should consider ways that they can help turn that "no" into a "yes." Public libraries are often in a unique position to learn about needs in the community and to coordinate an answer to those needs among other organizations. The public library does not always have to offer the resource or the service. But with an increased knowledge about the dos and don'ts of working with veterans, public librarians can help other organizations and advocates in the community increase their knowledge and begin to find ways to better meet the needs of the veteran and military communities.

Collection Development and Readers' Advisory

In addition to outreach efforts and programs, many public librarians will want to include materials related to the veteran and military communities in their library collections. Although there are a large number of books and other materials published each year that address the veteran and military communities, librarians must take care when selecting materials to support these patrons. There is also an abundance of books, novels, and movies that appear to be helpful but may be misleading. In this landscape, it can be challenging for librarians to be sure that the materials they are selecting for their collections are high-quality and accurate.

One common area of concern when evaluating materials related to the military and veteran communities is the issue of stolen valor. Memoirs and other nonfiction books can include elements of *stolen valor*, a term that indicates that someone is claiming military accolades that they did not earn. Librarians should be careful to evaluate such books before adding them to the collection and consider stolen valor as a factor when weeding materials.

Another common area of concern relates to books about the military family experience. A number of such books have been published recently, including many picture books on the topic. However, the quality of these picture books can vary widely, and it can be difficult to understand some subtleties in the content or illustration of picture books written for military children. Indeed, librarians and even parents who are unaware of the full spectrum of picture books about military families may unintentionally purchase something that is outdated, misleading, or even unintentionally harmful for a military child to read. Similarly, guides for new military spouses and for those who have recently joined the military may fail to represent important topics, such as diversity in the military.

Collection development related to the veteran and military communities is complicated by the overall lack of reviews by professional educators and librarians. In the absence of professional reviews, librarians can find it difficult to determine what has been published and to evaluate its quality. The library profession, in addition to the readers, needs more support and guidance to improve the quality of materials on the veteran and military communities found in public library collections. Until a reputable library journal or website can regularly recommend materials for the veteran and military communities, it is only possible to offer a few guidelines based on the authors' personal experiences interacting with these types of materials. It is beyond the scope of this book to provide an exhaustive list of recommended relevant materials for public library collections. It is also difficult to provide public librarians with guidelines for collection development or readers' advisory beyond what librarians already know. The following, therefore, is a list of some of the things librarians should consider when selecting books for a public library that would be helpful to the veteran and military communities.

Scope. Although authors may have personal experience with a particular topic, their experiences may not have provided them with the background to cover the full scope of that topic. For example, when looking at a book written by a military spouse that is meant to offer advice to other military spouses, does the author attempt to offer advice for military spouses in all branches of the military? If not, does the author explain the limited scope of the book in its title or description? If so, how does the author handle advice for spouses in other military branches? If the author includes testimonials from and interviews with other military spouses, the book may be adequate. If the scope of the book does not match what the title says it should be, keep looking for a better option.

Fact-checking. Does the publisher have a good reputation for fact-checking? This may be particularly relevant in relation to memoirs and other nonfiction works, especially when they describe experiences that seem too good to be true. Good fact-checking should alleviate some concerns related to stolen valor issues, and librarians should consider a publisher's reputation for fact-checking during collection development.

Evidence. If a book claims to cover a health issue, do the authors use sources that align with the issue that is covered? For example, if a book offers advice on PTSD, do the references and resources come from licensed professionals with expertise on mental health, anxiety, depression, and PTSD? Does the reference list include high-quality scholarly sources?

Timing. Books that give advice about specific VA benefits may become outdated quickly because DoD and VA policies and procedures for many issues can change annually. For example, if a book provides guidance for service members about accessing benefits when they transition out of the military, it may become out of date in as little as a year. Before adding a book to their collection, librarians should ensure that it reflects the most current information about the topics that are discussed.

Conclusion

The suggestions, guidelines, and examples in this chapter are only intended to be a starting point for public librarians interested in working with the veteran and military communities. In addition to the outstanding efforts made by the libraries mentioned in this chapter, there are new and creative library programs, services, and outreach efforts being developed all the time. Public librarians are encouraged to connect with one another to share their ideas and success stories. Because working with the veteran and military communities is particularly effective as a collaborative effort, librarians should also strive to connect with other organizations that serve these communities. By developing collaborations, partnerships, and programs that focus on the unique needs of the veteran and military communities, public libraries can play a major role in providing support for veterans, service members, and their families.

Many organizations, ideas, and worthy endeavors throughout the country may not have been included in this chapter due to limited space. It is also important to note that the programs suggested in this chapter may also be offered to military families, caregivers, and parents of veterans and service members, as well as the advocacy groups that support them. Other ideas for military families can be learned by reviewing research initiatives by organizations such as the Institute of Veterans and Military Families, RAND Corporation, Watson Institute, and Blue Star Families. As with all work of this nature, it is hoped that the public library profession will learn from the efforts of all librarians and through continued communication with each other online and at library conferences.

References

All Things Considered. (2009, March 21). Military families learn to live with "new normal" [Audio recording]. Retrieved from http://www.npr.org/templates/story/story.php?storyId=102211294

American Library Association. (2016). Money smart week. Retrieved from http://www.ala.org/offices/money-smart-week

Aurora Public Library. (2016). Veterans history project is not just for libraries. Retrieved from http://www.aurorapubliclibrary.org/veterans-history-project-is-not-just-for-libraries/

Blue Star Families. (2016). Our impact. Retrieved from https://bluestarfam.org/impact

Bradbard, D. A., Maury, R. V., Kimball, M., Wright, J. C. M., LoRe', C. E., Levingston, K., ... White, A. M. (2014). *2014 military family lifestyle survey*. Falls Church, VA: Blue Star Families. Retrieved from https://bluestarfam.org/survey

California Humanities. (2016). War comes home. Retrieved from http://www.calhum.org/initiatives/war-comes-home

California State Library. (2011, August 11). Library of California board meeting. Retrieved from https://www.library.ca.gov/loc/board/agendas/2011AugDocs/LoCBoardMeetingAgendaWebsitePacket_11Aug2011.pdf

Caroline County Public Library. (2016). Veterans resources @ your library! Retrieved from http://www.carolib.org/content/veterans-resources-your-library

Charity Navigator. (2016). Retrieved from http://www.charitynavigator.org

City of Chula Vista. (n.d.). Chula Vista's veteran community. Retrieved from http://www.chulavistaca.gov/residents/veteran-community

City of Commerce Public Library. (2016). Veterans coffee night. Retrieved from http://www.cityofcommercepubliclibrary.org/library/?q=content/veterans-coffee-night

Fesko, S. (2013). Teens learning from real life heroes. *Voice of Youth Advocates, 36*(3), 45.

Folsom Community Service Day. (n.d.). Military care packages needed! Retrieved from http://www.folsomcommunityservice.org/index.php/program-event/military-care-packages-needed

Library of Congress. (2016a). Veterans history project: About the project. Retrieved from http://www.loc.gov/vets/about.html

Library of Congress. (2016b). Veterans history project: How to participate in the project. Retrieved from http://www.loc.gov/vets/kit.html

Melrose Park Public Library. (2016). Operation care package [Blog post]. Retrieved from http://www.melroseparklibrary.org/operation-care-package

Moulton, K. (2013). Utah to celebrate Veterans Day with parades, tributes. *Salt Lake Tribune.* Retrieved from http://archive.sltrib.com/story.php?ref=/sltrib/news/55195705-78/veterans-utah-ceremony-guard.html.csp

My Escambia. (2016, March 4). Veterans services outreach events planned at West Florida Public Libraries. Retrieved from http://myescambia.com/home/news/veterans-services-outreach-events-planned-west-florida-public-libraries

National Association of County Veterans Service Officers. (n.d.). Find service officers. Retrieved from https://www.nacvso.org/find_service_officers

North Carolina Humanities Council. (2016). NC vets for words: Chapel Hill, NC. Retrieved from http://nchumanities.org/content/nc-vets-words-chapel-hill-nc-2016

Pharr, J. (2013, November 26). What deployed troops really want in their care packages. Retrieved from https://www.veteransunited.com/life/what-deployed-troops-really-want-in-their-care-packages

Pierson, J. (2015, October 13). Veterans history project at Sedona Public Library. Retrieved from http://www.sedonalibrary.org/news/2015_10_30.php

Smart Investing @ Your Library. (n.d.). San Diego public library. Retrieved from http://smartinvesting.ala.org/lessons-learned/san-diego-public-library-2

United Service Organizations. (2014, December 31). How to make the perfect care package for troops [Blog post]. Retrieved from https://blog.uso.org/2014/12/31/how-to-make-the-perfect-care-package-for-troops

United Service Organizations. (2016). About us. Retrieved from https://www.uso.org/about

U.S. Department of Defense. (2016a). Military installations. Retrieved from http://www.militaryinstallations.dod.mil/MOS/f?p=MI:ENTRY:0

U.S. Department of Defense. (2016b). Military OneSource. Retrieved from http://www.militaryonesource.mil

U.S. Department of Labor. Veterans' Employment & Training Service. (n.d.) Stand down. Retrieved from https://www.dol.gov/vets/programs/stand%20down

U.S. Department of Veterans Affairs. (2016a). Locations. Retrieved from http://www.va.gov/landing2_locations.htm

U.S. Department of Veterans Affairs. (2016b). Make the Connection. Retrieved from http://maketheconnection.net

Veterans Connect @ the Library. (2016). Retrieved from http://calibrariesforveterans.org

Veterans Village of San Diego. (2016). Stand Down meaning & history. Retrieved from http://vvsd.net/stand-down

Veterans Writing Project. (n.d.). What we do. Retrieved from https://veteranswriting.org

Virginia Library Association. (2016). VLA: Free webinars in partnership with the Department of Veterans Affairs. Retrieved from http://www.vla.org/index.php?option=com_content&view=article&id=433:vla--free-webinars-in-partnership-with-the-department-of-veterans-affairs&catid=21:latest-news

War Ink. (2014). Retrieved from http://www.warink.org

Webb, A. (2016, March 10). VA partners with Boise Public Library to locate, help homeless veterans. *Idaho Statesman.* Retrieved from http://www.idahostatesman.com/news/local/military/article65382287.html

Williams, J. F. & Needham, G. (2010). Strategic reality check: An Infopeople webinar [Webinar]. Retrieved from https://infopeople.org/civicrm/event/info?id=194 &reset=1

Witthaus, J. (2015, July 25). St. Louis library offers a writing boot camp for veterans. *St. Louis Post-Dispatch.* Retrieved from http://www.stltoday.com/news /local/metro/st-louis-library-offers-a-writing-boot-camp-for-veterans/article _f00828b6-1812-5fbe-aa92-b4b4f0e8ffd0.html

4

Veteran and Military Communities on College and University Campuses

Members of the veteran and military communities are enrolling in higher education in ever-increasing numbers, and colleges, universities, and their libraries are taking notice. However, the services, programs, and policies developed for veteran and military-affiliated students vary widely between academic institutions, which can be challenging for these students to navigate. Academic librarians can play a significant role in helping veteran and military-affiliated students traverse the higher education landscape to achieve academic success. Librarians who provide reference support can help ensure that veteran and military-affiliated students are aware of existing policies, programs, and resources that may support them on their path to a degree, especially on campuses without a veteran center. Instructional librarians can make classrooms more welcoming for veteran and military-affiliated students, and those librarians who teach credit-bearing courses can ensure that military-affiliated students receive necessary accommodations for military-related needs. Library administrators can consider the unique needs of veterans and service members when designing new spaces. And all librarians can advocate for veteran and military-affiliated students in higher education. They can share information about programs and policies available at other institutions, support policies that are friendly to veterans and service members, and increase the programs and resources available for veteran and military-affiliated students on their campuses.

This chapter will focus on providing information, suggestions, and resources for academic librarians interested in working with veteran and military-affiliated students, whether their campus has many or few resources devoted to these unique populations. Chapter 1 explained who is included in the veteran and military communities; this chapter will explain in more detail which members of the veteran and military communities are typically present on college and university campuses. It will also answer some of the common questions that academic librarians have about veteran and military populations: How large is the veteran and military population in higher education? What educational benefits are available for veterans and service members? How are veteran and military-affiliated students different from other student populations? What might a particular college or university be doing to support veteran and military-affiliated students? The second half of the chapter will provide specific ideas for library services, outreach, and collaborations to provide academic librarians with concrete ideas for how they can better support veteran and military-affiliated students on their campuses.

Who Are Veteran and Military-Affiliated College Students?

College and university campuses, and therefore academic libraries, tend to serve specific subsets within the larger veteran and military communities. Although it is common in higher education to use the term *veteran* as a general term that includes both veterans and service members, there are in fact a number of veteran and military-affiliated groups on college and university campuses, including the following:

- veterans and service members
- veteran and military spouses
- military dependents
- cadets and midshipmen
- survivors

This chapter will primarily focus on library services for veterans and service members as well as subpopulations such as women veterans, Reservists, and veterans with disabilities.

The Number of Veterans and Service Members on College Campuses

The veteran and military communities are very diverse and include everyone from service members still in their teens to centenarian World War II veterans. Although veterans and service members from any age group may enroll in colleges and universities, veteran and service member enrollments tend to follow common patterns. These patterns are important to recognize, but librarians should be careful to take a broad view of who veteran and military-affiliated students may be and not exclude anyone who has served, regardless of their period of service, number of deployments, or type of discharge.

Perhaps unsurprisingly, a narrow segment of the overall veteran population makes up the bulk of veterans attending colleges and universities nationwide. U.S. Department of Veterans Affairs (VA) data indicates that although Post-9/11 veterans made up only about 19 percent of the overall veteran population in 2015, almost 73 percent of individuals who used the GI Bill in 2014 used the Post-9/11 GI Bill, which requires beneficiaries to have served at least 90 days of service after September 10, 2011 (U.S. Department of Veterans Affairs. Veterans Benefits Administration, 2015d; U.S. Department of Veterans Affairs, 2014; U.S. Department of Veterans Affairs.

Veterans Benefits Administration, 2016a). This indicates that the majority of student veterans are recent veterans who may still be in the process of transitioning from military service into a civilian occupation.

Service member students also vary in age, often depending on the program they are using to attend college. A large number of service members attend college, typically part-time, using Tuition Assistance (TA) benefits. Research on Navy and Marine TA has shown that TA users vary in age and that women take advantage of these benefits at a higher rate than men (Buddin & Kapur, 2012). In addition to TA, programs such as Green to Gold, Advanced Civil Schooling, and many others send service members to civilian colleges and universities. The variety of programs available to current service members means that the characteristics of students who are still serving can vary widely. Some students may be just starting out in the military and share many attributes with traditional college student populations. Other students may have many years of experience in the military and be achieving a graduate degree to move to the next level in their military career.

Scope of the Issue

There is a significant number of student veterans and service members enrolled at colleges and universities across the country, but the exact number is impossible to know because veterans and service members are not obligated to disclose their status to the schools they attend. Different metrics and estimates, however, help represent the scope of veteran and service member participation in higher education. For example, according to one recent estimate, veterans and service members make up approximately 5 percent of undergraduate students nationwide (Molina & Morse, 2015). This number can vary dramatically from one institution to another, but it helps illustrate why colleges and universities are taking the influx of veterans and service members so seriously.

Exploring data from commonly used veteran and military education benefits can provide a picture of the extent to which veterans and service members are enrolling in higher education. More detailed information about these educational benefits can be found in the "Educational Benefits for Veterans and Service Members" section of this chapter.

Veterans using GI Bill benefits. According to VA data, in 2014, over 1 million students were using VA education benefits (U.S. Department of Veterans Affairs. Veterans Benefit Administration, 2015d). However, many of those receiving VA education benefits are not veterans. A significant number of GI Bill benefit recipients are veterans' spouses and children, as some benefits can be transferred.

Service members using TA benefits. The number of service members using TA is smaller than the number of veterans using the GI Bill, but is still a substantial number that impacts college and university campuses nationwide. In 2013, over 275,000 active-duty service members were receiving TA benefits (United States Government Accountability Office, 2014). This number does not include members of the National Guard and Reserves who are on ordinary drilling status and using TA benefits as well.

State benefits. In addition to federal benefits, some states also have benefits available. The number of students using state veterans' benefits can vary widely. For example, almost 39,000 students received Texas Hazlewood Exemption during fiscal year 2014. However, Texas is one of the states with the largest number of veterans, and it has an expansive benefit program for veterans. Therefore the number of students receiving state education benefits is likely to be smaller in other states that offer such benefits.

Veterans and service members without benefits. Although the numbers for veterans and service members receiving education benefits can be a helpful metric toward understanding the extent to which veterans and service members are enrolling in higher education, they also are incomplete. Many veterans are not receiving education benefits for a number of reasons, including that they may not be eligible for benefits, they may have already exhausted their benefits, or they may have transferred their benefits to a spouse or child. At Texas A&M University, the Veterans Resource and Support Center estimates that 33 percent of their veteran undergraduate students and 57 percent of their veteran graduate students are not receiving education benefits (J. Smith, personal communication, May 27, 2015). Similarly, service members may not be receiving benefits because they have already exhausted their TA benefits for the year, their service contract will be over before the end of the semester, or for other reasons.

Student veterans and service members who are not receiving education benefits, which must be verified through the college or university, are often difficult to track. Many institutions request that veterans and service members self-report their status to get an estimate of how many veteran and military-affiliated students are enrolled. But some veterans and service members may choose not to self-identify, and therefore the campus will not know about their veteran or military status.

Where to Find Numbers

Although veterans and service members are likely to be found at nearly any institution, the number of veterans, service members, and other military-affiliated students enrolled at any particular institution can vary widely. For example, a disproportionate number of veterans and service members using education benefits enroll at for-profit institutions (Altman, 2015). To determine how many student veterans and service members are likely to be enrolled at a particular institution, there are a few places to look for data.

- For aggregate data on student veterans, the VA publishes an Annual Benefits Report that includes trends on GI Bill usage as well as state-level data detailing how many users were enrolled at colleges and universities in a particular state using federal veteran education benefits (U.S. Department of Veterans Affairs. Veterans Benefits Administration, 2016d). This state-level data may help frame institutional veteran enrollment data in a larger context to determine whether a specific institution is attracting a significant percentage of student veterans in the state.

- Some institution-level data on military TA and GI Bill enrollment is available online. The Department of Defense's (DOD) TA DECIDE site allows users to search for institutions that will meet their academic and TA needs and provides some institutional-level data about previous TA use at that institution, including the number of users enrolled (U.S. Department of Defense. Voluntary Education Partnership Memorandum of Understanding, n.d.). Similarly, the VA's GI Bill Comparison Tool allows users to search at the institution level and provides some institution-level data about previous GI Bill use at that institution, including the number of GI Bill users enrolled (U.S. Department of Veterans Affairs, n.d.).

- For the most accurate and up-to-date information about veteran and military-affiliated students at a particular college or university, it is best to go directly to the source. If the college or university has a veteran center, that will be the librarian's first point of contact for finding data on student veteran and service member enrollment. Even if the college or university doesn't have a veteran center, administrators are likely still tracking the numbers of veterans and service members using education benefits. Any campus that has student veterans and service members using education benefits should have a designated point person for processing those benefits. This individual is often known as a school certifying official (SCO) and is often found in the campus veteran center, registrar's office, or financial aid office. The college or university website may have this information published for student veterans so they can find their certifying official each semester. If the college or university doesn't have a veteran center, the campus SCO would be a good point of contact for accessing student veteran and service member enrollment numbers.

Educational Benefits for Veterans and Service Members

The influx of veterans and service members in higher education correlates to the financial resources available for many veteran and military-affiliated students. The military and veterans' education landscape is a complicated one that many veterans and service members struggle to navigate without assistance. Because this complex network of educational benefits is exceptionally complicated and changes frequently, librarians should consider referring student veterans and service members with in-depth questions about educational benefits to an expert. Campus financial aid officers or veteran center employees may be able to answer some questions, while others may be referred to the VA or DoD. Vet Success on Campus (VSOC) counselors, if available on campus or in the region, are also an excellent option for referrals because they are VA employees and have expertise about VA education programs.

Many service members join the military specifically for the education benefits. The military is well-known as a career path that can lift people out of poverty and provide them with an opportunity to obtain a college degree. For this reason, understanding the educational benefits offered to veterans and service members in higher education is fundamental to supporting them. Veterans and service members have sacrificed to obtain a higher education, and their educational benefits are precious to them. Although many generous educational benefits are available to veterans and service members, they can still experience considerable financial pressure while in school. Some veterans and service members are not eligible for financial aid related to their military service, or they may have already exhausted their benefits. One report notes that only 38 percent of all veteran and service member undergraduates and 20 percent of all veteran and service member graduate students received GI Bill benefits in 2007–2008 (Radford, 2011). Some veterans may be eligible for benefits but at a reduced rate, especially if they served only a short period on active duty.

Most veterans are post-traditional students, which means that they are likely to have financial obligations that most traditional students do not. They are likely to be paying their own way through college, as opposed to having parental financial support. They may have mortgages and car payments as well as a spouse and dependent children who need support. Many veterans and service members work outside of school to help make ends meet (Kim & Cole, 2013). Even veterans and service members who are receiving full education benefits can find that their benefits may be inadequate to meet their needs and those of their families. The resulting financial pressure may discourage veterans and service members from completing their degrees.

Librarians should be aware that there are many programs available for veterans and service members, including traditional financial aid, and be prepared to refer veteran and military-affiliated students to campus and local resources for help if they are struggling financially.

Sarah and her husband, Sean, are both veterans for whom the Post-9/11 GI Bill has had tremendous impact. The Post-9/11 GI Bill's generous benefits covered their full tuition bills for graduate school. However, they had also recently become parents when they began graduate school. They soon found that the cost of childcare, even part-time, would far exceed the capacity of their Post-9/11 GI Bill stipends. Because they were already familiar with the higher education financial aid process, they knew to fill out the Free Application for Federal Student Aid (FAFSA) in addition to filing for GI Bill benefits. Sarah and Sean proved to be eligible for university scholarships and childcare subsidies that, along with help from extended family and a lot of schedule juggling, enabled them to manage the costs of childcare, avoid taking on student loans, and complete their degrees on time

---

GI Bill

The most common education benefit available to veterans is the Servicemen's Readjustment Act of 1944, commonly referred to as the GI Bill. The original GI Bill, instituted at the end of World War II, applied to service members who "were in active service after 16 September 1940, had 90 days or more of service and were released under conditions other than dishonorable, or who became eligible through service-incurred disability regardless of length of service" (Army Times Publishing Company, n.d.). The original GI Bill provided one year of education or training with the possibility of extension of up to three years or the length of service, whichever was shorter, and it included full tuition and a stipend (Army Times Publishing Company, n.d.). The impact of this first GI Bill was profound; over half of World War II veterans, a total of 7.8 million veterans, used the GI Bill to pursue higher education and training (Mettler, 2005, p. 7).

The GI Bill has had several updates since 1944, and its most recent overhaul created the Post-9/11 Veterans Education Assistance Act of 2008, commonly known as the Post-9/11 GI Bill. The Post-9/11 GI Bill is the education benefit most frequently used by veterans in higher education (U.S. Department of Veterans Affairs. Veterans Benefit Administration, 2015d). To be eligible for full Post-9/11 GI Bill benefits, veterans must have served on active duty in the military for at least 36 months, unless they were discharged due to a disability (Post-9/11 GI Bill, 2009). The Post-9/11 GI Bill's benefits are quite generous; veterans who are eligible for full benefits receive up to 36 months of full in-state tuition at public universities as well as a monthly housing stipend. The specific benefit available to each veteran varies based on a number of factors, including the school they are attending, the amount of time they served, and whether the program is online or in-person (U.S. Department of Veterans Affairs. Veterans Benefits Administration, 2016a). The Post-9/11 GI Bill can, under some circumstances, be transferred from the service member to a dependent.

In addition to the Post-9/11 GI Bill, there are a number of other federal education benefits provided by the VA. These benefits are often lumped together under the common term GI Bill, but they do have some distinct differences in compensation. For example, some student veterans use an earlier version of the GI Bill, commonly referred to as the Montgomery GI Bill or Chapter 30, especially if their service predates 9/11. However, some Post-9/11 veterans also choose to use the Montgomery GI Bill because it pays a flat amount directly to them regardless of the cost of their tuition. Students attending low-cost institutions may benefit more from receiving tuition dollars directly rather than having the VA send funds to the school.

Veterans with a disability may also be eligible for vocational rehabilitation, which can provide additional education and training benefits (U.S. Department of Veterans Affairs. Veterans Benefits Administration, 2016e). Many campuses have a VSOC counselor available to help veterans learn whether they may be eligible for vocational rehabilitation assistance and to help those using vocational rehabilitation benefits overcome any obstacles to their academic success (U.S. Department of Veterans Affairs. Vocational Rehabilitation & Employment, 2016). There are also federal education benefits specifically for Reservists, such as the Montgomery GI Bill Selected Reserve (MGIB-SR), which provides a monthly payment to members of the Reserves and National Guard to pursue education and training while they are in the military (U.S. Department of Veterans Affairs. Veterans Benefits Administration, 2015b). Finally, there are also VA benefits available to some dependents, including the Survivors and Dependents' Educational Assistance (DEA) program and the Marine Gunnery Sergeant John David Fry Scholarship. These benefits support those who lost a spouse or parent in the line of duty and, in the case of the DEA, who had a spouse or parent disabled in the line of duty (U.S. Department of Veterans Affairs. Veterans Benefits Administration, 2016b).

In addition to VA education benefits, there are several other sources of education benefits for veterans and service members. Some common programs are detailed below.

Tuition Assistance

Tuition Assistance (TA) is a program offered by each branch of the military to service members who wish to pursue higher education while still serving. The exact details and restrictions vary, depending on the branch of service, but in general, the DoD will pay up to a certain capped dollar amount per credit hour with an annual limit per service member (Military OneSource, 2016). TA is commonly used at colleges located on or near military installations and for fully online programs, a convenient option for service members with unpredictable schedules or inflexible work hours. TA is also frequently used by Reservists, and it can be used in conjunction with some other education benefits.

Reserve Officers' Training Corps

Many librarians may already be familiar with the Reserve Officers' Training Corps, or ROTC. Many colleges have Army, Air Force, or Naval ROTC programs on their campus, where student cadets (often called midshipmen for naval programs) participate in military training in hopes of commissioning as an officer in the military. ROTC cadets and midshipmen may be traditional undergraduate students, but they also may be service members who are planning to move from the enlisted to the officer ranks or students in graduate school. Although many ROTC cadets and midshipmen receive scholarships to fund their schooling in exchange for a commitment to the military after their education is complete, some students participate in ROTC without a scholarship or with a minimal stipend.

Green to Gold, Seaman to Admiral-21, and Marine Corps Enlisted Commissioning Educational Program

The Army, Navy, and Marine Corps have programs available to help enlisted personnel complete their undergraduate degrees to become a commissioned officer. Examples of these programs are the Army's Green to Gold program, the Navy's Seaman to Admiral-21 (STA-21) program, and the Marine Corps Enlisted Commissioning Educational Program (MECEP) (U.S. Army, 2015; U.S. Navy, 2016; U.S. Marine Corps, 2016). Each of these programs sends service members to civilian four-year colleges and universities, where they attend school full-time as part of an ROTC program. Once their degree is complete, they contract to serve in the military for a set number of years as commissioned officers. Service members who participate in these programs are likely to be a few years older than other ROTC cadets, who tend to be traditional college students.

Advanced Civil Schooling, Performance-Based Graduate School Incentive Program, and CSAF Captains Prestigious PhD Program

Some branches of the military also have programs that send commissioned officers to civilian colleges and universities full-time to achieve graduate degrees, often PhDs. Examples of these programs are the Army's Advanced Civil Schooling program, the Army's new Performance Based Graduate School Incentive Program, and the Air Force's CSAF Captains Prestigious PhD Program (U.S. Army Acquisition Support Center, n.d.; Tice, 2014; Gildea, 2014). Participants in these programs are midcareer officers who may have held positions with a great deal of responsibility and authority. They can be very dedicated students because their careers depend on their academic success and because they have been relieved of the majority of their military-related responsibilities so they can focus on their studies. These and other senior veteran and military-affiliated students can be an important resource for librarians who wish to learn more about the military and how they can help student veterans and service members.

State Veterans' Education Benefits

In addition to federal education benefits from the DoD or the VA, some states have their own education benefits available for student veterans and service members. The benefits available to veterans and service members can vary widely from one state to another. For example, the state of Minnesota offers the Minnesota GI Bill, which pays up to $1,000 per semester to eligible full-time veteran students (Minnesota Office of Higher Education, 2012). Some states offer more limited benefits for students who are Purple Heart recipients or who have a disability; for example, Indiana offers free tuition for Indiana residents who are Purple Heart recipients (Indiana Department of Veterans' Affairs, n.d.). Other states have broader benefits; for example, student veterans in Texas may be eligible for the Hazlewood Exemption, which is a tuition waiver offered to Texas veterans (those who entered their military service in Texas) for up to 150 credit hours' worth of classes.

Private Scholarships

In addition to government-sponsored education benefits, there are some privately funded veteran and military scholarships available. One of the most prominent is the Tillman Foundation scholarship, which is in memory of Pat Tillman, the Arizona Cardinals football player who joined the Army after 9/11 and served as an Army Ranger before he was killed (Pat Tillman Foundation, 2016b). The Tillman Foundation's prestigious and competitive scholarship program recognizes veterans whose service continues beyond their military contract and provides tuition and fees as well as living expenses to recipients (Pat Tillman Foundation, 2016a).

Although these educational benefits are the most commonly used financial resources for veteran and military-affiliated students in higher education, there are many more. Librarians who encounter student veterans and service members who are struggling financially should be prepared to help them research some of the most available options. They should also be aware that there are many other resources available through VSOs and other organizations nationwide and sometimes on individual college and university campuses. Librarians should be aware of the important role that education benefits play in helping veteran and military-affiliated students succeed on campus and be prepared to refer students in financial need to sources of help, both on-campus and off.

Characteristics of the Veteran and Military Communities in Higher Education

To support veteran and military-affiliated students effectively, it is important for librarians to understand how they differ from other students. Although each student veteran, service member, and family member is an individual, there is research available that can help librarians better understand common characteristics and trends among veteran and military-affiliated students.

Veteran and Service Member Students

According to research published by the American Council on Education in 2013, veterans differ from traditional students in a number of ways:

- Student veterans are older than their civilian counterparts, for obvious reasons—many of them spent their traditional college years in the military.

- They are overwhelmingly male, although women are actually over-represented among student veterans. Women make up only about 10 percent of the total veteran community but 25 percent of those in college.

- Student veterans are more racially diverse than their civilian counterparts, and they are more likely to be first-generation students.

- They tend to be transfer students, although they may have been away from the classroom for years before they returned to school. (Kim & Cole, 2013; National Survey of Student Engagement, 2010)

These demographic differences can help to explain why student veterans and service members do not always feel comfortable on college and university campuses, especially if the campus has a lot of traditional students. Veterans and service members can feel a lot older than their fellow students. It can be disorienting for a student veteran who may be recently returned from a combat deployment to sit in class next to a student who is still talking about going home for a high school homecoming football game. It isn't uncommon to hear student veterans complain about the perceived immaturity of their more traditional classmates, or to have young students asking them inappropriate questions, such as, "Did you kill anyone?" (Sander, 2012).

Research has also shown that veterans and service members behave in different ways than civilian students (Kim & Cole, 2013; National Survey of Student Engagement, 2010). Perhaps because they are older, they tend to live and work off-campus, and they often have spouses and care for children. They are likely to have less time to spend on extracurricular activities and high-impact learning practices. The heavy burden of responsibilities shouldered by student veterans can make it difficult for colleges and universities (and libraries) to connect with student veterans in the same ways that they do with traditional students.

However, despite all of the challenges they face, veterans tend to be very goal-oriented about their education. Veterans and service members often look at higher education as an obstacle that must be overcome to move forward to their futures, and this outlook helps them commit to their studies. Research confirms that despite the challenges of commuting, working, and caring for children, student veterans and service members spend more time than their civilian counterparts preparing for classes and are more likely to actually talk to faculty. Even though student veterans and service members may not spend a great deal of time on campus or engaging in extracurricular activities, they actually may spend more time on academics (Kim & Cole, 2013).

Although there has been a great deal of research about student veterans in recent years, there is little historical data about student veterans' academic outcomes and how they compare to their civilian counterparts. It is difficult to find such data because the experiences of veterans in higher education are quite complicated. The VA has historically tracked the number of veterans receiving benefits, but because many veterans exhaust their benefits before completing their degrees, they may fall off the VA's radar well before graduation. It is also common for veterans to take time off before completing a degree or to transfer schools, which makes it challenging for colleges and universities to track graduation rates. And, of course, not all veterans or service members identify themselves as veteran or military-affiliated and therefore cannot be tracked.

To get a better understanding of student veterans' educational outcomes, the Student Veterans of America recently partnered with the VA and the National Student Clearinghouse on the Million Records Project to capture and analyze the academic outcomes of student veterans using federal education benefits. Initial findings from this study suggest that while student veterans have lower completion rates than the national average, they do have better outcomes than many other post-traditional students. Veterans also take longer to complete their degrees, perhaps because they are shouldering family and work responsibilities while in school (Cate, 2014).

As was mentioned at the beginning of this chapter, it is common in higher education to use the term *veteran* to encompass both veterans and service members. Research on veterans and service members also tends to follow this pattern of considering veterans and service members to have similar experiences, challenges, and academic needs. For most academic librarians, there is little need to distinguish between student veterans and service members, but there are some distinctions of which librarians should be aware. For example, service members in higher education, because of their ongoing commitment to the military, can be called back to duty at any time, which means they may have to leave midsemester to deploy to a combat zone. Student service members in the National Guard and Reserves may have to miss the occasional day of classes to participate in their monthly drills. Librarians who teach, especially those teaching for-credit classes, should be aware of the possibility of military-related absences beyond the students' control as well as of campus policies related to those absences.

Some recent research has also found that there are some demographic differences between active-duty service members, National Guard and Reserves service members, and veterans in higher education (Molina & Morse, 2015). Although the level of granularity in this research is more appropriate for student services personnel, there are a few highlights that may help academic librarians understand the range of veteran and military-affiliated students they may encounter. For example, members of the National Guard are more likely to be in-state students, and the average age at which they enter college is 20, as opposed to 25 for veterans (Molina & Morse, 2015). National Guard members participate in the same initial training as their active-duty counterparts, but they are then released from active duty and return to drilling status. This means that many of these part-time service members remain in their state of residency, and their military obligation, which is typically one weekend a month and two weeks a year, allows for entry into higher education. It would not be uncommon for librarians to encounter service members from the National Guard or Reserves who are similar in age to traditional civilian students.

This research also reveals some of the academic challenges faced by active-duty service members. This group is most likely to enroll in classes part-time, to work full-time while in school, and to take online classes (Molina & Morse, 2015). This makes a lot of sense, because unless active-duty student service members are enrolled in a program such as Green to Gold, which sends them to school full-time, they tend to be taking classes one or two at a time using military TA benefits. These students tend to prefer online programs with classes that work around an unpredictable work schedule and that do not require transferring to a new school when they are moved to a new duty station.

Although librarians may not see enough veteran and service member students to begin to identify differences between current and former service members or active duty and Reservists, it may be helpful to understand that there can be some distinct differences and unique challenges associated with each type of veteran and military-affiliated student. Regardless of these differences, all veteran and service member students are likely to have additional challenges or academic risk factors related to their military service that librarians can help work to alleviate.

Veteran and Military Spouse Students

Although this chapter focuses primarily on student veterans and service members in higher education, there are other members of the veteran and military communities on college campuses of whom librarians should be aware. One significant population is that of veteran and military spouses. Like student veterans and service members, the higher education experiences of veteran and military spouses may be delayed and intermittent. When a military service member is moved to another duty station, their spouse may have to seek out a new college or university and arrange for a transfer. When a service member is sent for extended training or is deployed overseas, their spouse may have to put an academic career on hold to maintain the home or care for children.

Although veteran and military spouses can have some characteristics in common with student veterans and service members in higher education, there are some distinct differences. For example, active-duty military spouses are overwhelmingly female, with some estimates as high as 95 percent (Maury & Stone, 2014). For this reason, many civilians assume that veteran and military-affiliated women are military spouses, a mistake that can be frustrating for women veterans and service members. Compared with civilian spouses, military spouses are more likely to have young children at home. They are more likely than civilian spouses to not be employed, and "the majority of spouses interviewed who were neither employed nor seeking employment mentioned parenting responsibilities as their reason for not working" (Harrell, Lim, Castaneda, & Golinelli, 2004). A service member's military obligations can have a major impact on the career and educational opportunities of their spouse, but there tend to be fewer educational benefits available to spouses to offset the challenges.

Unlike veterans and service members, who often have access to GI Bill or TA benefits, veteran and military spouses have access to fewer and more limited educational programs. For example, the My Career Advancement Account (MyCAA) is a DoD-sponsored program aimed at supporting the educational needs of the spouses of early-career military members. However, this program caps support at $2,000 per person per fiscal year, and at $4,000 total per person. It also carries some restrictions on degree programs to further its goal of helping military spouses find "portable" careers (Friedman, Miller, & Evans, 2015). Other available scholarships include branch-specific funds, such as Army Emergency Relief's Spouse Education Assistance Program and the Navy-Marine Corps Relief Society's Education Assistance Program, both of which offer financial assistance to the spouses of active-duty and retired service members from their branches. Spouses of service members who lost their lives or were permanently disabled in the line of duty are eligible for VA education benefits, such as the Dependents Education Assistance Program (U.S. Department of Veterans Affairs. Veterans Benefits Administration, 2015a).

Although there is some financial aid directly available to veteran and military spouses, a popular option in recent years has been for eligible veterans and service members to transfer their GI Bill benefits to their spouses.

Service members can transfer all or part of their educational benefits to their spouses, who can begin using those benefits immediately (U.S. Department of Veterans Affairs. Veterans Benefits Administration, 2016c). Some service members may choose to try to complete their own education using TA funds to free up GI Bill funds for their spouse or dependent children. This means that many military spouses may be experiencing the same challenges of funding their educations as service members, or they may have even fewer resources available to them. Indeed, in some states, they may also be classified as out-of-state students until they establish residency, which is a financial burden and may cause some military spouses to put their education on hold (Harrell et al., 2004).

Once again, although this chapter focuses on the needs and challenges of student veterans and service members, military spouses remain an important additional population for colleges and universities to consider. Military culture frequently includes spouses, who play an important role by maintaining family life during the upheaval of trainings and deployments. When developing programming and outreach to student veterans and service members, librarians should remember that veteran and military spouses may also be interested in such programming. Librarians should consider taking steps to actively engage and include spouses when trying to connect with student veterans and service members.

Military Dependent Students

Military dependent students have little written about them in higher education literature. The children of military personnel do face obstacles to academic achievement due to parental deployments and transfers to new duty stations during their K–12 education (Card et al., 2011; Ruff & Keim, 2014), but there is little research exploring how military-related obstacles impact the children of military personnel at the college level. Although military dependent students may certainly have some academic challenges due to gaps in their education, their particular library-related needs may also differ greatly from those of student veterans and service members.

As military dependent students generally fit the profile of traditional students, their needs may be more in line with other at-risk traditional populations already served by the library than with other military-related populations. Military dependent students may be interested in military-related issues and are an excellent group to target regarding library programming related to military issues. However, because they have not served in the military themselves, their specific academic needs and information-seeking behavior may not resemble that of student veterans and service members.

Cadets and Midshipmen

There are major differences between veterans and service members, who are serving or have already served in the military, and cadets and midshipmen, who are in training to serve in the military. Cadets and midshipmen, unlike veterans and service members, tend to be a traditional population of students. They are likely to attend college straight out of high school, without any gaps in their academic résumés, and because their military service has not officially commenced, they have not yet experienced deployments or many of the stresses of military life. It is true that some cadets and midshipmen are actually veterans and service members who are training to move into the officer ranks, and they should be included in any library outreach or programming aimed at veterans and service members. However, the majority of cadets and midshipmen are traditional students, and not all of them will end up officially serving in the military. For librarians at a military academy (e.g., West Point), the vast majority of cadets and midshipmen will commission. However, many cadets and midshipmen in ROTC programs will not be offered an active-duty commission, instead either serving in the Reserves or not transitioning into military service. At some colleges and universities, students are encouraged to participate as cadets or midshipmen without ever intending to commission into the military. For example, at Texas A&M University, fewer than half of the members of the Corps of Cadets end up accepting a commission into the military. Instead, more than 60 percent of Texas A&M cadets participate in a leadership studies certificate program (Texas A&M University. Corps of Cadets, 2014a; Texas A&M University. Corps of Cadets, 2014b).

Some veterans and service members can be frustrated if they perceive their service and sacrifices as being conflated with cadet training because they know that cadet training is generally not considered to be equivalent to military service and that many cadets may not go on to serve in the military. Certainly, cadets and midshipmen function as another population on campus interested in military-related issues, and therefore they can be an important group to include if hosting an event, such as a lecture from a senior military official. But librarians should take care not to give the impression that veterans, service members, and cadets and midshipmen are a single group of students with similar or equivalent needs and experiences.

Information-Seeking Behavior of Veterans and Service Members

Student veterans and service members have many demographic differences from their civilian counterparts. Although there is little research exploring the information-seeking behavior of veterans and service members, there are a couple of studies that suggest that veteran and military-affiliated students may differ from civilian students when accessing information. Hannaford (2013) examined the information-seeking behavior of enlisted Army veterans and noticed that veterans were conditioned to seek out expert assistance. Hannaford, a service member herself, notes that "military culture has a profound influence on veteran information seeking behavior. While enlisted, soldiers are inundated with informational briefings and official orders that cover every aspect of life (to include behavior outside of official duty). According to the participants of this study, the major difference in seeking information outside the military versus seeking information while enlisted is in the Army there was 'always someone to ask'" (2013, p. 13). The military trains service members to begin the information-seeking process by consulting an expert, but they may have difficulty finding those experts once they transition to civilian life.

Hannaford's (2013) assertion that many veterans are accustomed to asking for in-person assistance from a designated authority is supported by Mills, Paladino, and Klentzin's (2015) study examining the library-related needs of student veterans. Mills et al. note that "the student veteran participants suggested that military training predisposes them to seek out specialists when looking for answers, rather than proceeding on their own and potentially 'wasting time'" (2015, p. 272–273). Military training conditions service members to seek out a designated authority for needed information, and this conditioning can carry into civilian life and impact how student veterans seek information as part of their academic experience. Mills et al. suggest that the unique information-seeking behavior of veterans and service members can serve as an asset for librarians to capitalize on, declaring that this behavior "bodes well for librarians interested in engaging with student veterans because librarians are especially well-suited in the educational community to serve students who have a strong preference for efficiency and time-saving strategies" (2015, p. 273).

Veterans and service members may be very receptive to librarians positioning themselves as one of the designated campus authorities for research support. However, for veterans and service members to benefit from librarian research expertise, these students must realize that they could benefit from research support. A student veterans needs assessment at Miami University in Oxford, Ohio, found that "only 15% felt they needed more help with conducting research for papers and presentations" (Atwood et al., 2015, p. 175). Additionally, student veterans and service members must first understand what librarians do and how they can help. Mills et al. recommend in-class library instruction as the most effective way to connect student veterans and service members with librarian expertise. They note that "all participants who received library instruction in one or more RMU classes asked for assistance by library faculty and staff at some later point, which points to the effectiveness of library instruction as a tool to increase library awareness with this population" (2015, p. 273). In-class library instruction targeting student veterans may not be feasible for all campuses, especially because a significant percentage of veteran and service member students are enrolled in online courses.

Academic librarians should consider that the information-seeking behavior of veteran and service member students predisposes them toward seeking out expert assistance. Therefore, they should make efforts to work with campus veteran centers and academic departments to help familiarize veteran and military-affiliated students with library resources and the research expertise offered by librarians.

Dos and Don'ts of Working with the Veteran and Military Communities

In addition to understanding who student veterans and service members are and how they tend to search for information, academic librarians who work with veteran and military-affiliated students should be aware of some common pitfalls of working with the veteran and military communities. This section gives just a few dos and don'ts to help librarians avoid common mistakes and also provides some basic strategies for making the library a welcoming place for student veterans and service members.

Don't: Make veterans and service members move to the front of the class. All teachers know how frustrating it can be to have students file into a classroom, only to have them cluster at the back of the room, sometimes rows and rows away from where the teacher is standing. While it is tempting to make students move up to the front of the room, librarians should remember that students who are veterans or service members may feel more comfortable sitting in the back. Veterans and service members are taught situational awareness, or to be aware of what is going on around them. In particular, veterans and service members who have recently returned from a combat zone may find it difficult to stop monitoring their surroundings for danger, and they may feel most comfortable and able to concentrate if they can easily observe their surroundings. Asking these students to move to another location may make it more difficult for them to focus on learning.

Do: Design space to allow people to sit with their backs to a wall. Instead of asking veterans and service members to move, work to create a space where they can be comfortable. For some veterans and service members, this may mean a space where they can sit with their backs to a wall, where no one can walk up behind them and surprise them with their presence.

Sarah began classes less than a year after returning from her deployment to Iraq. She remembers arriving at one of her classes very early each week to obtain a seat where her back could be against the wall and where she could easily see the door. There were two other student veterans in her class, and often the three of them would find themselves sitting side-by-side at least 10 minutes before class would start, joking about how they all arrived early to claim their seats because they couldn't quite relax in that particular room if they had to sit on the other side of the table with their backs to the door.

If the library's classrooms have spaces where student veterans and service members can position themselves to reduce the burden of situational awareness, librarians should let them use it. And if the library doesn't have such a space, it may be worth considering such needs the next time the classrooms are reconfigured. Further, librarians may wish to identify whether the library has study spaces that allow students to sit in such protected positions. If it does, consult with the campus veteran center to promote such spaces to veterans and service members. And if it doesn't have such spaces, it may be worthwhile to consider creating some alternative spaces that are quieter and more controlled, which may be helpful to these patrons and others with similar needs.

Do: Disclose veteran status if applicable. Librarians who are veterans or military-affiliated should be encouraged to disclose their military service to students if they feel comfortable doing so. Mentioning military service at the beginning of a library instruction session, for example, can challenge students' perceptions of librarians and of veterans. Persistent stereotypes surrounding both librarianship and military service can prevent students from anticipating that a librarian may have served in the military, and calling attention to a librarian's current or former military service can help dispel some of these stereotypes and give students a broader conception of the military and veteran communities. It can also lead to small interactions that help librarians build relationships with student veterans and service members on campus. For example, students may take a moment after class to mention their own military service or that of a friend or family member.

Similarly, librarians who serve as liaisons to veterans and service members should remember that it can be helpful to disclose any military affiliation they may have, whether they are veterans, service members, or close relatives of those who have served. Student veterans and service members may respond differently to a librarian if they perceive the librarian to be part of the veteran or military communities and therefore someone who understands what they are going through. They may be more likely to open up to a librarian who understands military terminology and jargon, who can empathize with the challenges of transitioning to higher education and navigating the bureaucracy of veterans' education benefits, and who will not be shocked if the student slips into the colorful language commonly heard in the military.

Do: Remain cognizant of your relationship to the veteran and military communities. Members of the veteran and military communities frequently poke fun at one another based upon their branch of the military or their type of service. For example, members of the Army or Marines might goad members of the Air Force by calling it the *Chair Force*, or those who serve in infantry positions might refer to those in support roles as *POGs*, or persons other than grunts. These types of nicknames and acronyms abound in the military community. But librarians should be aware that this type of ribbing is exclusively the province of those who have served. Service members and veterans are likely to resent a civilian, or even a military dependent, poking fun at another veteran or service member. Librarians should be aware of their own relationship to the veteran and military communities and refrain from participating in or perpetuating these types of categorizations of veterans and service members.

Don't: Assume all veterans and service members are alike. Just like everyone else, student veterans and service members are unique individuals. Each has their own experiences in the military and makes their own choices about how they relate to the military. Some veterans choose to close the door on their military service and do not disclose their veteran status. Other veterans are very open about their service and may even have military tattoos, T-shirts, and paraphernalia that make their veteran status readily apparent. Some veterans and service members have found the military to be a positive experience, and they may even consider their time in higher education to be a mere barrier to returning to a military unit full-time. Other veterans and service members found their military experience painful.

There is no right way for veterans and service members to feel about their service, and librarians should be careful to respect that some veterans and service members will not wish to include themselves as members of the veteran and military communities or even to avail themselves of services intended for their population. Librarians should take care to help all patrons, including veterans and service members, to feel included and supported by the library. They should also recognize that individual needs can vary widely and that services intended for veterans and service members may not be a good fit for everyone included in that category.

Do: Recognize the efforts and contributions of veterans and service members on campus. Student veterans and service members may feel like outsiders on a college campus, especially at schools with large populations of traditional students. Libraries, which often play a role as a social hub on campus, can help veterans and service members feel welcome on campus. Libraries can develop displays, exhibits, and programs that highlight the experiences and sacrifices of student veterans and service members and help the campus and the veterans and service members better understand how veteran and military-affiliated students add diversity to the campus community. Librarians can help lead the way toward recognizing student veterans and service members as an asset to campus, which can go a long way toward helping these students feel welcome.

College and University Support for Veterans and Service Members

As the number of veterans and service members enrolling in higher education has increased in the wake of the Post-9/11 GI Bill, many colleges and universities have responded by developing policies and services to support veterans and service members on campus. Academic librarians should be familiar with their campus's policies and services to effectively refer student veterans and service members to available sources of support. Librarians may also wish to become familiar with the policies and services being implemented at colleges and universities nationwide to serve as advocates for the veteran and military-affiliated students on their campuses.

Federal policies and guidelines inform the policies governing student veterans and service members in higher education to ensure that they receive the support they need to transition from the military into college and to achieve academic success. For example, President Obama's "8 Keys to Success: Supporting Veterans, Military and Military Families on Campus" describes the programs and initiatives that colleges and universities should offer to help support their veteran and military-affiliated students (Baker, 2013). The VA administers the Principles of Excellence program that outlines guidelines for supporting student veterans, such as accommodating military-related absences (U.S. Department of Veterans Affairs. Veterans Benefits Administration, 2015c). And the DoD's Voluntary Education Partnership Memorandum of Understanding (MOU) program establishes an agreement between a college or university and the DoD to make that institution eligible to receive funds from the TA program (U.S. Department of Defense, 2014). This MOU outlines policies, such as military-related readmission policies, as well as programs, such as a point of contact for TA, that are intended to ease transitions and help student service members find the resources they may need.

Student veterans and service members who are trying to select a college or university have the opportunity to identify schools that adhere to such guidelines as the 8 Keys to Success and the DOD's MOU program by using the DoD's TA DECIDE tool or the VA's GI Bill Comparison Tool (U.S. Department of Defense. Voluntary Education Partnership, n.d.; U.S. Department of Veterans Affairs, n.d.). Veterans and service members may also consult metrics such as the *Military Times'* "Best for Vets" designation, which considers factors such as availability of priority registration for student veterans (Altman, 2015). Colleges and universities that wish to attract veteran and military-affiliated students are likely to consider meeting federal guidelines and also exploring additional services and programs to support student veterans and service members. Although the specific efforts to support veteran and military-affiliated students may vary widely from one institution to another, there are some common trends across higher education that may help librarians identify what they can look for on their campuses.

Policies

Policies play a very important role in making colleges and universities more supportive of student veterans and service members. By developing policies that can help alleviate the strain of military-related absences and that recognize the knowledge and skills gained during military service, colleges and universities can provide invaluable support for military-affiliated students. Common policies are listed below.

Military withdrawals. Service members who are enrolled in classes run the risk of being called up to military service, sometimes with little to no warning, while classes are in session. Some colleges and universities offer a military withdrawal policy that will refund students' tuition and fees, even after a drop deadline, if the student is forced to withdraw for military reasons. For example, Indiana University Bloomington provides a full refund of tuition and fees to students who are "called to active duty, specialized training or as part of disaster relief efforts" (Indiana University Bloomington. Office of the Registrar, 2016). Librarians, especially those who teach credit-bearing courses, should be aware that students in this situation are often required to prepare very quickly to set their civilian life aside for a period of time, which involves a great deal of paperwork, logistics, and stress. Students may not be aware that they could be entitled to a refund, and in the stress of the moment, they may not even think to inquire about the possibility. Librarians can help by becoming familiar with their college's or university's policy so they can help students obtain any refund they may be due.

Excused absences for military training. In addition to policies regarding military activation, student service members in the National Guard and Reserves benefit from policies that set clear procedures for excusing absences for military training. Although military reserve units are known to train, or drill, one weekend a month and two weeks a year, those weekend drills often include Fridays and sometimes even Thursdays, which can result in missed classes. Because military orders are not provided for regular training, college and university policies that provide service members clear instructions on how to document drill or short-term training-related absences can help them juggle priorities successfully. These policies also provide instructors with information on how to accommodate absences related to military training, underscoring that students who miss military-related training face serious consequences, such as being declared Absent without Leave, or AWOL. Librarians who teach credit-bearing courses should be aware of their college's or university's policy regarding excused absences for military training in the event that they have a student who requires this accommodation.

Military leave for employees. Similar to student service members, college and university employees who are serving in the National Guard and Reserves benefit greatly if their institution provides military leave. Military leave policies provide a separate category of paid time off for employees so they are not forced to use all of their personal vacation time for their military service. Military leave is often sufficient for Reservist employees to attend their annual two-week trainings as well as the occasional three-day weekend training, although it is not unusual for Reservists to have to tap into vacation time to accommodate all required absences. Some colleges and universities, such as Texas A&M University and the University of Utah, offer paid military leave for their employees (Texas A&M University. Human Resources, 2016; University of Utah. Division of Human Resources, 2016). Longer-term military leave, such as for deployments or extensive training, is not usually covered by a college or university's military leave, but the Uniformed Services Employment and Reemployment Rights Act of 1994 (USERRA) does protect the civilian employment rights of service members who are called up to military duty (Employer Support of the Guard and

Reserve, n.d.). Librarians with students or colleagues who are eligible for military leave should be aware of such benefits if their college or university offers them.

Credit for military experience. Many civilians are unaware that service members spend a lot of time in what they call "the schoolhouse." Many members of the military spend a great deal of time in their initial training, which teaches them the knowledge and skills to perform their new job responsibilities. The military relies on a continuous cycle of training to develop its service members, who may learn not only combat skills but also foreign languages, new technologies, and medical skills. Until recently, many civilian institutions did not offer credit for military training or expertise; for example, an Arabic linguist could receive no credit toward a degree in Middle Eastern Studies or a medic could receive no credit toward a degree in the medical field (Schworm, 2008). Many schools have begun working to identify areas where academic credit can be granted for military experience to better recognize the expertise of student veterans and service members and to place them into what may be a more appropriate position on the path to a degree. For example, a college or university might grant language credits to a military linguist who can produce recent military language proficiency test scores. Or, upon considering the physical taxation of military basic training, a school may grant physical education credits to veterans and service members. Such credits can help alleviate student veteran and service member frustration at feeling like they are starting at square one in higher education, and they can also help veteran and military-affiliated students avoid redundant coursework and accomplish their academic goals sooner. Librarians may be able to advocate on their campuses for policies allowing student veterans and service members to substitute relevant alternate experience for some courses and therefore extend the usefulness of their educational benefits.

Priority registration. Many colleges and universities have begun to provide veterans and service members with priority registration, while some states have even enacted legislation requiring state colleges and universities to provide this service (Pennsylvania Department of Education, 2016). Priority registration allows student veterans and service members to register for their classes ahead of the general student body, which makes it less likely that they will be unable to enroll in the classes they need. Because military educational benefits last for a limited time period and many restrict the types of courses they cover, priority registration can play an important role in helping student veterans and service members complete their education. Priority registration also gives students in the National Guard or Reserves flexibility to select classes that interfere less with military drill responsibilities, helping them to attend class more. Librarians at colleges and universities that have priority registration for veteran and military-affiliated students can help direct students to this program. And librarians whose campuses do not have such a policy may be able to advocate for their campus to adopt priority registration for student veterans and service members.

Resources and Programs

In addition to policies enacted to support student veterans and service members, many colleges and universities are also devoting substantial resources toward helping veteran and military-affiliated students transition to campus life and succeed academically. Common resources and programs are listed below.

School certifying official. Colleges and universities with students receiving GI Bill benefits will have an SCO who is responsible for coordinating veterans' benefits with the VA (U.S. Department of Veterans Affairs, 2015b). This individual is often located in the campus registrar's office, veteran center, or financial aid office. Student veterans submit their GI Bill paperwork to the SCO each semester to receive their veterans' education benefits. Librarians can work with the SCO to better understand how many veteran and military-affiliated students are present on their campus.

Veteran centers. It is increasingly common for colleges and universities, especially those with high numbers of student veterans and service members, to have an office dedicated to supporting the needs of veteran and military-affiliated students. According to one study, over 70 percent of colleges and universities that offer services or programs for student veterans and service members have such an office available (McBain, Kim, Cook, & Snead, 2012). Some veteran centers act as a single service point for student veterans and service members. In these offices, veteran and military-affiliated students can submit for benefits certification, attend veteran-oriented programming, connect with other student veterans and service members, and even receive referrals for counseling and disability services. Other veteran centers and offices may have a more limited scope and focus heavily on specific support areas, such as military admissions or developing policies to support veterans and service members. Veteran centers are a great resource for librarians seeking information about current programs and services for veteran and military-affiliated students at their colleges and universities.

Financial aid. Although there are a number of veteran and military-related education benefits, paying for college remains a significant barrier for student veterans and service members. Lopez (2013) conducted interviews of student veterans and service members that "underscored the significance of financial aid assistance and how it results in uncertainties regarding how and if the student veteran [sic] are able to afford their college or university education" (pp. 202–203). One common financial barrier student veterans and service members can experience is gaps in veterans' or military financial assistance. Some schools help veterans and service members in this situation by providing access to short-term financial aid to help students pay their bills while waiting for their benefits to be paid. But veteran and military-affiliated students can also find that they are not eligible for education benefits or that their benefits will expire or be exhausted before their degree is complete.

Colleges and universities can help student veterans and service members in this situation by educating students about their eligibility for civilian financial aid benefits. Many student veterans and service members may not even fill out the FAFSA because they are unaware that they are eligible to apply for traditional financial aid. Colleges and universities can also connect students with scholarships, especially those that target students with a military service background. Because financial pressure remains a major issue for veteran and military-affiliated students, librarians may frequently refer student veterans and service members to the financial aid office.

Orientations for veteran and military-affiliated students. Many colleges and universities have developed orientations specifically for student veterans and service members (McBain et al., 2012). These orientations familiarize student veterans and service members with the resources available to them, including common student services such as tutoring, counseling, and disability services. At Texas A&M University, this orientation is called Vet Camp, and departments and programs from across campus are invited to set up resource tables and share information about their services and resources with incoming veteran and military-affiliated students. If the campus has an orientation for veteran and military-affiliated students, involving the library in this orientation can be a simple but effective strategy toward increasing student veteran and service member awareness of library resources.

Student veteran organizations. Student veterans and service members can feel isolated on college and university campuses, especially campuses with a large number of traditional college students. One way that colleges and universities help student veterans and service members overcome this feeling of isolation is by helping them connect with one another. A common place for student veterans and service members to connect is in a campus student veteran organization. The Student Veterans of America (SVA) is a national organization of student veterans with chapters on over 1,300 college campuses nationwide (Student Veterans of America, 2016). These chapters are student-led, but colleges and universities can support these organizations by providing access to meeting spaces and funding to help the groups get started and then to maintain momentum. For example, attendance at student veteran organization meetings may increase if the organization has the budget to provide refreshments.

The college or university can also help support the organization by providing a staff or faculty advisor who can give advice and guidance to student leaders and also connect them with additional resources on campus and in the community. Some academic libraries step in to fill this role. At West Texas A&M University's Cornette Library, the library director serves as cosponsor for the campus SVA chapter, and the library's Friends organization sponsors a monthly luncheon meeting for the group (S. Kennedy-Witthar, personal communication, October 20, 2015).

Veteran-oriented classes. Another common strategy is to offer classes specifically for student veterans and service members, but the success of these classes has been mixed (Grasgreen, 2012). While student veterans and service members may appreciate opportunities to connect with other veteran and military-affiliated students, they also often have scheduling limitations due to work and family responsibilities as well as limited flexibility in selecting classes due to education benefit program regulations. Classes for veterans and service members have been structured as transitional classes aimed at orienting veteran and military-affiliated students to college life (Fawley & Krysak, 2013), but they also may be offered in disciplinary areas such as writing or history. Librarians at colleges and universities that offer classes that limit enrollment to student veterans and service members may find that enrollment numbers are quite low for those classes. Despite these challenges, librarians may also find that these classes can present an opportunity to connect with student veterans and service members in an academic context and to embed information literacy instruction.

Campus celebrations of veteran holidays. Veteran-related holidays, and Veterans Day in particular, are an opportunity for colleges and universities to recognize the contributions of the veterans on their campuses. Colleges and universities remember Veterans Day in a number of ways; some colleges may have a large-scale recognition ceremony, like the University of Utah's Veterans Day Commemoration Ceremony, while others may host events, such as panel discussions or film showings that delve into military and veteran issues and experiences (University of Utah, 2016). College and university libraries can support campus efforts to recognize veteran-related holidays by creating exhibits or book displays that focus on the military or combat.

Staff Training

In addition to other services and programs to support veteran and military-affiliated students, many colleges and universities offer training for faculty and staff to help them better support student veterans and service members. Recognition programs such as the *Military Times'* "Best for Vets" designation consider whether such training is available; if the college or university is considered a "Best for Vets" school, it likely offers such training (Altman, 2015). This training is frequently led by the staff at the campus veteran center, and it may be offered on an ad hoc basis to individual colleges or departments that request training or may be consolidated into an annual campus-wide training that staff and faculty from across campus can attend. If the campus makes training on student veterans and service members available, hosting the training in the library or sending librarians and staff to a campus training may be a very helpful way to provide library employees with the tools they may need to serve student veterans and service members effectively.

Although the staff members from the campus veteran center are probably very comfortable conducting training for academic departments, they may be unsure about how to translate their presentation materials to make them relevant for the library. Librarians may wish to suggest that the presentations focus on a few particular areas, such as the following:

- *The student veteran and service member profile.* This chapter has explored some of the characteristics of student veterans and service members in general, but the staff from the veteran center may be able to provide more granular demographic information about the veteran and military-affiliated students on campus. They may also be able to give librarians and library staff a basic understanding of how the experiences of student veterans and service members are different from those of traditional students. For example, student veterans and service members have been given astounding levels of responsibility at a very young age; it is not uncommon for officers in their early 20s to be responsible and accountable for millions of dollars of equipment, not to mention the lives of the service members reporting to them.

- *Importance of remaining unbiased.* Fawley and Krysak note that "another challenge for both faculty and librarians is to separate personal feelings on military and war from professional obligations to the students" (2013, p. 530). Although veterans of the wars in Iraq and Afghanistan have received a more supportive response than veterans of Vietnam, many people do have strong antiwar and antimilitary feelings that occasionally manifest as anger or frustration toward individual veterans or service members. Veterans and service members have a wide variety of political beliefs, and many veterans may also disagree with the decision to enter into a particular military conflict. However, most veterans and service members feel that their sacrifices and service deserve respect, even if the war in which they served was unpopular. Instructors, including librarians, who convey a strong disdain for the military and service members risk alienating veteran and military-affiliated students.

- *Best practices for working with veterans.* Librarians can also request that the campus veteran center help them develop some best practices for working with veteran and military-affiliated students. For example, best practices in the classroom may involve refraining from unnecessarily dismissive or disdainful comments about the military or military service, permitting veteran and military-affiliated students to select a seat in the classroom where they will not be distracted by a need to maintain situational awareness, and remaining flexible about working with students who may need to miss a few classes due to military responsibilities. Best practices in reference support may involve promoting online reference services to help student veterans and service members who spend limited time on campus due to work and family responsibilities or perhaps promoting the library's veteran liaison as the expert who can work with the student one-on-one by appointment. And best practices for working with student veterans and service members as student workers may include maintaining flexibility to accommodate military-related absences as well as recognizing the experience and expertise of student veterans and service members by giving them options to engage in more interesting or challenging work.

If the college or university does not have faculty and staff training available, the library may wish to seek out additional resources. There may be opportunities to invite a veteran librarian in the area or state to conduct training for the library, or librarians may be able to take advantage of upcoming or recorded webinars as a starting point for a conversation on veteran and military-affiliated students in the library. For example, in 2015, the Texas State Library held a series of four free webinars on veterans in libraries (DiTullio, 2015). Other state libraries may make similar webinars or webinar series available for librarians in their states. Participating in these types of trainings can help librarians gain a better understanding of student veterans and service members, their unique challenges, and the strengths that they bring to college and university campuses.

Library Services for Student Veterans and Service Members

Although many colleges and universities have developed services and programs to support their veteran and military-affiliated students, only recently have academic libraries begun evaluating the needs of student veterans and service members. Because libraries play a key role as academic and social centers on campus, they are uniquely positioned to welcome and support student veterans. Recent research supports the importance of library support for student veterans, as Mills et al. declare that there is "a clear need for academic libraries to make a particular and specific effort to reach this population" and that "this outreach is likely to be well-received" (2015, p. 273).

One way that academic librarians can meet the needs of student veterans and service members is to develop services tailored to support veteran and military-affiliated students. Many of the services that academic libraries have developed to support student veterans and service members, such as LibGuides or library instruction, are the same services that they offer to other student groups. Others, however, are newly and specifically created for veteran and military-affiliated students. As an added benefit, these newly developed services aimed at veteran and military-affiliated students may also support other post-traditional students and students and faculty researching veteran and service member issues.

Liaison to Veteran and Military-Affiliated Students

One of the simplest strategies that libraries can employ to better serve student veterans and service members is to officially designate a library liaison to this group of students. Depending on the size of the campus and librarian workload, libraries can designate a single liaison or build a team of librarians and library staff who are interested in student veteran and service member issues and can work together to provide support. A number of libraries have designated veteran liaisons, including the University of Dubuque, Manhattan College, and the University of West Florida (University of Dubuque, n.d.; Manhattan College, 2015; McGowan, 2016). Library liaisons may work with the campus veteran center and other veteran-related organizations on campus to identify the needs of veterans and service members and identify ways that the library can help to fill those needs. Liaisons may also perform a number of other roles pertaining to support for student veterans and service members; for example, they may provide information literacy instruction and outreach to veterans' classes and groups, and they may build the library's collection of military-related materials.

Successful liaisons to veteran and military-affiliated students may be veterans or service members themselves, as veterans and service members often have a sense of camaraderie with others who have served. However, a military background should not be a prerequisite to serving as a liaison to veteran and military-affiliated students, and neither should the lack of a librarian or staff member with a military background prevent a library from designating a liaison to these students. Liaisons who have close family members or friends who have served are also commonly called upon, as these relationships have made them familiar with military culture. However, the most fundamental characteristic of a successful liaison, whether or not they have a military background, is that they should have an interest in and even passion for veteran and service member issues and a respect for the sacrifices inherent to military service.

Office Hours

If the college or university has a veteran center or a veterans' study lounge, librarians may wish to consider holding office hours in that location. If a librarian or team of librarians has been designated as liaison, holding weekly office hours in the veteran center may be an opportunity for the liaison to begin developing a relationship with the veteran center staff and the student veterans and service members themselves. Although librarians may not receive a large volume of questions during office hours, they can benefit greatly from sitting down in a room full of student veterans and service members and listening to their conversations. By listening patiently, librarians can begin to understand where student veteran and service members' frustrations lie and may identify some challenges that the libraries can help overcome.

Librarians may find themselves present in opportune moments, such as when student veterans and service members instinctively turn to one another for research support instead of turning to the library. Librarians can take advantage of these moments to demonstrate their research expertise and begin building confidence among the student veterans and service members. Atwood et al. astutely note that "word of mouth is a critical tool for earning veterans' trust" (2016, p. 176). Spending some time in a military-oriented space on campus and waiting patiently to help students when the opportunities arise is one way that librarians can begin to build trust with veteran and military-affiliated students.

LibGuides

One of the more common services developed for student veterans and service members is that of a LibGuide created for collecting resources that may be helpful to veteran and military-affiliated students. LibGuides can be developed relatively quickly and, although they require maintenance to keep links and information up-to-date, they do not require a substantial long-term investment of time.

Veteran and military-related LibGuides draw together a number of resources for student veterans and service members, including on-campus and community resources as well as research materials on veterans and service members. The following are examples of LibGuides academic librarians have developed for student veterans and service members on their campuses:

- USC Libraries' Veterans Services @ USC: http://libguides.usc.edu/uscveterans

- Austin Community College District's Veterans (U.S.): http://research-guides.austincc.edu/Veterans

- Western Washington University's Veterans Resource Guide: Welcome WWU Veterans!: http://researchguides.austincc.edu/Veterans

- University of Utah's Veterans at the U: http://campusguides.lib.utah.edu/veterans

Spaces

Space is at a premium in academic libraries as library gate counts reflect students' ever-increasing need for study space (American Library Association, 2012). But the physical space of some academic libraries can be off-putting to some student veterans and service members. When a student veteran or service member walks in the front door of the library and sees a crowded, noisy space with teenage college students socializing, they may think that the library is not a place for serious study or for post-traditional students. Furthermore, the open-concept floor plans that have become popular in libraries can be problematic for veterans and service members whose military service has left them with a need to constantly monitor their surroundings. But student veterans and service members can benefit greatly from use of the physical library because they may have work and family responsibilities that can make studying off-campus challenging. Libraries have adopted a few different strategies for making the physical library space more appealing for veterans, some of which require no actual changes to the library's layout.

Library spaces for veteran and military-affiliated students. A few libraries have been able to create a space in the library specifically for veteran and military-affiliated students. A dedicated space for veterans, service members, and other members of the veteran and military communities is helpful because it provides a location where student veterans and service members can study with fewer distractions from people passing through or students chatting. The additional benefit of a dedicated space is that it can serve as a place where veterans and service members can connect with one another and provide peer support. The following are examples of library spaces for veterans and service members:

- Washington State University WSU Veterans Center: https://va.wsu.edu/services

- UMass Dartmouth Veterans Reading Room: http://www.lib.umassd.edu/about/veterans-reading-room-claire-t-carney-library

- Washburn University's Veterans Success Center: http://www.washburn.edu/academics/center-student-success/veterans-success-center/index.html

When libraries can't provide dedicated space. For many libraries, a dedicated space for veteran and military-affiliated students may not be feasible due to space constraints. Even if the library can't provide space for a veteran center or reading room, it may be able to facilitate student veteran and service member use of the library space. For example, librarians at Miami University in Oxford, Ohio, recommend that librarians "offer space in your facility for them to meet or work together in groups" (Atwood et al., 2016, p. 176). Mills et al. confirm that many of the student veterans they interviewed expressed interest in having student veteran organization meetings and veteran study sessions in the library (2015). Even if the library is unable to provide dedicated space to student veterans and service members on a permanent basis, these types of intermittent uses may be feasible.

Alternatively, the library may want to consider working with the campus veteran center to identify study spaces in the library that are particularly military student friendly. These study spaces could be in low-traffic areas where student veterans and service members can easily monitor their surroundings and may allow them to position themselves so people can't walk up behind and inadvertently surprise them. Although the library may not be able to guarantee that military student–friendly spaces would be available or exclusive to student veterans and service members, the library could highlight such areas on a map and provide copies to the campus veteran center to hand out to veterans and service members who need help finding a good place to study (LeMire, 2015).

Information Literacy Instruction

Reaching student veterans within an academic context is a challenging proposition for librarians. Campuses that have a class for veterans may be open to an embedded librarian model within their classes; for example, Fawley and Krysak note that the University of Alabama's veteran liaison

> embeds two library classes per semester into the 'Military to College' course.... The library session outcomes are to introduce students to an academic library environment, give a brief

overview of the research process and locating and evaluating sources, and establish a foundation for subsequent instruction to build upon. There is also an online course guide with links to key library resources, contact information for assistance, and web resources for veterans. (2013, p. 528)

Other campuses have developed fully online instruction for veterans, which can be a great model for veteran and military-affiliated students who may be relying heavily or completely on online learning to complete their education. One such example is the University of Toledo's distance learning course for veterans and post-traditional students (Atwood et al., 2016). Librarians can contribute to these online courses by developing online instruction modules and embedding them within the online course to connect with veteran and military-affiliated students.

Library instruction in veteran-oriented classes provides a great opportunity for librarians to connect with groups of student veterans and service members in an academic context, which can be an important step to helping students recognize the benefits of working with a librarian. A survey administered to student veterans at Miami University in Oxford, Ohio, indicated that student veterans may underestimate their need for research support. It determined that "only 15% felt they needed more help with conducting research for papers and presentations" (Atwood et al., 2016, p. 175). Library instruction can help student veterans and service members develop a better assessment of their research skills and establish the librarian as an expert available to be consulted for research help.

However, not all campuses have veteran-only courses that librarians can embed into, and the longevity of the programs that do exist is uncertain (Grasgreen, 2012). If the college or university does not have veteran-only classes, librarians can also work to connect with student veterans and service members through traditional library instruction sessions. If they are comfortable doing so, librarians who are veterans or otherwise military-affiliated may wish to self-identify in library instruction sessions as a way to open the door to conversations with students about their military service or the service of a loved one. Even if there are no veteran or military-affiliated students in a class, librarians may find that students are researching military-related topics and appreciate knowing that the librarian has expertise in this area. For example, a common topic in some first-year writing classes recently has been women in combat arms due to the new military policy opening up all military occupations to women. Simply mentioning any military experience as part of the standard librarian introduction can be an easy way to help student veterans and service members see the librarian as a potential ally and can also lead to research consultations with students researching military issues.

Distance Education Support

Flexibility is a major factor in veterans' and service members' choice of college or university. Many veterans and service members end up attending for-profit colleges and universities, likely because these institutions are more likely to provide flexibility so veterans can fit classes around their other responsibilities (Field, 2008). This flexibility can be particularly crucial for service members who may work irregular schedules, be sent for long-term training exercises, or be deployed overseas while attending classes. One way that librarians can support veteran and military-affiliated students' need for flexibility is by highlighting and expanding services that support distance education students. For example, librarians can market the availability of early-morning and evening chat hours and email reference, which may better coincide with the availability of students physically located in another time zone.

But librarians should also consider providing accommodations specifically aimed at veteran and military-affiliated students. Because deployed service members may have limited or intermittent access to an Internet connection, librarians can work with instructors to ensure that students are able to download library resources efficiently (Lorenzetti, 2004). Murphy (2009) notes that "deployed students who will face enough obstacles trying to complete their educations do not need additional problems with downloading documents or e-mailing the worldwide services librarian" (p. 54). Librarians, especially those with significant numbers of active-duty students, should consider creating accommodations such as downloadable versions of tutorials or prepackaged required reading articles in smaller file sizes to minimize the time and frustration associated with accessing library materials while overseas.

Finally, librarians may wish to explore developing policies that govern library access for students whose studies are interrupted by military service. For example, such policies could allow the library to extend remote access to students who are working on an altered academic schedule to finish classes left incomplete due to a deployment or military-related action.

Collections

Many libraries may wish to build their collections as another strategy for supporting the veteran and military communities on their campuses. Some academic libraries have even created separate collections for veteran and military-related resources (e.g., Sopiarz, 2016). The types and quantity of resources for and about veterans and service members that the library may wish to acquire are dependent on many factors: size and type of college or university, number of veterans and service members enrolled, characteristics of the student veteran and service member population, and so on. This section is not intended to provide an exhaustive list of the materials that any given library should have in its collection, nor is it intended to endorse any particular resources. Instead, this section provides some general suggestions for the types of resources that veterans and service members on campus may need or want, as well as the types of resources that individuals researching veteran- and service member–related issues may want to access. Individual titles are listed only as examples.

Military resource guides. Some libraries, especially libraries at colleges and universities with many veterans and service members who are in transition or who have recently transitioned from the military, may want to provide access to guides to military resources. There are an abundant number of these guides, which are aimed at providing practical support for veterans, service members, and their families, and they may be particularly helpful for students at schools without a robust veterans' support system. The following are some examples:

Moore, J., Lawhorne, S. C., & Philpott, D. (2011). *Life after the military: A handbook for transitioning veterans.* Lanham, MD: Government Institutes.

Philpott, D. & Moore, J. (2009). *The wounded warrior handbook: A resource guide for returning veterans*. Lanham, MD: Government Institutes.

The military experience. Library collections should include materials about the experiences of veterans, including the generations of veterans and service members frequently found on the campus. The presence of these materials signals that the experiences and sacrifices of veterans and service members are not forgotten in the library, which is a message important to student veterans and service members, many of whom served overseas and returned to the United States to realize that the civilian population was largely disconnected from the wars in Iraq and Afghanistan.

When acquiring military-related materials, bear in mind that it can be difficult for civilians to capture the nuances of the military experience. High-quality civilian publications about war and military life abound, but some works that are well-received by other civilians can be received skeptically by veterans and service members. To appeal to veterans and service members, libraries should consider seeking out materials that are authentic to the military experience. For example, documentaries about the wars in Iraq and Afghanistan (e.g., *Gunner Palace, Restrepo*) or films based on a true story (e.g., *Generation Kill*) may be better received by a veteran and military-affiliated audience than popular Hollywood films (e.g., *Hurt Locker*).

Similarly, although there are many civilian works exploring the experiences and impact of war and military service, it may be helpful to include some works written by military veterans. In particular, works by Post-9/11 veterans investigating the wars in Iraq and Afghanistan may be helpful to include in the library collection. There are several books available that fit this category, many of which have been very well-reviewed. The following are fiction examples:

Gallagher, M. (2016). *Youngblood: A novel*. New York: Atria.

Klay, P. (2014). *Redeployment*. New York: Penguin.

Powers, K. (2012). *The yellow birds: A novel*. New York: Little, Brown and Co.

The following are nonfiction examples:

Busch, B. (2012). *Dust to dust: A memoir*. New York: Ecco.

Luttrell, M. & Robinson, P. (2007). *Lone survivor: The eyewitness account of Operation Redwing and the lost heroes of SEAL Team 10*. New York: Little, Brown and Co.

Williams, K. & Staub, M. E. (2005). *Love my rifle more than you: Young and female in the U.S. Army*. New York: W. W. Norton.

Military-related research. In addition to supporting veterans and service members by providing access to materials about the military and the military experience, academic librarians should also be prepared to support students and researchers investigating the needs and experiences of veterans and service members. For example, students may be interested in writing a research paper on common military topics, such as the challenges of incorporating women into combat roles in the military or the health disparities of military veterans. To support student research needs, libraries may wish to purchase materials that focus on these topics. For example, some undergraduates may find resources such as the *Praeger Handbook on Veterans' Health* to be a helpful first step toward exploring their topics.

If there are researchers on campus exploring veteran and military issues, librarians may wish to become familiar with more in-depth sources of data on veterans. For example, researchers investigating post-traumatic stress disorder (PTSD) will likely want to become familiar with the PILOTS database sponsored by the VA (U.S. Department of Veterans Affairs. National Center for PTSD, 2016). Researchers may also be looking for data resources, including the resources below:

- VA Open Data: http://www.va.gov/data
- VA Information Resource Center: http://www.virec.research.va.gov
- VA Office of Research & Development: http://www.research.va.gov
- VA Health Services Research & Development: http://www.hsrd .research.va.gov/default.cfm
- National Center for Veterans Analysis and Statistics: http://www .va.gov/vetdata
- Pew Veterans Survey: http://www.pewsocialtrends.org/2012/11/27/the -veterans-survey

In addition to data sets, researchers may want to become familiar with the organizations researching and reporting on veteran and military issues. A small sampling of these organizations is listed below:

- Institute for Veterans and Military Families: http://vets.syr.edu
- National Center for Veterans Studies: http://veterans.utah.edu
- Pew Research Military & Veterans: http://www.pewresearch.org/topics /military-and-veterans
- RAND Corporation Military Veterans: http://www.rand.org/topics /military-veterans.html
- USC Center for Innovation and Research on Veterans & Military Families: http://cir.usc.edu/about

Primary sources. In addition to published accounts and research data sets, academic libraries may want to include primary sources in their military and veteran-oriented collections. If the library has an archives or special collections, it may want to explore developing a veteran collection, especially if those veterans are alumni. Such a collection can bring together veteran artifacts such as photographs, letters, and other memorabilia to inform the research of future generations. Some veteran collections may also wish to include veteran oral histories. Librarians from Bowling Green State University assert that "collecting oral history is a time-honored role for libraries and would raise awareness on campus of the contribution that student veterans have made with their military service as well as the richness that their diversity of experience and perspectives offer to the campus community. Other academic libraries have had considerable success with this strategy for building bridges to the military/veteran community" (Atwood et al.,

2016, p. 177). For example, the University of Utah's American West Center and Fort Douglas partner on a veteran oral history project that is archived in the University's Marriott Library Special Collections (University of Utah. American West Center, 2014).

Libraries that do not have an archives or the capacity to collect and preserve oral histories may want to explore the Library of Congress' Veterans History Project, which preserves oral histories collected by veteran family members and other volunteers (Library of Congress, 2016). Regardless of where they are preserved, primary source materials from local veterans and service members can be an invaluable resource for students and researchers trying to understand the experiences of combat and the impact of military service on individuals and their families.

The above-listed resources are just a small sampling of the types of resources that the library should consider including in its collection. There is a wide variety of resources that can support veterans and service members, including materials intended to answer their direct questions, materials intended to represent and explore their experiences, and materials that support research into their needs. The materials that will best support veterans and service members in the library will depend on who the veterans and service members are on campus as well as the mission and purpose of the library.

Library Outreach to Student Veterans and Service Members

Student veterans and service members are often post-traditional students, and like other students outside of the traditional demographic, they may experience barriers to library usage. Research has indicated that one significant barrier to library usage by post-traditional students is unfamiliarity with library resources and services (Aagard, Antunez, & Sand, 2015, p. 222). To familiarize post-traditional students with library resources and services, libraries have developed a number of outreach strategies (Cannady, King, & Blendinger, 2012; Ismail, 2011). Academic librarians can use these and additional outreach strategies to connect with student veterans and service members and to familiarize veteran and military-affiliated students with library resources and services.

Outreach Events

If the college or university has a large number of student veterans and service members, one strategy to connect with them is to develop or participate in outreach events aimed at veteran and military-affiliated students. A number of colleges and universities have begun sponsoring campus veterans' events, especially orientation events. There are a number of different ways that libraries can get involved in these events. For example, Columbus State Community College developed a mini-presentation that was embedded within the campus student veteran orientation (Atwood et al., 2016). And at Texas A&M University, librarians staff a resource table at the campus's Vet Camp orientation for incoming student veterans and service members each semester.

Even if it is not feasible for librarians to have an in-person presence at veteran orientation events, there are other strategies that the library can employ. For example, at Bowling Green State University, the library "supplied a well-crafted one-page information sheet about the Library and Learning Commons to include in the orientation packet of newly enrolled veterans" (Atwood et al., 2016, p. 177). Service members are frequently handed packets of information and required to learn their content, so veterans are often very familiar with this method of information dissemination.

Displays and Exhibits

Another common outreach strategy aimed at student veterans and service members is to create military-related library displays. For example, some librarians may choose to do a military-themed book display in November to coincide with Veterans Day. This type of display can help to spotlight some of the library's military-related collections and encourage all patrons to become more familiar with the challenges, sacrifices, and victories of military service. If the library has archival materials related to the military, displaying unique photographs, letters, and memorabilia related to military history can also be a popular way to connect the library's collections to veteran-related holidays and events.

Librarians should also consider developing displays or exhibits that feature the veterans and service members on their campus, especially the student veterans. Librarians can work to collect photographs, memorabilia, and biographical sketches of student veterans and service members on their campus and build a display that highlights their unique experiences. Such a strategy can be a particularly effective way to demonstrate that the library is interested in and sees value in student veterans and service members. For example, when such a display was constructed at the University of Utah's Marriott Library, student veterans responded very positively, and a follow-up display was created to specifically highlight the women veterans on campus (LeMire, 2015). Student veterans and service members may appreciate the opportunity to share a little bit about their service with the rest of the campus, and other students can be surprised to find out that the person who sits behind them in chemistry has completed multiple combat tours.

Veteran and Military-Affiliated Students in the Library Collection

In addition to highlighting student veterans and service members through library displays, librarians can work to show the library's appreciation for student veterans and service members by including their voices in the library collection. Many campuses have creative writing programs, and some may have a course that focuses on war stories and personal narratives related to the military experience. For example, the University of Utah offers a Writing about War course that brings together both civilians and veterans to read, analyze, and write about military and combat experiences (Moulton, 2012). The University of Utah's Marriott Library collaborated with the Writing and Rhetoric Studies Department to collect stories written in the class, format them into a book, and print them on the library's Espresso Book Machine (LeMire, 2015). If the college or university doesn't offer such a class, librarians may be able to partner with creative writing faculty to develop a writing workshop for veterans and service members on campus and in the local community. Librarians also may be able to use an online platform to collect the stories of workshop participants who wish to share their work.

Promotional Materials

In addition to more time-consuming outreach efforts, librarians should consider whether their budgets would allow them to purchase promotional items aimed at veteran and military-affiliated students. Some military-oriented promotional items can be rather expensive; for example, Bowling Green State University purchased a copy of a resource guide aimed at student veterans for all incoming student veterans in Fall 2015. They furnished each book with "a bookplate bearing contact numbers for the University Libraries" (Atwood et al., 2016, p. 177). However, promotional items for veteran and military-affiliated students can also be simple and inexpensive. Librarians at Texas A&M University purchased small, inexpensive spiral-top notebooks with attached pens and gave them to incoming student veterans and service members at the university's resource fair for incoming veteran and military-affiliated students. This type of notebook is commonly used in the military because it fits easily in uniform pockets, and librarians were hoping to use this item to subtly reference military culture and to provide students with a useful tool branded with the library logo. Student veterans and service members responded very positively to these mini-notebooks, and they remain a popular item at resource fairs for veteran and military-affiliated students.

Collaborations and Partnerships

Campus Collaborators

A number of different resources and organizations for veterans were discussed in chapter 2. Although these resources remain relevant for academic librarians, some colleges and universities also have veteran and military-related resources and organizations specific to the campus with which librarians can collaborate.

Librarians whose college or university has a veteran center should consider this office to be the most likely collaborator in supporting veteran and military-affiliated students. As mentioned earlier in this chapter, this office serves as a point of contact not just for veterans but also for service members, survivors, dependents, and sometimes even for cadets and midshipmen who plan to commission into the military. Academic librarians interested in working with student veterans and service members should make it a priority to meet with the director of their campus veteran center.

Campus veteran centers are commonly led by a military veteran, often a former commissioned officer who has retired from the military. This means that the leader of the veteran center has a great understanding of veterans and service members and their particular needs, but it may also indicate that they are not likely to be familiar with the myriad services, programs, and collections available in modern academic libraries. They may be surprised to hear from a librarian and unsure how the library could support the veteran center in their mission to help student veterans and service members succeed. For example, they may know that many veterans and service members on campus are parents of minor children and struggle to balance family responsibilities with their academic workload, but they may not mention this challenge because they don't see how that relates to the library—after all, the students don't often mention the need for research support. But by discussing student needs with the veteran center leadership, librarians may discover that student veterans and service members with children may be having difficulty accessing librarian support, print resources, or a quiet study area in the evenings.

Librarians may be able to help these students by marketing online reference services to this group, by directing students to the library's document delivery service, or by designating a study space in the library where students can study with their children. Because veteran center directors may not be aware of the extent of the library's resources and services, they may not immediately recognize that the library can be a valuable campus partner, so it often pays off for librarians to ask questions, be persistent, and bring their own ideas for what the library can do to help.

In addition to a veteran center, some campuses may have other departments and faculty interested in veterans and service members. For example, at the University of Utah, there is a committee dedicated to planning the annual Veterans Day Commemoration (University of Utah, 2016). Membership on such committees can bring librarians into contact with other staff and faculty who are passionate about veterans' issues and therefore open up opportunities for partnership. Some campuses have faculty researching veterans' issues; at Texas A&M University, the campus Veteran Resource and Support Center organized the Veteran Research and Assessment Coalition, which brings together researchers studying veterans' issues to foster collaboration and share information (Texas A&M University. Veteran Resource and Support Center, 2015). Librarian participation in such groups can lead to increased library involvement in veteran-related research projects and can also help inform library collection development efforts.

Student Organizations

Many college and university campuses have SVA chapters. As previously mentioned, these chapters are student-led groups of veterans who work together to help one another transition to college and succeed academically. These groups also often empower veterans by working collaboratively to advocate for veterans' needs on campus and to serve others, especially veterans in need. Large campuses may have other formal student veteran organizations; for example, some law schools have a veterans' organization for law student veterans. If the college or university has a student veteran organization, whether or not it is a chapter of SVA, this can be a great group for librarians to consult with to gain insight into the needs of student veterans on campus. Librarians can ask to attend one of the group's regular meetings as a way to start a conversation about student veteran needs, or they can invite the group to the library for a special event or program.

In addition to an SVA chapter, the college or university may also have other student groups interested in veterans and veterans' issues. For example, Texas A&M University's Aggie Shields student organization is a group of students that collects donated textbooks and checks them out to veterans, service members, and their dependents ("Aggie Shields," 2016). This unique group has some natural areas for partnership and collaboration with the library. Other campuses may have additional student groups interested in veterans' issues that may offer new and interesting ways that the library can support student veterans and service members.

Local Partners

In addition to on-campus partners such as a campus veteran center and student veteran organization, many communities have organizations in the local area that are interested in veterans' issues. For example, the local area may have branches of large veterans service organizations such as the Veterans of Foreign Wars (VFW) or American Legion that may be interested in partnering on programming (U.S. Department of Veterans Affairs, 2013a). Some areas may have local military museums that may be natural partners; for example, just down the highway from Texas A&M is the Museum of the American GI ("Museum of the American G.I.," n.d.). Some areas may even have regular gatherings of local veterans' organizations, such as the San Diego Veterans Coalition or the Coalition of Brazos Valley Veterans Organizations ("San Diego Veterans Coalition," 2016; TexVet, 2016). These coalitions can be a great place to learn about some of the different organizations in the area that are interested in veterans' and service members' issues and to identify potential partners for programming.

Larger veteran and military organizations, such as the state department of veterans' affairs, local chapters of the federal VA, and military installations, may also be potential partners for libraries working to support veterans and service members (U.S. Department of Veterans Affairs, 2013b; U.S. Department of Veterans Affairs, 2015a; U.S. Department of Defense, 2016). However, librarians should be aware that larger organizations may have less capacity for partnerships with individual libraries or librarians.

Conclusion

Student veterans, service members, and other military-affiliated students make up a small but significant part of many college campuses. This chapter covered only a few of the many ways that academic librarians can play a role in helping these veteran and military-affiliated students succeed in college. Librarians can support student veterans and service members by helping them feel welcome in the library and on campus and by providing them with library programs, services, and collections. They can also make an impact by facilitating referrals to the campus veteran center and other available resources and by advocating for campus and library policies that are friendly to the veteran and military communities. Colleges and universities have made great strides in making their campuses a more welcoming and supportive place for student veterans and service members, and it is time for libraries not only to catch up, but to lead the way.

References

Aagard, M. C., Antunez, M. Y., & Sand, J. N. (2015). Learning from degree-seeking older adult students in a university library. *Reference Services Review, 43*(2), 215–230. doi:10.1108/RSR-06-2014-0017

Aggie Shields. (2016). Retrieved from https://maroonlink.tamu.edu/organization/tamushields

Altman, G. (2015, July 15). Most popular colleges for TA & GI Bill—latest trends. Retrieved from http://www.militarytimes.com/story/veterans/best-for-vets/2015/07/15/most-popular-colleges-for-ta-gi-bill-fiscal-2014/30124063

American Library Association. (2012). *State of America' libraries report 2012: Academic libraries.* Chicago, IL: American Library Association. Retrieved from http://www.ala.org/news/mediapresscenter/americaslibraries/soal2012/academic-libraries

Army Times Publishing Company. (n.d.) The GI Bill of Rights and how it works. *Army Times.* Retrieved from http://www.nationalww2museum.org/learn/education/for-students/national-history-day/gi-bill-of-rights.pdf

Atwood, T., Farmer, M., McDonald, K., Miller, B., Theodore-Shusta, E., & Wood, E. J. (2016). On the front lines: Serving Ohio's best. *Journal of Academic Librarianship, 42*(2), 172–180. doi:10.1016/j.acalib.2015.12.011

Baker, S. (2013). 8 keys to success: Supporting veterans, military and military families on campus [Blog post]. Retrieved from https://www.whitehouse.gov/blog/2013/08/13/8-keys-success-supporting-veterans-military-and-military-families-campus

Buddin, R. & Kapur, K. (2002). *Tuition assistance usage and first-term military retention* (No. RAND-MR-1295-OSD). Santa Monica, CA: RAND National Defense Research Institute. Retrieved from https://www.rand.org/content/dam/rand/pubs/monograph_reports/2005/MR1295.pdf

Cannady, R. E., King, S. B., & Blendinger, J. G. (2012). Proactive outreach to adult students: A department and library collaborative effort. *Reference Librarian, 53*(2), 156–169. doi:10.1080/02763877.2011.608603

Card, N. A., Bosch, L., Casper, D. M., Wiggs, C. B., Hawkins, S. A., Schlomer, G. L., & Borden, L. M. (2011). A meta-analytic review of internalizing, externalizing, and academic adjustment among children of deployed military service members. *Journal of Family Psychology, 25*(4), 508–520. doi:10.1037/a0024395

Cate, C. A. (2014). *Million records project: Research from Student Veterans of America*. Washington, D.C.: Student Veterans of America. Retrieved from http://studentveterans.org/images/Reingold_Materials/mrp/download-materials/mrp_Full_report.pdf

DiTullio, N. (2015, October 6). Providing library services for military and veteran communities in Texas webinar series begins October 28 [Blog post]. Retrieved from https://www.tsl.texas.gov/ld/librarydevelopments/?p=19137

Employer Support of the Guard and Reserve. (n.d.). USERRA. Retrieved from http://www.esgr.mil/USERRA/What-is-USERRA.aspx

Fawley, N. & Krysak, N. (2013). Serving those who serve: Outreach and instruction for student cadets and veterans. In Mueller, D. (Ed.) *Imagine, innovate, inspire: The proceedings of the ACRL 2013 conference* (pp. 525–531). Chicago, IL: Association of College and Research Libraries.

Field, K. (2008, July 25). Cost, convenience drive veterans' college choices. *Chronicle of Higher Education.* Retrieved from http://chronicle.com.lib-ezproxy.tamu.edu:2048/article/Cost-Convenience-Drive/20381

Friedman, E. M., Miller, L. L., & Evans, S. E. (2015). *Advancing the careers of military spouses: An assessment of education and employment goals and barriers facing military spouses eligible for MyCAA*. Santa Monica, CA: RAND Corporation. Retrieved from http://www.rand.org/content/dam/rand/pubs/research_reports/RR700/RR784/RAND_RR784.pdf

Gildea, D. (2014, June 25). CSAF to sponsor three captains for PhD program. Retrieved from http://www.af.mil/News/ArticleDisplay/tabid/223/Article/485786/csaf-to-sponsor-three-captains-for-phd-program.aspx

Grasgreen, A. (2012, January 4). Veterans only [Blog post]. Retrieved from https://www.insidehighered.com/news/2012/01/04/veterans-only-classes-both-expanding-and-closing

Hannaford, L. (2013). *Transitioning from the out date: Information seeking behavior of junior enlisted army veterans of Operation Iraqi and Enduring Freedom* (Master's thesis). Retrieved from ProQuest Dissertations & Theses Global (Order No. 154926).

Harrell, M. C., Lim, N., Castaneda, L. W., & Golinelli, D. (2004). *Working around the military. Challenges to military spouse employment and education*. Santa Monica, CA: RAND Corporation. Retrieved from http://www.rand.org/content/dam/rand/pubs/monographs/2004/RAND_MG196.pdf

Indiana Department of Veterans' Affairs. (n.d.). Applications/forms. Retrieved from http://www.in.gov/dva/2357.htm

Indiana University Bloomington. Office of the Registrar. (2016). Military withdrawal. Retrieved from http://registrar.indiana.edu/policies/withdrawal/military-withdrawal.shtml

Ismail, L. (2011). Getting personal: Reaching out to adult learners through a course management system. *Reference Librarian, 52*(3), 244–262. doi:10.1080/02763877.2011.556993

Kim, Y. M. & Cole, J. S. (2013). *Student veterans / service members' engagement in college and university life and education*. Washington, D.C.: American Council on Education. Retrieved from https://www.acenet.edu/news-room/Documents/Student-Veterans-Service-Members-Engagement.pdf

LeMire, S. (2015). Beyond service: New outreach strategies to reach student veterans. In *Creating sustainable community: The proceedings of the ACRL 2015 conference* (pp. 66–71). Chicago, IL: Association of College and Research Libraries.

Library of Congress. (2016). Veterans history project. Retrieved from https://www.loc.gov/vets

Lopez, E. S. (2013). *The effectiveness of university programs, services, and practices in retaining student veterans transitioning to higher education: Voices of student veterans—a case study analysis approach at two universities* (Doctoral dissertation). Retrieved from ProQuest Dissertations & Theses Global (Order No. 3599497).

Lorenzetti, J. P. (2004). Lessons from the field: What eArmyU can teach distance education providers. *Distance Education Report, 8*(12), 1–6.

Manhattan College. (2015). Veteran services & contacts. Retrieved from https://inside.manhattan.edu/student-life/veteran-services/services-and-contacts.php

Maury, R. & Stone, B. (2014). *Military spouse employment report*. Syracuse, NY: Institute for Veterans and Military Families.

McBain, L., Kim, Y. M., Cook, B. J., & Snead, K. M. (2012). *From soldier to student II: Assessing campus programs for veterans and service members*. Washington, D.C.: American Council on Education. Retrieved from http://www.acenet.edu/news-room/Documents/From-Soldier-to-Student-II-Assessing-Campus-Programs.pdf

McGowan, B. (2016). Military & veterans: A guide to the library. Retrieved from http://libguides.uwf.edu/military

Mettler, S. (2005). *Soldiers to citizens: The G.I. Bill and the making of the greatest generation*. Oxford: Oxford University Press.

Military OneSource. (2016). How to use the military tuition assistance program. Retrieved from http://www.militaryonesource.mil/voluntary-education?content_id=268274

Mills, C. P., Paladino, E. B., & Klentzin, J. C. (2015). Student veterans and the academic library. *Reference Services Review, 43*(2), 262–279. doi:10.1108/RSR-10-2014-0049

Minnesota Office of Higher Education. (2012). Minnesota GI Bill. Retrieved from https://www.ohe.state.mn.us/mPg.cfm?pageID=1803

Molina, D. & Morse, A. (2015). *Military-connected undergraduates: Exploring differences between National Guard, Reserve, active duty, and veterans in higher education*. Washington, D.C.: American Council on Education. Retrieved from https://www.naspa.org/rpi/reports/military-connected-undergraduates-exploring-differences

Moulton, K. (2012, May 9). Veterans, fellow students connect while writing on war. *Salt Lake Tribune*. Retrieved from http://archive.sltrib.com/story.php?ref=/sltrib/news/54051347-78/war-class-says-writing.html.csp

Murphy, E. W. (2009). Delivery to the sharp end of the spear: Responding to the need for library support to the deployed and downrange military community. *Journal of Library Administration, 49*(1/2), 51–57. doi:10.1080/01930820802310676

Museum of the American G.I. (n.d.). Retrieved from http://americangimuseum.org

National Survey of Student Engagement. (2010). *Major differences: Examining student engagement by field of study—annual results 2010*. Bloomington: Indiana University Center for Postsecondary Research. Retrieved from http://nsse.indiana.edu/nsse_2010_results/pdf/nsse_2010_annualresults.pdf

Pat Tillman Foundation. (2016a). Apply to be a Tillman scholar. Retrieved from http://pattillmanfoundation.org/apply-to-be-a-scholar

Pat Tillman Foundation. (2016b). Writing the story of a better future. Retrieved from http://pattillmanfoundation.org/our-story

Pennsylvania Department of Education. (2016). Veteran's education. Retrieved from http://www.education.pa.gov/Postsecondary-Adult/Veterans%20Education/Pages/default.aspx#.VuGid_krLIU

Post-9/11 GI Bill, 38 C.F.R. § 33 (2009).

Radford, A. W. (2011, September). *Military service members and veterans: A profile of those enrolled in undergraduate and graduate education in 2007–08.* Washington, D.C.: National Center for Education Statistics. Retrieved from http://nces.ed.gov /pubs2011/2011163.pdf

Ruff, S. B. & Keim, M. A. (2014). Revolving doors: The impact of multiple school transitions on military children. *The Professional Counselor, 4*(2), 103–113. doi:10.15241/sbr.4.2.103

Sander, L. (2012, March 11). Out of uniform: At half a million and counting, veterans cash in on Post-9/11 GI Bill. *Chronicle of Higher Education.* Retrieved from http://chronicle.com/article/At-Half-a-Million-and/131112

San Diego Veterans Coalition. (2016). Retrieved from http://sdvetscoalition.org

Schworm, P. (2008). Vets often denied academic credits. *Boston Globe.* Retrieved from http://archive.boston.com/news/local/articles/2008/02/05/vets_often_denied _academic_credits/

Sopiarz, J. (2016). Library outreach to veterans: Opportunities, challenges, examples. *Active Librarian, 1*(2), 1–14.

Student Veterans of America. (2016). Chapter directory. Retrieved from http:// studentveterans.org/index.php/chapter/directory

Texas A&M University. Corps of Cadets. (2014a). 2014 state of the Corps. Retrieved from http://corps.tamu.edu/2014-state-of-the-corps

Texas A&M University. Corps of Cadets. (2014b). Academic certificate in leadership studies. Retrieved from http://corps.tamu.edu/leadership

Texas A&M University. Human Resources. (2016). Military leave. Retrieved from http://employees.tamu.edu/benefits/leave/military

Texas A&M University. Veteran Resource and Support Center. (2015). TAMU veteran research & assessment coalition. Retrieved from http://aggieveterans.tamu.edu /faculty-outreach

TexVet. (2016). Coalition of Brazos Valley veterans organizations. Retrieved from http://www.texvet.org/partners/coalition-brazos-valley-veterans-organizations

Tice, J. (2014, December 15). Army launches new graduate school program. *Army Times.* Retrieved from http://www.armytimes.com/story/military/careers/army/officer /2014/12/08/performance-based-grad-school/19843661

United States Government Accountability Office. (2014). *DOD education benefits: Action is needed to ensure evaluations of postsecondary schools are useful.* Washington, D.C.: U.S. Government Accountability Office. Retrieved from http://gao .gov/assets/670/665580.pdf

University of Dubuque. (n.d.). Library liaisons. Retrieved from http://www.dbq.edu /library/aboutus/libraryliaisons

University of Utah. (2016). Veterans Day commemoration. Retrieved from http:// veteransday.utah.edu

University of Utah. American West Center. (2014). Saving the legacy: An oral history of Utah's veterans. Retrieved from http://awc.utah.edu/oral-histories/veterans .php

University of Utah. Division of Human Resources. (2016). Paid leave time. Retrieved from https://www.hr.utah.edu/benefits/paidLeave.php

U.S. Army. (2015). Green to gold scholarship option. Retrieved from http://www.goarmy .com/careers-and-jobs/current-and-prior-service/advance-your-career/green-to -gold/green-to-gold-scholarship.html

U.S. Army. Acquisition Support Center. (n.d.). Advanced civil schooling (ACS). Retrieved from http://asc.army.mil/web/career-development/programs/advanced -civil-schooling

U.S. Department of Defense. (2014). *DOD MOU between DOD Office of the USD (P&R) and educational institution and service-specific addendums.* Washington, D.C.: U.S. Department of Defense. Retrieved from https://s3.amazonaws.com/dodmou /dodmouwebsite/documents/DODMOU+3+SAMPLE+July_10_2015.pdf

U.S. Department of Defense. (2016). Military installations. Retrieved from http:// www.militaryinstallations.dod.mil

U.S. Department of Defense. Voluntary Education Partnership Memorandum of Understanding. (n.d.). Tuition assistance (TA) decide. Retrieved from https:// www.dodmou.com/TADECIDE

U.S. Department of Veterans Affairs. (n.d.). GI Bill comparison tool. Retrieved from https://www.vets.gov/gi-bill-comparison-tool

U.S. Department of Veterans Affairs. (2013a). Directory of veterans service organizations. Retrieved from http://www.va.gov/vso

U.S. Department of Veterans Affairs. (2013b). State veterans affairs offices. Retrieved from http://www.va.gov/statedva.htm

U.S. Department of Veterans Affairs. (2014). VETPOP 2014: Living veterans by period of service, gender, 2013–2043. Retrieved from http://www.va.gov/vetdata/docs /Demographics/New_Vetpop_Model/2L_VetPop2014.xlsx

U.S. Department of Veterans Affairs. (2015a). Locations. Retrieved from http://www .va.gov/landing2_locations.htm

U.S. Department of Veterans Affairs. (2015b). *School certifying official handbook.* Washington, D.C.: U.S. Department of Veterans Affairs. Retrieved from http:// www.benefits.va.gov/GIBILL/docs/job_aids/SCO_Handbook.pdf

U.S. Department of Veterans Affairs. National Center for PTSD. (2016). What is the PILOTS database? Retrieved from http://www.ptsd.va.gov/professional /pilots-database

U.S. Department of Veterans Affairs. Veterans Benefits Administration. (2015a). Dependents education assistance program. Retrieved from http://www.benefits .va.gov/GIBILL/DEA.asp

U.S. Department of Veterans Affairs. Veterans Benefits Administration. (2015b). Montgomery GI selected reserve (MGIB-SR). Retrieved from http://www.benefits .va.gov/gibill/mgib_sr.asp

U.S. Department of Veterans Affairs. Veterans Benefits Administration. (2015c). Principles of excellence. Retrieved from http://www.benefits.va.gov/gibill/principles _of_excellence.asp

U.S. Department of Veterans Affairs. Veterans Benefits Administration. (2015d). *VBA annual benefits report fiscal year 2014—education.* Washington, D.C.: U.S. Department of Veterans Affairs. Retrieved from http://www.benefits.va.gov /REPORTS/abr/ABR-Education-FY14-10202015.pdf

U.S. Department of Veterans Affairs. Veterans Benefits Administration. (2016a). Post-9/11 GI Bill. Retrieved from http://www.benefits.va.gov/gibill/post911_gibill.asp

U.S. Department of Veterans Affairs. Veterans Benefits Administration. (2016b). Survivors and dependents assistance. Retrieved from http://www.benefits.va.gov /gibill/survivor_dependent_assistance.asp

U.S. Department of Veterans Affairs. Veterans Benefits Administration. (2016c). Transfer Post-9/11 GI Bill to spouse and dependents. Retrieved from http://www .benefits.va.gov/gibill/post911_transfer.asp

U.S. Department of Veterans Affairs. Veterans Benefits Administration. (2016d). Veterans benefits administration reports. Retrieved from http://www.benefits .va.gov/reports/annual_performance_reports.asp

U.S. Department of Veterans Affairs. Veterans Benefits Administration. (2016e). Vocational rehabilitation and employment (VR&E). Retrieved from http://www .benefits.va.gov/vocrehab

U.S. Department of Veterans Affairs. Vocational Rehabilitation & Employment. (2016). VetSuccess on campus. Retrieved from http://www.benefits.va.gov/vocrehab/vsoc .asp

U.S. Marine Corps. (2016). Commissioning programs. Retrieved from https://www .marines.com/becoming-a-marine/commissioning-programs/enlisted-to-officer /mecep

U.S. Navy. (2016). STA-21: Seaman to admiral-21 program. Retrieved from http://www .sta-21.navy.mil

5

School and Special Libraries and the Veteran and Military Communities

The veteran and military communities are broad populations and include individuals from all ages and walks of life. Due to this diversity, members of the veteran and military communities can be encountered in any environment, including any library environment. Previous chapters have focused on the needs of veterans, service members, and their families in general and in public and academic libraries, but there are a number of other library settings in which librarians and library staff are likely to encounter members of the veteran and military communities as library patrons. This chapter will discuss the information needs of veteran and military-affiliated patrons and provide suggestions for librarians in five library settings: elementary and secondary school libraries, health sciences libraries, military libraries, law libraries, and prison libraries.

This chapter focuses on only some of the issues faced and success stories told by librarians working in these library settings. It is not a complete or thorough examination of what these librarians should say or do, but rather it is an effort to begin a conversation about how all librarians can serve the veteran and military communities. Librarians whose library context is described in this chapter may want to seek additional information through such professional organizations as the American Association of School Librarians or the Special Libraries Association to identify emerging strategies for helping members of veteran and military communities feel welcome in libraries. The future of serving those who served should be full of new endeavors, increased knowledge, and collaborations that allow the library profession to demonstrate its ability to evolve and respond to the needs and interests of veterans, military personnel, and their families.

School Libraries

Although this book primarily focuses on the needs of veterans and service members, school librarians are more likely to interact with a different military-affiliated population: military children. This section will provide school librarians with background information about the challenges experienced by the dependent children of military personnel, as well as offer suggestions for collaborations, services, and programs to support these children in the kindergarten through twelfth grade (K–12) school environment.

This section first provides demographic information about military children to help school librarians understand the number of military children in U.S. public schools. Next, it will discuss some characteristics of military children and military families, including the impact a service member's deployment can have on their family. Then this section will offer some ideas for collaborations and partnerships, and it will provide some additional ideas for programs, services, and collection development strategies to support military children. The section will end by covering some resources that school librarians and other educators can use to learn more about supporting the needs of military families.

School Libraries and Military Children

In 2014, U.S. military families included over 1.8 million military children (U.S. Department of Defense, 2015). Some military children attend Department of Defense Education Activity (DoDEA) schools, which are federally administered schools for military children on military installations around the world and in the United States (U.S. Department of Defense, n.d.). However, approximately 80 percent of military children attend U.S. public schools (U.S. Department of Education, n.d.). Although many of these military children are clustered in schools located near military installations, many others can be found in any school district. Members of the National Guard and Reserves may live hundreds of miles from their military units in communities with very few resources dedicated to military families.

In cities with large military populations, some branches of the Armed Forces fund Morale, Welfare, and Recreation (MWR) organizations known as family support centers that provide resources for many facets of military family life. The Department of the Navy's Fleet and Family Support Centers, for example, provide new parenting workshops, counseling, and employment assistance for military dependents (Commander, Navy Installations Command, n.d.). However, military families who live far away from a military installation may have difficulty accessing in-person military resources. For this reason, the military also provides some online resources that military families can access regardless of their location. Military OneSource provides service members and their family members with remote access to research databases, eBooks, audiobooks, and electronic resources for managing finances, relocating, or transitioning from military to civilian life (U.S. Department of Defense, 2016). However, many military families may still benefit from the in-person support that K–12 schools and school librarians can offer military children.

Characteristics of Military Children and the Children of Veterans

Some of the challenges faced by military children may be readily apparent, but others are not. Military children's education may have been interrupted by multiple long-distance moves as their families repeatedly transferred to new military bases. Also, many military children experience significant upheaval in their family life when a parent is deployed overseas, often for up to a year at a time. Deployments can impact every member of the family, both during the deployment and after the deployed parent returns. The affected family must adapt to new roles in the parent's absence and then has to strike a new balance to incorporate the deployed parent back into the family routine. Up to 2 million children have a military parent who has deployed at least once, and many may have a military parent who has deployed multiple times (Clever & Segal, 2013; Baiocchi, 2013). As a result, reports show that "uncertainty is the one constant in the military lifestyle" (Bradbard et al., 2014, p. 1).

Although military children do experience significant challenges as a result of a parent's military service, they can also develop a unique set of strengths. Park (2011) observes that "the available evidence suggests that military children typically function as well as or even better than civilian children on most indices of health, well-being, and academic achievement" (p. 67). Adolescents report "generally positive educational experiences, peer relations, and involvement with daily life activities" (Jeffreys & Leitzel, 2000, p. 225). Military children have to learn to be resilient and flexible, to take on new challenges, to be loyal, and to take responsibility very seriously (Hall, 2008). School librarians should be aware not only of the challenges that military children face, but also of the strengths that they can bring to the classroom. Librarians and teachers should work with military children not only to help them overcome their challenges but also to build upon their burgeoning strengths.

K–12 schools and librarians should also consider the needs of children of military veterans. When service members separate from the military, their children face additional challenges. For instance, spouses, parents, and other family members often serve as primary caregivers for wounded veterans (Watson Institute for International and Public Affairs, 2015). The children of these veterans may have difficulty coping with the impact of injuries and the stress of caregiving on their parents. The children of veterans also may still be dealing with past military-related hardships, even though their family is no longer likely to be moved to a new duty station or to have a parent deployed. For example, they may continue to experience separation anxiety as a result of a parent's earlier deployment. Additionally, children of veterans may be managing the challenges related to the transition from military to civilian life as they and their families adjust to a civilian lifestyle and identity. For example, the children of veterans who have moved away from a military installation may have a hard time adjusting to a lack of classmates who share and can identify with their experiences as military children.

The impact of deployments on military families. When military service members are deployed, they are given orders and sent to an assigned location. Although many deployments are combat-related, service members may also be deployed for other reasons, such as assisting organizations in disaster relief or working with United Nations or other joint task forces to participate in civil affairs activities. Military OneSource offers a guide for military families preparing for deployment that summarizes deployments in terms of a cycle that consists of four phases: predeployment, deployment, postdeployment, and reintegration (U.S. Department of Defense, 2012). This section is intended to help school librarians understand the challenges associated with each phase as well as its potential impact on military children.

Predeployment. During the initial phase of the deployment cycle, military personnel prepare travel documents, develop packing lists, and make plans for keeping in touch with family members. Families with children begin to implement their family care plan, a document outlining who will care for dependent children while the service member is deployed. Often this individual is a nondeploying parent, but sometimes children are sent to live with grandparents or other caregivers. Family members may prepare by connecting with local organizations that offer emotional support, coordinating responsibility for financial and household tasks while the service member is away, and processing information about the deployment. Researchers note that "before a parent's deployment, a child may become emotionally withdrawn, apathetic, or exhibit regressive behavior" (Flake, Davis, Johnson, & Middleton, 2009, p. 272). Children may cope by asking questions about what is going to happen, and families may help children feel some semblance of control by making plans for activities during the deployment. Predeployment activities can be stressful and require great effort by parents and caregivers to prepare for the logistics of the deployment in addition to the communication and emotional support that is needed as soon as the service member is notified of the deployment.

Deployment. The deployment phase begins when military personnel leave home, even if they are relocated to a staging area before traveling overseas. For service members, this is the phase when they begin performing their missions. Children's caregivers are responsible for running the household and representing the deployed service member in any legal or financial transitions. Meanwhile, caregivers continue to manage their own professional and social obligations and commitments. During this period, caregivers may seek professional help for their children, including consulting a therapist or psychologist, even though they may be reluctant to ask for help for themselves (Bradbard et al., 2014). Research indicates that the beginning of the deployment phase is characterized by a combination of feelings, including anger, sadness, and abandonment. And as the deployment continues, children's behavior can begin to change as a result of the stress of the deployment, including their academic performance (Fitzsimons & Krause-Parello, 2009).

Schools and school librarians should be cognizant of the stressors that military children face during the deployment phase and prepare to provide support to help military children cope during this difficult time. Research suggests that "a parental deployment disrupts a child's academic performance, particularly if the absence occurs during the month in which the child is tested" (Engel, Gallagher, & Lyle, 2010, p. 80). School librarians should be prepared for students with a deployed parent to experience some academic challenges and respond by providing access to academic support materials to help students engage academically and to catch up if they fall behind.

Postdeployment. The postdeployment period includes the service members' homecoming and the time period after the homecoming when military personnel reunite with family members and friends. This period may be one of the most challenging phases of the deployment cycle, as military personnel and their families must adapt both emotionally and physically. Service members must adjust to civilian routines and surroundings that differ greatly from high-tempo and high-stress deployment routines and surroundings, while "the service member must be reintegrated into a family that is not the same as the one that was left" (Johnson et al., 2007, p. 24). During this period, school librarians may wish to offer students books and other resources that help them understand and process the conflicted feelings they may be experiencing during what is often assumed to be a happy occasion.

Reintegration. Librarians should be aware that the deployment cycle does not end when service members return home from deployment.

Although the postdeployment period can be a stressful one, the period that follows can be equally challenging as the military family reintegrates into a family unit. Family life begins to return to normal, and the service members resume their normal military responsibilities. For many older children, this can be a particularly challenging period. During the deployment phase, older children may have been asked to take on some of the absent parent's responsibilities. When the parent returns, these older children experience mixed feelings when the parent takes back their responsibilities. In focus groups with teenagers with military parents, this is one of the greater challenges after a parent has returned from deployment (Bradbard et al., 2014).

During periods of sustained military conflict, the reintegration period can be complicated by the next deployment looming ahead on the family's horizon. Educators should know that academic challenges experienced by military children as a result of a parent's deployment may linger for an extended period of time. Research indicates that "children experience a decline in academic achievement that results from deployments from as far back as 5 years" (Engel, Gallagher, & Lyle, 2010, p. 80). Even after the deployed service member returns home and the family transitions back to a semblance of normalcy, family members can struggle to recover lost ground both academically and emotionally (Marek et al., 2014).

Although the deployment of a service member parent is a uniquely stressful experience for a child, there are number of other reasons that military personnel may be separated from their families. In addition to initial entry (basic) training, occupational schooling, and other entry-level educational courses that new service members attend, all service members are encouraged to seek additional opportunities to learn new skills. Officers may even be sent to attend graduate courses at locations away from their families. In addition, most service members participate in large-scale or small-scale joint training exercises that simulate deployments, both within the United States and overseas. Attending skills training, undergoing weekend survival workshops or unit exercises, and participating in advanced courses, such as language learning or advanced skills in the use of equipment, may also separate service members from their families for extended periods. Military children experience stress and anxiety during these absences even though the level of concern for the safety of the service member parent is likely to be diminished.

School librarians who collaborate with military family support organizations can learn more about the deployment cycle and the timing of deployments and large-scale training obligations among military units in the community. Through these collaborations, school librarians can host different types of activities to support military children through all phases of a deployment. Storytimes with military-related stories, collections featuring military children, and other programs and resources can help military children feel supported by their schools. Because studies show that military children also thrive when able to interact socially with their peers, school librarians may want to offer book clubs that provide opportunities for military children to interact and sometimes to read experiences like their own (Bradbard et al., 2014). Additionally, activities such as creating homemade photo albums, memory boxes, and dream jars, among other ideas, can be used by school librarians and teachers to help ease the difficulties of a student coping with a parent's absence. School librarians can coordinate with the parents of military children or support organizations to identify opportunities to host activities like these in the library setting.

Collaborations and Partnerships

Developing partnerships and collaborations with organizations interested in veteran and military issues can inform a school librarian's efforts to better understand the needs of military children and also to connect students with available resources. School librarians who work in areas near a major military installation may have large populations of military children in their schools. These librarians should take advantage of the additional resources available to help them further understand their students' needs. In cities near a major military installation, the DoD may have assigned school liaison officers to work with local schools to better assist military children (U.S. Department of Defense. Education Activity, n.d.). The school liaison officer is an excellent resource to help librarians better recognize the immediate needs and challenges of military children in the school, including keeping librarians apprised of upcoming training and deployment cycles.

Even school librarians located far from any military installation have access to resources they can use to better identify the needs of the children of military veterans. County veterans service officers (CVSOs) can be an excellent resource for learning more about school-aged children of veterans, particularly the challenges that children of veterans with a disability or mental health condition face. In addition to the CVSO, librarians may be interested in collaborating with local veterans service organizations (VSOs). VSOs often seek opportunities for outreach to educate the public about veteran and military communities. For example, the Veterans of Foreign Wars (VFW) sponsors a VFW in the Classroom event that any school can request from their local chapter (Veterans of Foreign Wars, 2016).

Finally, school librarians may have a tremendous resource for understanding the needs of their military children—the military service members, veterans, and military spouses or partners who are parents of children within their own school districts. Military and veteran parents may be able to suggest strategies that they have seen employed in other schools, as well as concrete suggestions about what has worked for them in the past. In any school with military children, librarians will find passionate, resilient, and caring parents who may be able to advise them on approaches to better supporting their families.

Programs, Services, and Collections

In addition to seeking increased knowledge about military families, particularly children, school librarians can focus on several types of services and programs that can help school libraries better identify and support the needs of military children in their schools.

Strategies and Approaches

- *Recruit.* Invite military parents to become informal advisers, members of an advisory council, or volunteers. Depending on the number of military parents at the school and their level of interest, the school library can communicate periodically with them for advice on specific projects, as time permits, or go so far as to create an online or in-person advisory group. Many schools already have parent organizations outside of the library. And some school libraries may already have a volunteer group that includes both nonmilitary and military parents. It might be helpful, depending on the number of military children in the school, to ask both types of parents to assist military children. This allows nonmilitary parents an opportunity to get to know military parents and vice versa. Word of mouth is essential in assisting parents with learning new skills and reducing isolation that might further challenge their efforts to manage a military family while a service member parent is deployed. Social opportunities, such as volunteering and advisory groups, assist both parents and children.

- *Host.* The physical space of the school library may be helpful for a number of purposes. Some school librarians report offering their library space as a "safe room" or "de facto counseling center" where students can process their feelings about a family member's deployment or a military-related bereavement ("Iraq War's Toll on Our Kids," 2007). Where feasible, school librarians may also want to consider whether their library space could be made available to external groups as a strategy to support military families. For example, school librarians could offer to host a new or existing local chapter of a military family organization or a veterans service organization, such as Blue Star Families. Many support groups struggle to meet regularly simply because they cannot find a space to meet at the same time or place each week or month, and group members quickly lose interest when the meeting place or time changes too frequently. By providing space to these organizations, school librarians can begin to build relationships with veteran and military organizations that can lead to new opportunities to collaborate on programming for military children.

- *Coordinate and promote.* Remember that some organizations may already be very active in hosting events and providing support to military families. School librarians can connect with these organizations, learn about their goals, and seek opportunities to assist them. The school library might promote events hosted by a local chapter of a VSO, for example, or provide flyers from any nearby military family support centers that host events in the community. For example, military teens might notice promotional materials about peer groups if they are posted on a school library bulletin board or in a display case.

- *Respond.* Be aware of the branches of the military with a presence in the local area and their deployment cycles and ensure that the school library is responsive to the needs of military children experiencing any of the phases of the deployment cycle. If it is difficult to learn about upcoming deployment cycles through formal channels, librarians can seek some assistance through direct contact with military parents. Although service members and military spouses are not permitted to disclose many details for security reasons, librarians do not need to know specific details that family members are not permitted to share. Instead, librarians can emphasize that they would like to understand the general time frame for when any phase of the deployment cycle will take place so that the library can make sure to offer books and other resources that might be helpful to the military children attending the school. Even if service members and military spouses cannot share this information directly, they may be able to connect the librarian with a unit ombudsman or other representative who could keep them informed.

- *Develop programming.* Depending on the demographics of military families in the school district, school library programming about military issues can fulfill two needs: it can provide emotional or academic support to military children and also familiarize nonmilitary students with the strengths and challenges of military families. For example, a school library could partner with a VSO to host an art project activity to send to deployed service members, especially deployed parents of children at the school. Another fun and educational activity is to invite a military service member, especially a parent from the school, to speak at an event hosted by the library. This type of activity gives military children in the class a time to shine, and it also gives nonmilitary children a chance to learn more about the military.

  For example, the library could host a storytime with a veteran who has a disability. Both schools and public libraries have hosted Luis Carlos Montalván, the author of the children's book *Tuesday Tucks Me In*, and his service dog, Tuesday ("Tuesday," 2016). This type of event provides all students with the opportunity to learn more about military service, people with disabilities, and service animals. It can also help military students feel as though their lifestyle is represented in the school and the school library, and it can be educational for all students.

- *Engage.* Librarians and other educators can also develop events and programming that engage not only military children but also their family members. Librarians in Fayetteville, North Carolina, home of the Army's 82nd Airborne Division, found that military spouses "valued family-oriented events that allowed family members to spend unstructured time together" (Taft & Olney, 2015). Many schools already host events, such as carnivals and picnics, that encourage the entire family to spend time together and to develop a sense of community with the school and with other students' families. By using strategies such as additional marketing materials that target military families or coordinating with local veterans' organizations to include military-related activities such as a tabling event to write cards to deployed service members, librarians can play a role in ensuring that military families are able to participate in this type of program.

- *Honor.* Schools, and school libraries in particular, can participate in events that recognize and honor the sacrifices of veterans and service members, such as Veterans Day and Memorial Day. Librarians can collect and display materials that illustrate the experiences of military families or host programs honoring their students' family members who have served in the military. For example, students could contribute photographs of their military-affiliated relatives to slide shows or displays, which could be shared with the entire school. This provides an opportunity for military children to share their experiences and also helps nonmilitary children connect with their military children classmates by uncovering any history of military service in their own families.

Collection development. Another way that school librarians can support the needs of military children in their schools is by building collections that include materials that reflect the interests, strengths, and challenges of the veteran and military communities. As with any group that is considered underserved or unique, military children may find solace and confidence through reading books that feature people with similar backgrounds. In addition to books that feature military children, the library can also incorporate the reading interests of military children into the library's collection management plan. For example, some military teenagers who are already avid readers might be knowledgeable about young adult novels that feature issues they can identify with, such as separation, grief, or sharing adult responsibilities in the family.

School librarians can consult a number of resources to help them build their veteran and military-related collections. They can seek advice from military parents and children about books that interest military families. They can communicate their collection development goals with the school liaison officers who work with schools in the area. Also, through collaboration with local businesses, librarians may find financial support to improve the library's collection, especially with regard to books and materials that demonstrate gratitude for and support of military families. Websites and blogs by other school librarians and military parents also make recommendations for books for military children in all age groups. As librarians learn more about the unique interests and needs of military children in their schools, they can customize the resources they prefer to use or recommend through the school library.

Although a comprehensive list of resources is beyond the scope of this book, this section includes some examples of the types of books and online materials that school librarians may wish to consider including in their collections. These specific materials are intended to serve as examples, and their inclusion should not be construed as a recommendation.

Deployments. Books for children and young adults that explore the feelings and challenges related to deployments and other long-term parental absences can be helpful for students who have a parent leaving on military duty, especially for the first time. The following are some examples:

Bunting, E. & Life, K. (2005). *My red balloon*. Honesdale, PA.: Boyds Mills Press.

LaBelle, J. & Rodriguez, C. (2009). *My dad's deployment: A deployment and reunion activity book for young children*. St Paul, MN: Elva Resa Publishing.

McElroy, L. T. & Paterson, D. (2005). *Love, Lizzie: Letters to a military mom*. Morton Grove, IL: Whitman.

Tomp, S. W. & Barrow, A. (2005). *Red, white, and blue good-bye*. New York: Walker & Co.

Military life. Materials for children and young adults about military lifestyle and culture can help military children feel represented in a school library and can also help nonmilitary children better understand the struggles of their classmates. The following are some examples:

Appel, A., Rothmiller, M., & Schwarzkopf, H. N. (2008). *My hero: Military kids write about their moms and dads*. New York: St. Martin's Press.

Ellis, D. (2008). *Off to war: Voices of soldiers' children*. Toronto: Groundwood Books.

Scillian, D. & Juhasz, V. (2006). *H is for honor: A military family alphabet*. Chelsea, MI: Sleeping Bear Press.

Ward, S. (2000). *I live at a military post*. New York: PowerKids Press.

People with disabilities. Many veterans and service members experience challenges related to their service, some of which may be related to a service-connected disability. Books and materials that help students understand a parent or loved one's disability may be helpful to include in the library collection. The following are some examples:

Kastle, S. & Gonzales-Othon, K. (2015). *Why is dad so mad?: A book about PTSD and military families*. Hays, KS: Tall Tale Press.

Maxwell, S., Biggers, L., & Maxwell, A. (2010). *Our daddy is invincible!* Bowie, MD: 4th Division Press.

Montalván, L. C. & Witter, B. (2014). *Tuesday tucks me in: The loyal bond between a soldier and his service dog*. New York: Roaring Brook Press

Resources for educators. In addition to collecting books and other resources for military children, some school librarians may wish to add selected print and electronic materials to their collections to help teachers and school administrators better understand the needs of military children.

1. *Print resources.* Although many school libraries have limited space to provide print resources for educators, librarians may wish to include a small number of resource guides for teachers and administrators working with military families. Such resource guides can be helpful to teachers who are committed to ensuring that the school is a welcoming environment for military-affiliated students. Examples of such resources include the following:

Astor, R. (2012). *The school administrator's guide for supporting students from military families*. New York: Teachers College Press.

Astor, R. (2012). *The teacher's guide for supporting students from military families*. New York: Teachers College Press.

2. *Online resources.* School librarians, especially those without space for print materials, can provide information and resources for teachers and administrators by connecting them to online resources. A few examples of these types of resources are listed below:

Blum, R. (2007). *Best practices: Building blocks for enhancing school environment*. Johns Hopkins. Baltimore, MD: Bloomberg School of Public Health. Retrieved from http://www.jhsph.edu/research/centers-and-institutes/military-child-initiative/resources/Best_Practices_monograph.pdf

This report includes helpful engagement ideas such as hosting a military care package night or scheduling an event to celebrate military children.

Defense Centers for Excellence for Psychological Health and Traumatic Brain Injury (2011). *Children of military service members resource guide*. Silver Spring, MD: Defense Centers for Excellence for Psychological Health and Traumatic Brain Injury. Retrieved from http://www.nctsn.org/sites/default/files/assets/pdfs/children_of_military_service.pdf

This online resource guide has reading recommendations and suggested activities for military children during and after deployment of a military parent.

U.S. Department of Veterans Affairs (2016). *Make the Connection.* Retrieved from http://maketheconnection.net

This website offers testimonials by veterans and their families from different age groups and eras. Viewers can watch short excerpts of longer veteran interviews about almost any topic. It can be a great way to expose students to stories from veterans.

President of the United States (2011, January). *Strengthening our military families: Meeting America's commitment.* Washington, D.C.: The White House. Retrieved from http://www.dol.gov/dol/milfamilies/strengthening_our_military_families.pdf

Additionally, educators may wish to review the information and resources provided by the Department of Education for veteran and military families (U.S. Department of Education, n.d.). The Department of Education has supported a number of initiatives to benefit children of military families; for example, the Interstate Compact on Educational Opportunity for Military Children provides protections for military children who change schools across state lines due to a parent's military service (Council of State Governments, 2013). These resources provide insight into the logistical challenges faced by military children in K–12 schools and provide guidance for school personnel working with military children and their families.

School librarians can play an important role in helping military children and the children of veterans feel included and supported in their elementary and secondary educational experiences. School librarians can learn about the unique characteristics of these children and can also help their fellow educators, the classroom teachers and administrators in their schools, learn strategies for better connecting with and supporting military children and the children of veterans in their schools. And school librarians have a unique opportunity to develop their own programs, services, and collaborations to make the school library in particular a welcoming place for veteran and military-affiliated children.

Health Sciences Libraries

Librarians and library staff at health sciences or medical libraries may encounter veterans and service members in a variety of circumstances. Veterans and service members may be clinicians, especially in VA and military hospitals, but also in civilian medical settings. They may be students studying nursing or medicine. They may be patients being treated by the clinicians the library serves, or they may be members of the public using library resources to research their own medical difficulties. Although health sciences librarians may see veterans and service members in a number of different contexts, this section will focus on veterans and service members as patrons or patients who may have unique medical needs related to their military service.

This section will begin by offering some answers to one simple question: what are some of the ways that veterans and service members may be different than other health sciences library patrons? It will provide some information about military and veteran health disparities and military service-related ailments. Next, the section will provide some information for health sciences librarians who specialize in veterinary medicine. Finally, the section will include some information about health care resources for veterans and service members.

Veteran and Service Member Health Disparities

Veterans and service members may experience the same health-related needs as civilians, but health sciences librarians should be aware of some of the exceptional needs of veteran and service members to support these patrons and their family members as well as the clinicians who may be serving them. Research has indicated that both men and women veterans experience health disparities in comparison with their civilian counterparts and that within the veteran population some groups experience worse health outcomes.

Health disparities between veterans, service members, and civilians. Researchers have been investigating the health and health behavior of veterans, service members, and civilians in an effort to identify problems and areas for potential intervention. One recent study found that male veterans reported "poor overall health, health-related functional limitations, and lifetime health conditions (i.e., cardiovascular disease, arthritis, cancer, depression, and anxiety) more frequently than civilian men" (Hoerster et al., 2012, p. 487). The same study also found that the health status of active-duty men was comparable to that of veterans (Hoerster et al., 2012). Some of the same researchers engaged in a separate study analyzing the health outcomes of women veterans, active-duty service members, Reservists, and civilians and found that while women service members had more favorable health outcomes, women veterans "reported consistently poorer health compared with the other three groups, including poorer general health, greater likelihood of health risk behaviors (e.g., smoking), and greater likelihood of chronic conditions and mental health disorders" (Lehavot, Hoerster, Nelson, Jakupcak, & Simpson, 2012, p. 475).

Research also indicates that veterans of all ages are more likely than nonveterans to have a disability, with some age groups nearly twice as likely (Holder, 2016). The Watson Institute's Costs of War Project suggests that at least 970,000 veterans have some degree of officially recognized disability as a result of the wars in Iraq and Afghanistan, and many more veterans endure chronic health issues without a disability status (Watson Institute for International and Public Affairs, 2015). The most common service-connected disabilities for all veterans were tinnitus, hearing loss, and post-traumatic stress disorder (PTSD), and the most common service-connected disabilities for new VA disability compensation recipients in 2014 were tinnitus, hearing loss, and knee flexion limitation (U.S. Department of Veterans Affairs. Veterans Benefits Administration, 2015b).

Health disparities within the veteran and military community. In addition to health disparities between veterans, service members, and civilians, there are also disparities within the myriad intersections of the veteran and military communities. For example, an analysis of retirement payroll data indicates a disparity in the mortality rates of officer and enlisted retirees (Edwards, 2008, p. 1666). Another study found that "veterans who lived in rural settings had lower health-related quality-of-life scores than their suburban and urban counterparts" (Weeks et al., 2004, p. 1762). Researchers found that although the VA has reduced racial disparities in process-of-care, it has not yet effected "meaningful reductions in racial disparity for important clinical outcomes such as blood pressure, glucose, and cholesterol control" (Trivedi, Grebla, Wright, & Washington, 2011, p. 713). Disparities can also exist between men and women veterans and based on sexual minority status; for example, one study found that "elevated odds of frequent mental distress, sleep problems, smoking, and poor physical health were noted in sexual minority veteran women as compared with both sexual minority non-veterans and heterosexual veterans" (Blosnich, Foynes, & Shipherd, 2013, p. 634).

The studies identified above are only a few examples of the many research studies that have explored health-related disparities between civilians and veterans as well as disparities within the veteran and military communities. Veterans and service members can experience health outcomes that vary significantly from those of civilians and from other groups within the veteran and military population, and librarians supporting veteran and military-affiliated patrons and the clinicians treating them should be aware that veterans and service members can have health outcomes that diverge from the general civilian population.

Military-Related Ailments

Veterans and service members can be vulnerable to diseases and other health issues directly related to their service. Some military service-related health issues, such as acute combat injuries, may be readily apparent before the individual separates from the military. However, other military service-related issues may not manifest until months, years, or even decades after the individual has separated from the military. As a result, veterans may seek out information in a health sciences library, and they may or may not be aware that their symptoms could be related to their military service. Approximately 7 million service members are still alive from the Vietnam War era, while some 700,000 veterans from World War II are still living (U.S. Department of Veterans Affairs, 2014). These veterans may consider their military service part of their distant past, yet they may be eligible for newly created benefits, depending on the location and the period in which they served.

Agent Orange. Vietnam-era veterans may have been exposed to Agent Orange or other herbicides that were sprayed on vegetation over the course of the Vietnam War. The VA recognizes specific health issues as presumptively related to Agent Orange exposure, including such diseases and conditions as Hodgkin's disease, Parkinson's disease, prostate cancer, and multiple myeloma (U.S. Department of Veterans Affairs. Public Health, 2015). Veterans who served in Korea or Vietnam may be interested in researching the known health effects of Agent Orange or other defoliants and whether they may be entitled to compensation and treatment for any related difficulties in their own health.

Gulf War Syndrome. Veterans of the first Gulf War (also referred to as Operation Desert Shield/Operation Desert Storm) as well as the second Gulf War (also referred to as the Iraq War or Operation Iraqi Freedom) may experience what is commonly referred to as Gulf War Syndrome and what the VA refers to as "Gulf War Veterans' Medically Unexplained Illnesses"

(U.S. Department of Veterans Affairs. Public Health, 2016c). The VA recognizes specific health issues as presumptively related to Gulf War Syndrome, including such illnesses as chronic fatigue syndrome, fibromyalgia, and functional gastrointestinal disorders (U.S. Department of Veterans Affairs. Public Health, 2016c). Veterans who served in the Persian Gulf may be interested in researching the presumed health effects of Gulf War Syndrome and whether they may be entitled to compensation and treatment for any related difficulties in their own health.

Burn pit exposure. Veterans of the first Gulf War as well as those who served in the wars in Iraq and Afghanistan may experience health effects related to burn pit exposure. Burn pits were open-air pits commonly used on military bases in combat zones to burn all types of waste and refuse, including trash, medical waste, plastics, and a wide variety of other materials (U.S. Department of Veterans Affairs. Public Health, 2016a). Although the VA has developed an Airborne Hazards and Open Burn Pit Registry to allow veterans and service members to report their exposure and resulting health concerns, the VA has not yet recognized any specific health issues as presumptively related to burn pit exposure. Veterans and service members of the wars in Iraq and Afghanistan, as well as those from the first Gulf War, may be interested in following the ongoing research on the health effects of burn pit exposure as well as identifying any progress toward presumptive recognition of resulting health issues.

Post-traumatic stress disorder (PTSD). PTSD is a challenge that can be faced by any individual, not just a veteran, who has been through a traumatic event. Many veterans, especially combat veterans, of every generation may struggle with PTSD. The VA has developed its National Center for PTSD to provide veterans and their family members with information about PTSD and to help connect them with local VA PTSD resources as well as specialized VA PTSD treatment programs around the country (U.S. Department of Veterans Affairs. National Center for PTSD, 2016). Veterans and family members who are interested in researching PTSD effects and treatment options may wish to review ongoing research into PTSD treatments as well as VA treatment options in the local area.

Traumatic brain injuries. Veterans and service members may suffer from a service-related traumatic brain injury (TBI), even if they did not suffer a direct head injury. Veterans and service members who were exposed to concussive explosions, especially repeated ones, may suffer from TBI (U.S. Department of Veterans Affairs. Health Care, 2015). Combat troops in Iraq and Afghanistan were frequently exposed to such blasts, and those in combat-support roles may have also been exposed, especially via improvised explosive devices (IEDs). The VA's Polytrauma System of Care is intended to provide rehabilitation for veterans and service members who suffer from TBI (U.S. Department of Veterans Affairs. Health Care, 2016b). Veterans and family members who are interested in researching the short- and long-term effects of TBI and rehabilitation options may wish to review ongoing research into TBI as well as VA treatment options in the local area.

Military sexual trauma. Military sexual trauma (MST) is the term used by the VA "to refer to experiences of sexual assault or repeated, threatening sexual harassment that a Veteran experienced during his or her military service" (U.S. Department of Veterans Affairs. Mental Health, 2015). Both men and women can experience MST, and although the rates of women who have reported experiencing MST are far higher (approximately 1 in 4 for women versus 1 in 100 for men), there are far fewer women in the military. Furthermore, because the VA's Veterans Health Administration (VHA) treats fewer women, the numbers of men and women treated by the VHA for MST are similar (U.S. Department of Veterans Affairs. Mental Health, 2015; Suris & Smith, 2011). Each VA Health Care System has an MST coordinator who can connect veterans with care, even if they are not otherwise eligible for VA care.

Veterans, Service Members, and Veterinary Medicine

Veterinary medicine librarians may also receive veteran and military-related questions. Service animals are becoming an increasingly popular treatment option for service-connected disabilities. For example, some veterans and service members are turning to service dogs as a treatment for PTSD (Yount, Olmert, & Lee, 2012). Veterinary medicine librarians may receive questions from patrons interested in learning how to acquire a service animal, locate organizations that train service animals, or care for service animals. Librarians should be aware that the VA does provide service dogs for some veterans, although the VA does not cover all associated expenses (U.S. Department of Veterans Affairs. Rehabilitation and Prosthetic Services, 2016). There are also a number of veterans service organizations (VSOs) that provide service animals to veterans, including such organizations as Patriot PAWS ("Patriot PAWS," 2016).

Veterans, service members, and civilians may also be caring for retired military working dogs. Military working dogs, like military service members, may have been deployed overseas, exposed to chemicals and radiation, and survived explosions. Retired working dogs may have health issues related to their work in the military, such as spinal compression and degenerative joint disease (Linn, Bartels, Rochat, Payton, & Moore, 2003; Banfield & Morrison, 2000). Some dogs may also have behavioral problems related to their military service, with some exhibiting symptoms akin to PTSD (Dao, 2011). Veterinary medicine librarians receiving health-related questions from patrons caring for retired working dogs should consider inquiring about an animal's military history during reference interviews.

Health Care Resources

Although veterans and service members do have some additional health-related challenges, they also may have access to additional health care resources. Research conducted prior to the Affordable Care Act indicated that veterans and active-duty service members were more likely than civilians to have health insurance and less likely to have financial barriers to care (Lehavot, Hoerster, Nelson, Jakupcak, & Simpson, 2012; Hoerster et al., 2012). Active-duty service members are automatically enrolled into TRICARE, formerly known as the Civilian Health and Medical Program of the Uniformed Services (CHAMPUS). TRICARE is a health care program for military personnel and their qualified family members, giving them access to military health service providers. Those in the National Guard and Reserves receive access to military medical care while on active-duty orders and also have the option of purchasing access to military health insurance, TRICARE Reserve Select, when on drilling status.

Service members are also likely to seek out civilian medical care, however, if they live in a remote location, need to seek a second opinion for a chronic health problem, require discreet medical care for a condition that might not be covered by the military health system, or are referred to a civilian specialist. Members of the National Guard and Reserves, because they have limited access to military medical treatment, are also likely to use civilian health care providers for most of their care, including routine treatment.

Unlike service members, veterans are usually not eligible to receive care at military treatment facilities and may be unaware of VA-sponsored health care options that they qualify for based on income or other factors. Military retirees may be eligible for care at military treatment facilities, although that care is subject to availability. They may maintain their TRICARE insurance coverage to receive care from civilian providers. The vast majority of military veterans, nevertheless, are not retirees and therefore do not maintain access to military health treatment facilities or to TRICARE. Instead, they may seek eligibility for health care treatment from the VA immediately after leaving military service. Depending on the VA's decision about what kind of disability compensation the veteran qualifies for, a veteran may instead seek health care through insurance coverage with an employer. Even if the veteran is eligible for VA health care, the demand for VA health care far outstrips the VA's capacity.

The VA determines each veteran's eligibility status based on several criteria, such as whether there was documentation of an injury while the veteran was on active duty, when and where the veteran served and for how long, and the veteran's level of income. These criteria are established and reviewed by Congress annually, allowing the VA to prioritize groups of veterans and their health care according to those criteria. For example, former prisoners of war, Purple Heart recipients, and veterans with a disability compensation rating of at least 10 percent are given "enhanced eligibility status" that affords them increased access to care (U.S. Department of Veterans Affairs. Health Care, 2016a).

A veteran with a chronic health condition unrelated to military service would usually not seek health care from the VA. A veteran whose chronic health condition management costs more than the family income might still seek health care through the VA to augment the coverage offered by employer insurance plans. Low-income veterans, for example, may use the VA to acquire prescription medications that are not covered by an insurance plan or are too costly. Each case is decided on a case-by-case basis by a veterans service representative (VSR) or a board of representatives at the VA. Due to the complexity of the eligibility ratings and the VA's annual revision of criteria, no one outside the VA is permitted to advise a veteran on precisely what is covered. Practitioners and health sciences librarians outside of the VA can encourage a veteran to learn more, but they are often cautioned not to speak on behalf of the VA due to the legal nature of determining eligibility ratings.

Many veterans may believe that they are not eligible for VA care because they do not fall into one of the commonly known categories, such as having a service-connected disability or a Purple Heart. However, veterans who are within five years of deployment to a combat zone as well as those with a low income threshold receive enhanced eligibility status. As a result, many veterans who thought they were ineligible or who have been ineligible in the past now have access to VA health care services, yet they may not know that they are now eligible (U.S. Department of Veterans Affairs. Health Care, 2016a). Health sciences librarians who are working with veterans or service members should suggest that they contact the VA or their military service provider to determine whether they may be entitled to care of which they were unaware.

One of the most pivotal moments in Kristen's experience with VA health care was the result of learning about programs from other veterans. For the first several years after leaving the Army, Kristen did not seek VA health care because she was under the impression that she was ineligible for any VA services. Although she had served four years in the military, she did not realize that she would be eligible for VA benefits and services because she believed that only military retirees and veterans with a disability were eligible for most VA benefits and services. Shortly after her marriage, her father-in-law mentioned that another relative, also a veteran, loved to go the VA just to interact with other veterans. Kristen was surprised to learn that this relative was permitted to seek health care at the VA even though he had private health insurance.

Kristen returned to the VA and learned that her personal circumstances qualified her for VA health care services that year. She soon found that interacting with other veterans at the VA had a profound impact on her daily life. While sitting in a waiting room some weeks later, a serendipitous conversation with another veteran informed Kristen of another much-needed veterans' benefit: the VA provides hearing aids free-of-charge to veterans who qualify for this benefit. Within two months, Kristen was wearing a hearing aid, which dramatically improved her ability to communicate with coworkers and friends.

Visiting the VA has also had other benefits for Kristen; she has derived a sense of community from the veterans who welcome her and engage with her each time she visits the VA. Her sense that she was not a veteran was replaced by a sense of belonging. And it all began with a conversation over dinner with her father-in-law.

Military-related health sciences resources. Health sciences librarians and library staff should consider evaluating their collections to determine whether patrons, both clinicians and the general public, have adequate access to research related to the health issues and disparities veterans and service members may face. Although a substantial amount of the research on these issues is available in standard medical databases, such as PubMed, librarians may want to consider including databases such as the Published International Literature on Traumatic Stress (PILOTS) database, which is sponsored by the VA and publicly available. Libraries who receive a significant number of veterans and service members researching military-related health issues may also wish to consider acquiring or aggregating resources on common military health ailments, such as Agent Orange and Gulf War Syndrome, either within the print collection or within a web page or LibGuide. Communication with the VA Environmental Health Coordinator should yield many other resources based on the veteran and military-affiliated patrons served by the library (U.S. Department of Veterans Affairs. Public Health, 2016b).

Librarians can obtain more information by meeting with representatives of Disabled American Veterans (DAV), Paralyzed Veterans of America (PVA), or similar organizations. This type of VSO specializes in various issues related to health care for veterans. In some cases, the organization uses different criteria for determining a veteran's eligibility for assistance, or the organization may even have a legal team to assist veterans who wish to submit an appeal for their disability status. By connecting with the VA, local VSOs, and online research tools, librarians can help empower veterans and service members to decipher the health implications of their military service and to seek out appropriate care and compensation from the VA.

Military Libraries

One of the most important resources for service members, military family members, and military retirees is military libraries, which can be large research libraries, midsized libraries on individual military installations, or small libraries in combat zones or onboard ships. However, this section will refer to the military libraries sponsored through the military's Morale, Welfare, and Recreation (MWR) programs, which include those libraries on military installations, in deployment zones, and onboard ships (Military OneSource, 2016).

Although military libraries and their collections are not available to all members of the veteran and military communities, they play a key role in supporting the needs of service members and their families by serving not only the needs of those stationed at a particular military installation but also those who are more distant, including those on ships or on deployments. Because virtually all of their users are military-affiliated, military librarians often have extensive knowledge of the unique characteristics, needs, and challenges of the military community.

This section will review some of the barriers that prevent service members and their families from fully utilizing military libraries, describe some strategies that military librarians can employ to raise awareness about military libraries, and suggest organizations that military librarians can collaborate with to extend their reach into the military community.

Access to Military Libraries

Both civilians and service members may have misconceptions about who has access to military libraries. Access to military libraries is typically given only to current military service members and their dependents, including both active-duty service members and Reservists. Libraries are located on military installations and typically only available to those who have permission to enter a military installation. However, military librarians should still connect with public librarians who may be in a position to refer military-affiliated patrons to the local military library. Military librarians can also remind service members that they have access to resources beyond those in their installation's physical library, such as online resources (U.S. Army MWR, 2016).

Due to confusion over who has access to military libraries, some well-intentioned individuals and organizations may make incorrect referrals to military libraries. For example, many civilians do not realize that veterans who did not complete the 20 years of service required to retire from the military are not typically granted routine access to military installations, preventing them or their families from using military libraries. Military librarians may increase the effectiveness of referrals by working with other local libraries and organizations to help them understand which veterans are eligible to access military library resources and where they can refer patrons who can no longer access military libraries.

Awareness

As with many other types of libraries, one of the major challenges that military librarians face is ensuring that patrons are aware of the libraries' collections and services. Military families may have inconsistent and demanding work schedules and may relocate often, making it harder for them to visit libraries to learn more about services and collections. Military libraries have grown in recent years, and many have developed excellent online resources that help them reach service members deployed overseas as well as service members and their families who are stateside but far from the nearest military library, such as members of the National Guard and Reserves (Jowers, 2008). However, many military libraries struggle to market their resources to patrons who are unaware that they are available. As many military families live "off-post" or "off-base," meaning that their homes are not located within the confines of a military installation, some military families may find it more convenient to visit their local public libraries for their library needs. They may not even realize that their military installation's library provides many of the same services as a public library, including such common services as storytimes for young children.

Additionally, other centers and organizations on the military installation may have overlapping missions that can inadvertently lead service members to miss opportunities to benefit from military library services. For example, many Army posts have an Education Center that facilitates service member access to academic examinations, such as the SAT or CLEP, so many service members may not realize that they also have access to academic examination preparation materials via their military library. Because of these challenges, military librarians may have to work harder to market their libraries to potential patrons. One way that military librarians build awareness and increase access is by developing collaborations and partnerships.

Collaborations and Partnerships

Although military librarians have strong expertise in working with military communities, they may wish to collaborate with public libraries, academic libraries, and other organizations to connect with patrons who are not taking full advantage of military library resources. For example, members of the National Guard and Reserves who live far from a military installation may be unaware that they have access to military library resources, even if they never set foot in a military library. To better connect with these potential patrons, military librarians may benefit from building partnerships with other libraries and organizations.

Public library partners. Public libraries are a natural partner for many military libraries. In communities near military installations, members of the veteran and military communities may be patrons of the local military library, the local public library, or both. But because many public librarians have never visited a military library, they may not be familiar with all of the services, programs, and collections available at military libraries. This lack of familiarity means that public librarians may not recognize some opportunities to refer military-affiliated patrons to military library resources.

To encourage referrals from public libraries to military libraries, military librarians should initiate relationships with local public librarians. These relationships can be particularly beneficial when they engage not only public library managers but all front-line staff at the public library.

For example, military librarians can arrange for all interested local public librarians to take a tour of the military library to learn more about its facility, services, and programs. Alternatively, military librarians can supply local public libraries with bookmarks or brochures that public librarians can share when referring military-affiliated patrons to their local military library resources. Military and public libraries may also benefit from developing joint programming opportunities. For example, an information fair that promotes the assets of both libraries could help patrons learn about the resources available to them at each type of library, or the libraries could collaborate on efforts to support military personnel and families who are preparing to transition out of the military.

Academic library partners. Military librarians may also profit from developing partnerships with academic libraries. Many service members enroll in college classes while in the military but may have limited access to their college libraries because they often take classes online or at satellite campuses. By connecting with academic librarians, especially those at institutions frequently used by service members at their installation, military librarians can identify and then respond to gaps in support between the academic library and the military library. Increasing academic librarians' understanding of what military libraries can provide will facilitate referrals for appropriate patrons from the academic library to the military library. Military librarians and academic librarians can work collaboratively to help service member students better understand and use the full extent of the resources available to them.

Other partners. As military librarians strive to connect with service members and their families at a distance, whether they are at another base or far from any military installation, they must consider developing strategic partnerships to reach potential patrons. These partners may be military or civilian and may be located near the military installation or far away, depending on the patrons that military librarians are trying to reach. For example, one potential source for military librarian partnerships is with National Guard and Reserves' Family Readiness Groups (FRGs).

FRGs are officially sponsored networks that provide information and support to military families, including spouses and children. These organizations can be a great partner for marketing military library resources because their members are likely to be eligible patrons of military libraries. Many FRG resources online include Military OneSource, a military-sponsored website that includes links to military library resources. But because Military OneSource includes information about counseling, financial and legal resources, and many other resources, in addition to library resources, the information about military libraries can easily be overlooked. Military librarians can advocate for military library resources to be explicitly included on FRG websites to increase discoverability by FRG members. Military librarians may also wish to review official FRG leaders' handbooks and suggest potential additions that highlight military library resources and activities (U.S. Navy, 2011). By reaching out to patrons such as the National Guard and Reserves FRG, military librarians can leverage the power of an existing network to connect with eligible patrons.

Law Libraries

Law librarians may encounter members of the veteran and military communities as patrons in a variety of contexts. Veterans and service members may be attorneys doing research for a case, law students, or members of the general public. Public law libraries in particular may encounter veterans and service members investigating legal questions. Regardless of which category veteran and service member patrons may fall into, it is important to understand that veterans and service members may experience the same types of legal issues as civilians, but they also can have specific legal needs related to or influenced by their service.

This section will begin with an overview of some of the legal difficulties that are commonly faced by some members of the military and veteran communities. Next, this section will cover some of the legal resources available to veterans and service members to help law librarians direct patrons to appropriate resources. Finally, this section provides information about online resources that law librarians can use to help patrons find the information they need.

Common Legal Issues Faced by Veterans and Service Members

It is not uncommon for veterans or service members to face legal issues. For example, one study of Maine veterans identified that 70 percent of their veteran survey respondents had experienced a legal issue in the last 12 months (Liscord & Elliott, 2013). Many of these legal issues, such as divorce, child support negotiation, or housing disputes, parallel those experienced by civilians. However, even legal issues not directly related to the military can be complicated by veteran status. For example, child support and custody questions can be complicated by out-of-state moves, which are common among military families. Additionally, veterans and service members can have legal issues directly related to their military service. Common veterans' issues are listed below.

VA disability appeals. Veterans who have applied for disability compensation and had their claims denied may wish to do some legal research or consult with an attorney when filing an appeal. Attorneys who assist veterans in preparing their claims for benefits are required to be certified by the VA (U.S. Department of Veterans Affairs. Office of General Counsel, 2016). Law librarians should be aware that the VA provides a searchable database of VA-certified attorneys, which may be a helpful resource for veterans seeking legal help in filing an appeal (U.S. Department of Veterans Affairs, 2010).

Military discharge upgrades. The character of a service member's discharge from the military can have a profound effect on their future. Military discharges fall within a spectrum. The highest discharge status is honorable, which entitles a veteran to all VA benefits for which their service renders them eligible. The most unfavorable discharge status is dishonorable, which is a punitive discharge rendered only after a court martial, and leaves the veteran ineligible for any veterans' benefits (Oregon Department of Veterans' Affairs, 2010).

Veterans who receive a discharge status below honorable may wish to apply for a discharge upgrade, often to become eligible for a particular category of veterans' benefits. For example, while a general discharge would be sufficient to render a veteran eligible for VA disability compensation, the veteran would have to receive a discharge upgrade to become eligible for GI Bill benefits (U.S. Department of Veterans Affairs. Veterans Benefits Administration, 2015a). Veterans who wish to upgrade their discharge status must apply to the discharge review board for their branch of service (e.g., Army, Navy), often with the guidance of an attorney.

Workplace protections. Veterans and service members are entitled to certain legal protections in the workplace as a result of their military service. Some veterans, depending on such factors as disability rating and the period of time in which they served, may be eligible for veterans' preference in federal hiring (United States Department of Labor. Veterans' Employment & Training Service, n.d.). States may also have veteran's preference laws; Texas, for example, gives preference in hiring for state jobs to veterans, including those with disabilities, and the surviving family members of deceased service members (Veteran's Employment Preferences, 2015). Furthermore, veterans cannot be discriminated against during the hiring process or in the workplace. Section 1002.18 of the Uniformed Services Employment and Reemployment Rights Act of 1994 (USERRA) protects past, present, and future service members from employment discrimination: "An employer must not deny initial employment, reemployment, retention in employment, promotion, or any benefit of employment to an individual on the basis of his or her membership, application for membership, performance of service, application for service, or obligation for service in the uniformed services" (Regulations Under the Uniformed Services Employment and Reemployment Rights Act of 1994, 2005, p. 75297).

Veterans Treatment Courts. Veterans who are facing criminal charges related to mental health or substance abuse problems may be eligible to participate in a Veterans Treatment Court (U.S. Department of Veterans Affairs. Veterans Health Administration, 2015). Research from the Bureau of Justice Statistics indicates that approximately 60 percent of veterans in state and federal prisons meet criteria for substance dependence or abuse (Noonan & Mumola, 2007), and, as the Office of National Drug Control Policy declares, "many of these issues can be connected to the trauma of combat and other service related experiences" (Office of National Drug Control Policy, 2010, para. 1). Veterans, whether or not they live in areas with Veterans Treatment Courts, may also wish to be familiar with the VA's Veterans Justice Outreach Program, which aims to "avoid the unnecessary criminalization of mental illness and extended incarceration among Veterans by ensuring that eligible, justice-involved Veterans have timely access to Veterans Health Administration (VHA) services, as clinically indicated" (U.S. Department of Veterans Affairs. Office of Public and Intergovernmental Affairs, 2016b).

In addition to veterans' legal questions, law librarians may receive patrons interested in exploring military-related legal questions. Military legal issues can be very different from veteran or civilian legal issues because service members are subject to the Uniform Code of Military Justice, or UCMJ, in addition to the civilian legal code. Common military legal issues are discussed below.

UCMJ. Military service members are subject not only to the civilian penal code but also to the complex military penal code. The Uniform Code of Military Justice (UCMJ) is the legal code that applies to all branches of the U.S. military. UCMJ was enacted by Congress and applies to all active-duty personnel as well as Reservists when they are on active status (Uniform Code of Military Justice, 1951). UCMJ covers offenses that can lead to court martial, including serious offenses such as desertion and espionage. It also covers minor offenses that typically lead to nonjudicial punishments rather than court martial. Law librarians who support service members should offer access to information about both criminal and military law, as criminal charges against service members can involve both civilian and military legal proceedings (Tomasovic, 2008).

Servicemembers Civil Relief Act. The Servicemembers Civil Relief Act (SCRA) is legislation intended to "strengthen and expedite national defense by giving service members certain protections in civil actions" (United States Courts, n.d.). It provides service members with protections in many different aspects of civilian life in order to minimize potential distractions, such as an eviction, especially during deployments or long-term training responsibilities. For example, the SCRA provides protections against default judgments, caps on interest rates for debts incurred prior to military service, and the ability to terminate leases when the service member receives military orders (Servicemembers Civil Relief Act, 2003). Service members may not be aware of the full extent of the protections available to them under SCRA, so librarians should consider recommending SCRA as a resource to service members who have civil legal difficulties.

Uniformed Services Employment and Reemployment Rights Act. The Uniformed Services Employment and Reemployment Rights Act of 1994 (USERRA) is legislation that protects service members who temporarily leave their jobs for military service (Uniformed Services Employment and Reemployment Rights Act, 1994). USERRA covers involuntary absences, such as when a Reservist is given deployment orders, but it also covers voluntary absences, such as when a soldier in the National Guard volunteers for training. Under USERRA, service members who leave their workplace for military duty are, in many cases, entitled to return to their civilian position or a comparable position when their military duty has ended (U.S. Department of Labor, 2008). Service members who are having difficulty returning to their civilian workplace after a deployment or training and service members who believe they are being discriminated against as a result of their military service may benefit from exploring the protections and limitations of USERRA.

Legal Resources Available for Veterans and Service Members

Although the legal issues veterans and service members may face can be complicated by their relationship to the military, law librarians should be aware that veterans and service members may have access to certain resources based on their military status.

JAG. Service members may be eligible for support from the Judge Advocate General Corps (JAG) for their military branch. JAG provides many different types of supports for service members and their dependents, including such common services as drafting wills and powers of attorney and reviewing contracts and leases. JAG also provides defense services to service members facing a court martial. Although JAG provides support for a wide range of service member legal issues, they do not cover all service member legal needs; for example, they may not represent service members in family court. In addition, some services provided by JAG are subject to availability of resources, so service members are not guaranteed JAG support ("U.S. Navy Judge Advocate General's Corps," n.d.). Despite these limitations, law librarians may consider suggesting JAG to service members researching legal issues.

Low-cost and pro bono resources for veterans. Most veterans, with the exception of retirees, are not eligible for JAG support. However, there are a number of free resources available for veterans that librarians can share with them. Both the VA and the American Bar Association maintain pages on legal resources for veterans and military families (U.S. Department of Veterans Affairs. Office of General Counsel, 2015; American Bar Association, 2016a; American Bar Association, 2016b). Individual states also maintain a list of local legal resources for veterans, such as the *Michigan Military and Veterans Legal Services Guide*, which provides contact information for both low-cost and free legal resources for veterans and service members in Michigan. Some law schools also offer legal clinics for veterans, such as Yale Law School's Veteran Legal Services Clinic or Emory Law's Volunteer Clinic for Veterans (Yale Law School, n.d.; Emory University School of Law, 2016).

Public law libraries. Veterans and service members who are researching their own personal legal issues may benefit from visiting a public law library. Public law libraries are available in many states, although the number of libraries and the resources they have available can vary widely from one state to another. Although many academic law libraries provide support for members of the general public, public law libraries may be more likely to include resources that are tailored to help people navigate the legal system on their own as they focus on supporting laypeople.

Online Resources for Veteran and Military-Affiliated Patrons

Because the laws and regulations related to veterans and service members change often, print resources may not be the most helpful tools for patrons or for the librarians helping them. However, a number of law libraries around the United States, such as John Marshall Law School's Louis L. Biro Library and Regent University's School of Law, have developed LibGuides or web pages that aggregate electronic resources to support veteran and military-affiliated patrons (John Marshall Law School. Louis L. Biro Law Library, 2015; Regent University School of Law Library, 2016). Such guides can serve as a toolkit that offers information to answer military-related legal questions as well as links to resources to support military-related legal needs. Successful resource guides for veterans and service members may include such resources as the following:

- Literature on military-related legal issues, such as legal databases and journals, to include the VA's Veterans Law Review (U.S. Department of Veterans Affairs, 2016);

- Links to military-related primary sources, such as USERRA, UCMJ, SCRA, and other veteran-related legislation;

- Links to information and resources for common military and veteran-related issues, such as the Board of Veterans Appeals for disability compensation claim appeals or the Application for Review of Discharge for military discharge upgrades;

- Links to local veteran legal support organizations such as a veteran clinic at a nearby university and low-cost or pro bono legal resources in the local area; and

- Websites to assist service members and military spouses with divorce, such as Military OneSource's "Rights and Benefits of Divorced Spouses in the Military" or a legal guide to understanding the military spouse's rights under the Uniformed Services Former Spouses' Protection Act (Legal Assistance for Military Personnel, 2001).

Librarians should review existing LibGuides and websites from other institutions before developing their own resources for veteran and military-affiliated patrons. The legal needs of veterans and service members may vary to some degree from one region to another, depending on proximity to military installations and other local factors, but most communities and their law libraries will encounter veteran and military-affiliated patrons with legal issues. By familiarizing themselves with military and veteran-related legal issues, state bar association legal guides for military or veteran communities, and the resources available to veteran and military-affiliated patrons provided by local organizations or VSOs such as Disabled American Veterans, law librarians will be prepared to effectively support their veteran and service member patrons.

Prison Libraries

Prison librarians play a crucial role in the lives of incarcerated veterans by helping them find information to help them make sense of their military service, to learn to cope with and seek help for military-related health concerns, to maintain connections with the veteran and military communities, and to transition back into everyday life. By familiarizing themselves with veteran-related resources and information, prison librarians help ensure that incarcerated veterans have access to needed resources during their incarceration, transition, and life outside prison.

This section is focused on providing information to support librarians who work with military veterans who are incarcerated. Although the bulk of the section is focused on information that will primarily be helpful to prison librarians, there is also some information that may be helpful to librarians providing support to veterans in local and county jails. This section begins with some basic information about the size of the incarcerated veteran population before providing some suggestions about information and resources that may be helpful for librarians who are trying to meet the information needs of incarcerated veterans. This section then will include some suggestions for how librarians can help incarcerated veterans feel connected with the larger military and veteran communities and will conclude by suggesting some additional resources for prison librarian collaboration and partnerships.

Incarcerated Veterans

Unfortunately, some veterans and service members run into trouble with the criminal justice system. According to the Bureau of Justice Statistics, 8 percent of inmates in state and federal prisons had once served in the military (Bronson, Carson, Noonan & Berzofsky, 2015). Incarcerated veterans have a number of demographic differences from incarcerated nonveterans. For example, incarcerated veterans tend to be older than nonveterans (Bronson et al., 2015). Research suggests that "male veterans in the age group that entered military service in the early years of the All Volunteer Force (AVF) were at greater risk of incarceration than nonveterans of similar age and ethnicity, whereas veterans who enlisted in later years of the AVF had less risk of incarceration than nonveterans" (Greenberg & Rosenheck, 2012, p. 1). Data indicates that although incarcerated veterans are more likely to be convicted of a violent sexual offense, they also tend to have fewer prior offenses than their civilian counterparts (Bronson et al., 2015).

Many incarcerated veterans' legal issues may be related to mental illness issues. The Bureau of Justice Statistics reports that "an estimated 48% of veterans and 36% of nonveterans in prison were ever told they had a mental disorder. Veterans in prison (23%) were twice as likely as nonveterans

(11%) to report that a mental health professional ever told them they had post-traumatic stress disorder (PTSD)" (Bronson et al., 2015, p. 8).

Information and Resources for Incarcerated Veterans

Prison librarians play a unique role in helping incarcerated veterans. They connect incarcerated veterans with the information and resources available to help them succeed after they leave prison. They help incarcerated veterans achieve lifelong educational goals, and they also provide access to books and other materials for veterans who may never reenter civilian life. Like all library patrons, however, some incarcerated veterans may be unaware of the extent of the support available to them in their library.

Learning whether someone who visits a prison library is a veteran will help prison librarians connect the veteran with unique resources available to them. Prison librarians knowledgeable of resources for veterans may benefit from learning about new efforts elsewhere in the country to market the full extent of prison library services to incarcerated veterans. For example, prison librarians may choose to emulate a program offered by the Washington State Penitentiary. Librarians at the Washington State Penitentiary give a presentation at the prison's annual Help and Program Fair to help familiarize inmates with library resources and services (Washington Secretary of State, 2015). Such efforts can benefit both the general population as well as incarcerated veterans. But librarians should also be aware of the unique needs of incarcerated veterans, which may require that prison librarians maintain knowledge of VA and state veterans' benefits, educational resources, information about exposures and other military-related medical conditions, as well as where to find and how to share information with a veteran who is about to reenter society and relocate to a new community.

Veterans' benefits and incarcerated veterans. Prison librarians may be asked to assist veterans with benefit-related questions whose answers can vary greatly depending on the individual's specific circumstances. Prison librarians should be knowledgeable of what the VA has to offer to dispel myths and correct misconceptions about incarcerated veterans' eligibility for VA benefits. Many veterans may assume they are not eligible at all for any benefits from the VA, although that may not be true. More than 75 percent of incarcerated veterans received an honorable or general discharge (Bronson et al., 2015). This suggests that they may be eligible for some VA benefits, even while incarcerated, depending on the circumstances of their legal issues.

Even veterans who would otherwise be eligible for VA benefits may believe that incarceration disqualifies them for benefits. However, prison librarians can help incarcerated veterans understand that eligibility for federal veterans' benefits can be complicated, but not necessarily out of reach:

- Eligibility for certain benefits may be affected by incarceration, sometimes depending on the length of the incarceration period or the type of offense for which the individual is incarcerated. For example, VA disability compensation payments are reduced, but not cut off, for veterans convicted of a felony and incarcerated for more than 60 days (U.S. Department of Veterans Affairs. Benefits Assistance Service, 2015). However, eligibility to receive VA benefits while incarcerated varies and depends on the specific benefit, so librarians should be familiar with the information the VA makes available about benefits for incarcerated veterans.

- Depending on the type of discharge and the nature of a veteran's incarceration, they may be eligible for homeless benefits when the veteran's prison sentence ends. As part of the prison library's support for those transitioning out of prison, librarians should be familiar with resources for homeless veterans, such as the VA's online guides for its homeless reentry program (U.S. Department of Veterans Affairs. Office of Public and Intergovernmental Affairs, 2016a). In fact, the U.S. Department of Labor regularly solicits proposals from support organizations to develop grant-funded programs that would assist veterans who will essentially be homeless upon leaving prison as part of the Homeless Veterans Comprehensive Assistance Act (HVCAA).

Education for incarcerated veterans. Incarcerated veterans, like many other veterans, may wish to further their education once leaving the military. Eligibility for GI Bill benefits is possible for incarcerated veterans, although the exact availability of benefits will depend on whether the veteran was otherwise eligible for VA education benefits and the type of conviction. Even veterans who are not eligible for GI Bill benefits may wish to further their education, however, and prison librarians can help incarcerated veterans connect with existing prison educational programs, distance education programs, and informal learning resources to support their educational development. Prison librarians may wish to develop partnerships with academic librarians whose institutions may be enrolling incarcerated veterans to facilitate access to information and help academic librarians better understand the challenges and limitations of incarcerated students.

Incarcerated veterans and health. According to the Bureau of Justice Statistics, 61 percent of veterans in state prisons and 57 percent of veterans in federal prisons meet the criteria for drug or alcohol dependence (Noonan & Mumola, 2007). As the Office of National Drug Control Policy notes, "many of these issues can be connected to the trauma of combat and other service-related experiences" (2010). Some veterans, for example, may have attempted to self-medicate themselves for depression or anxiety after leaving the military. These efforts might have resulted in alcoholism or drug use that contributed to their legal problems. Although some veterans may receive treatment via Veterans Treatment Courts, others may need to seek alternate resources for treatment, especially as they transition out of prison.

Incarcerated veterans may also need to use library resources to investigate other health conditions related to their military service, such as chronic health conditions or exposures that may have contributed to some of the problems they experienced after leaving the military. Librarians can help incarcerated veterans gain access to resources to learn more about PTSD and other stressors related to transitioning from military to civilian life to identify potential avenues for support and treatment. Prison librarians, therefore, can benefit from becoming familiar with the myriad resources available for veterans, including incarcerated veterans, to provide veterans with the information and resources they need. Examples of the resources librarians can use to find this type of information include the following:

- The Environmental Health Registry Evaluation for Veterans provides information about assessing a veteran's criteria for VA benefits related to exposure to environmental hazards and other conditions (U.S. Department of Veterans Affairs. Public Health, 2016d).

- The Veterans Justice Initiative is an effort by the VA to help veterans with legal problems related to a mental health or substance abuse issue avoid unnecessary incarceration by connecting them with treatment (U.S. Department of Veterans Affairs. Office of Public and Intergovernmental Affairs, 2016b).

Relocation after prison. Although there are resources available to veterans who are transitioning out of prison, accessing these resources can take research and planning. Information varies significantly based on the area in which the veteran will be settling. Prison librarians may be asked to help veterans find information and resources for different locations all around the country, including areas where policies and resources are very different from the local area. These challenges represent some of the most difficult tasks faced by prison librarians in assisting incarcerated veterans with finding information about the community in which they plan to live after reentering society

To identify resources in the area to which the veteran will be relocating, prison librarians should seek out resources at the state and local level. For example, the VA provides a guidebook for incarcerated veterans for many states and VA regions (U.S. Department of Veterans Affairs. Office of Public and Intergovernmental Affairs, 2016a). These guidebooks provide information about federal, state, and local resources for veterans as well as contact information for social service organizations in the local areas. Librarians may wish to facilitate access to a number of guidebooks to support incarcerated veterans who will be leaving the state upon their release. Incarcerated veterans also may qualify for the Homeless Veterans Reintegration Program (HVRP) (Homeless Veterans Reintegration Programs, 2001). The Department of Labor hosts a website about the resources available via HVRP in addition to a downloadable guide for service providers (U.S. Department of Labor, 2005).

Prison librarians may find additional help in contacting chapters of a veterans service organization (VSO) that is established where the veteran plans to relocate. To learn which VSOs are active in any city or zip code in the United States, librarians can visit the National Resource Directory at www.nrd.gov. This website lists organizations, county veterans service officers (CVSOs), and VA facilities for all states in the United States. For additional help, librarians can contact the CVSO for the area in which the veteran is planning to relocate. CVSOs help connect veterans in their area with available resources and benefits, and they often have considerable knowledge of the VSOs in their local area. To find a CVSO, librarians can visit the National Association of County Veterans Service Officers at https://www.nacvso.org/find_service_officers.

Empowering Incarcerated Veterans

Although prison librarians play a very important role in the lives of incarcerated veterans by connecting them with needed information, prison librarians can also help incarcerated veterans connect to the larger veteran and military community. One important aspect of military culture is the instilled sense of responsibility for contributing to the welfare of other service members. This desire to support other veterans and service members leads many veterans to volunteer or assist other veterans after they transition out of the military. Incarcerated veterans may feel this same need, and prison librarians can help empower incarcerated veterans by giving them the opportunity to volunteer and connect with other veterans or even with those who may serve in the future.

One way that prison librarians have been empowering incarcerated veterans is through oral history interviews. Incarcerated veterans, just like all other veterans, may have stories to share about their military experiences. Librarians at the Maryland Correctional Institution, for instance, have trained inmates who are veterans to conduct oral history interviews with other incarcerated veterans as part of the Library of Congress' Veterans History Project (Julius, 2008). This project allows veterans to connect with other veterans through the interview process, and it also allows veterans to give back by sharing their stories and experiences with the larger community, including those who may serve in the military in the future. To learn more about the Veterans History Project, see the online toolkit at https://www.loc.gov/vets/kit.html.

Collaborations and Partnerships

Prison librarians can partner with other libraries to find appropriate resources for incarcerated veterans. The state library may be a good starting point for prison librarians seeking support from other librarians. For example, the Colorado State Library's Institutional Library Development unit provides library support for both adult and juvenile inmates in state correctional facilities, including programs intended to smooth the transition back into everyday life (Colorado Department of Education, 2016). Prison librarians can work with the state library to develop resources to answer frequently asked questions by incarcerated veterans, which the state library can then disseminate to other prison librarians and prison library workers statewide. State libraries may also develop an online guide to help all veterans, including those who are incarcerated, connect with needed resources. For example, the South Carolina State Library's WorkSC.org site connects veterans and service members with a variety of useful resources (South Carolina State Library, 2016). In addition to state libraries, prison libraries may want to connect with public librarians, academic librarians, law librarians, health sciences librarians, or librarians from other types of libraries to help connect incarcerated veterans with the resources and information they may need.

Prison librarians, like all of the other types of librarians mentioned in this chapter, have an important role to play in connecting veterans to the information they need. Regardless of the type of library in which librarians serve, they can support the veteran and military communities by learning more about who these patrons are in their libraries, by making connections with other libraries and with other organizations that support veterans and service members, and by using their creativity to develop programs, services, and collections that meet the unique needs of the veteran and military-affiliated patrons in their communities.

References

American Bar Association. (2016a). ABA home front. Retrieved from http://www.americanbar.org/portals/public_resources/aba_home_front.html

American Bar Association. (2016b). Pro bono resources for veterans. Retrieved from http://www.americanbar.org/groups/committees/veterans_benefits/pro_bono_resources_for_veterans.html

Baiocchi, D. (2013). *Measuring Army deployments to Iraq and Afghanistan.* Santa Monica, CA: RAND Corporation. Retrieved from http://www.rand.org/content/dam/rand/pubs/research_reports/RR100/RR145/RAND_RR145.pdf

Banfield, C. M., & Morrison, W. B. (2000). Magnetic resonance arthrography of the canine stifle joint technique and applications in eleven military dogs. *Veterinary Radiology & Ultrasound, 41*(3), 200–213. doi:10.1111/j.1740-8261.2000.tb01479.x

Blosnich, J., Foynes, M. M., & Shipherd, J. C. (2013). Health disparities among sexual minority women veterans. *Journal of Women's Health, 22*(7), 631–636. doi:10.1089/jwh.2012.4214

Bradbard, D. A., Maury, R. V., Kimball, M., Wright, J. C. M., LoRe', C. E., Levingston, K., ... White, A. M. (2014). *Military family lifestyle survey*. Falls Church, VA: Blue Star Families. Retrieved from https://bluestarfam.org/survey

Bronson, J., Carson, E. A., Noonan, M., & Berzofsky, M. (2015, December). *Veterans in prison and jail, 2011–2012*. Washington, D.C.: Bureau of Justice Statistics. Retrieved from http://www.bjs.gov/content/pub/pdf/vpj1112.pdf

Clever, M., & Segal, D. R. (2013). *Future of Children, 23*(2), 13–39.

Colorado Department of Education. (2016). Prison libraries. Retrieved from https://www.cde.state.co.us/cdelib/prisonlibraries/index

Commander, Navy Installations Command. (n.d.). Fleet & family support program. Retrieved from http://www.cnic.navy.mil/ffr/family_readiness/fleet_and_family_support_program.html

Council of State Governments. (2013). MIC3: Military interstate children's compact commission. Retrieved from http://www.mic3.net

Dao, J. (2011, December 1). After duty, dogs suffer like soldiers. *New York Times*. Retrieved from http://www.nytimes.com/2011/12/02/us/more-military-dogs-show-signs-of-combat-stress.html?pagewanted=all

Edwards, R. (2008). Widening health inequities among U.S. military retirees since 1974. *Social Science & Medicine, 67*(11), 1657–1668. doi:10.1016/j.socscimed.2008.07.003

Emory University School of Law. (2016). Volunteer clinic for veterans. Retrieved from http://law.emory.edu/academics/clinics/volunteer-clinic-for-veterans.html

Engel, R. C., Gallagher, L. B., & Lyle, D. S. (2010). Military deployments and children's academic achievement: Evidence from Department of Defense Education Activity schools. *Economics of Education Review, 29*(1), 73–82. doi:10.1016/j.econedurev.2008.12.003

Fitzsimons, V. M. & Krause-Parello, C. A. (2009). Military children: When parents are deployed overseas. *Journal of School Nursing, 25*(1), 40–47. doi:10.1177/1059840508326733

Flake, E. M., Davis, B. E., Johnson, P. L., & Middleton, L. S. (2009). The psychosocial effects of deployment on military children. *Journal of Developmental & Behavioral Pediatrics, 30*(4), 271–278. doi:10.1097/DBP.0b013e3181aac6e4

Greenberg, G. A. & Rosenheck, R. A. (2012). Incarceration among male veterans: Relative risk of imprisonment and differences between veteran and nonveteran inmates. *International Journal of Offender Therapy and Comparative Criminology, 56*(4), 646–667. doi:10.1177/0306624X11406091

Hall, L. K. (2008). The children. In *Counseling military families: What mental health professionals need to know* (pp. 101–128). New York: Routledge.

Hoerster, K. D., Lehavot, K., Simpson, T., McFall, M., Reiber, G., & Nelson, K. M. (2012). Health and health behavior differences: U.S. military, veteran, and civilian men. *American Journal of Preventive Medicine, 43*(5), 483–489. doi:10.1016/j.amepre.2012.07.029

Holder, K. A. (2016). The disability of veterans. Retrieved from https://www.census.gov/content/dam/Census/library/working-papers/2016/demo/Holder-2016-01.pdf

Homeless veterans reintegration programs 38 U.S. Code § 2021 (2001).

Iraq War's Toll on Our Kids. (2007). *School Library Journal, 53*(11), 18–20.

Jeffreys, D. J. & Leitzel, J. D. (2000). The strengths and vulnerabilities of adolescents in military families. In J. A. Martin, L. N. Rosen, & L. R. Sparacino (Eds.), *The military family: A practice guide for human service providers* (pp. 225–240). Westport, CT: Praeger.

John Marshall Law School. Louis L. Biro Law Library. (2015). Veterans' benefits and issues: home. Retrieved from http://libraryguides.jmls.edu/c.php?g=261818

Johnson, S. J., Sherman, M. D., Hoffman, J., James, L. C., Johnson, P. L., Lochman, J. E., ... Stepney, B. (2007, February). *The psychological needs of U.S. military service members and their families: A preliminary report.* Washington, D.C.: American Psychological Association. Retrieved from http://www.apa.org/about/policy/military-deployment-services.pdf

Jowers, K. (2008). Military libraries expand reach, offerings to troops. *Navy Times, 58*(2), 24.

Julius, E. (2008, November 10). Behind Md. prison walls, veterans participate in history preservation project. *Herald-Mail.* Retrieved from http://articles.herald-mail.com/2008-11-10/news/25056868_1_fellow-inmates-veterans-history-project-navy-veteran

Legal Assistance for Military Personnel. (2001). Uniformed services former spouses' protection act (USFSPA). Retrieved from http://www.nclamp.gov/l_usfspa.pdf

Lehavot, K., Hoerster, K. D., Nelson, K. M., Jakupcak, M., & Simpson, T. L. (2012). Health indicators for military, veteran, and civilian women. *American Journal of Preventive Medicine, 42*(5), 473–480. doi:10.1016/j.amepre.2012.01.006

Linn, L. L., Bartels, K. E., Rochat, M. C., Payton, M. E., & Moore, G. E. (2003). Lumbosacral stenosis in 29 military working dogs: Epidemiologic findings and outcome after surgical intervention (1990–1999). *Veterinary Surgery, 32*(1), 21–29. doi:10.1053/jvet.2003.50001

Liscord, R. M. & Elliott, C. S. (2013). *Serving those who served: Understanding the legal needs of Maine's veteran community.* Portland, ME: Pine Tree Legal Assistance. Retrieved from http://ptla.org/sites/default/files/maine-veteran-legal-needs-study.pdf

Marek, L. I., Hollingsworth, W. G., D'Aniello, C., O'Rourke, K., Brock, D. P., Moore, L., ... Wiles, B. (2014). Returning home: What we know about the reintegration of the deployed service members into their families and communities. *NCFR Report Magazine.* Retrieved from https://www.ncfr.org/ncfr-report/focus/military-families/returning-home

Military OneSource. (2016). Morale, welfare, and recreation programs and eligibility. Retrieved from http://www.militaryonesource.mil/on-and-off-base-living/recreation-and-travel?content_id=281032

Noonan, M. E. & Mumola, C. J. (2007). *Veterans in state and federal prison, 2004.* Washington, D.C.: Bureau of Justice Statistics. Retrieved from https://www.bjs.gov/content/pub/pdf/vsfp04.pdf

Office of National Drug Control Policy. (2010). Fact sheet: Veterans treatment courts. Retrieved from https://www.whitehouse.gov/sites/default/files/ondcp/Fact_Sheets/veterans_treatment_courts_fact_sheet_12-13-10.pdf

Oregon Department of Veterans' Affairs. (2010). Military discharge in the United States. Retrieved from http://www.oregon.gov/odva/docs/pdfs/criminal_justice_portal/military_discharge.pdf

Park, N. (2011). Military children and families: Strengths and challenges during peace and war. *American Psychologist, 66*(1), 65–73.

Patriot PAWS. (2016). Retrieved from http://www.patriotpaws.org

Regent University School of Law Library. (2016). Veterans law: Introduction. Retrieved from http://libguides.regent.edu/veteranslaw

Regulations Under the Uniformed Services Employment and Reemployment Rights Act of 1994, 20 Fed. Reg. 1002 (December 19, 2005).

Servicemembers Civil Relief Act, 50 U.S. Code § 3901–4043 (2003).

South Carolina State Library. (2016). Resources for military and veterans. Retrieved from http://worksc.org/start-here/resources-military-and-veterans

Stanford Law School. (2016). Stanford law veterans organization (SLVO). Retrieved from https://law.stanford.edu/stanford-law-veterans-organization-slvo/

Suris, A. M. & Smith, J. C. (2011). Sexual assault in the military. In B. A. Moore & W. E. Penk Eds.), *Treating military personnel for PTSD: A clinical handbook* (pp. 255–269). New York: Guilford Press.

Taft, J. & Olney, C. (2015, January 20). Library services for the "new normal" of military families. *Public Libraries, 53*(6), 28–33.

Tomasovic, B. (2008, August 27). Army Trial Defense Service protects soldiers. Retrieved from http://www.army.mil/article/11927/Army_Trial_Defense_Service_protects_Soldiers

Trivedi, A. N., Grebla, R. C., Wright, S. M., & Washington, D. L. (2011). Despite improved quality of care in the Veterans Affairs Health System, racial disparity persists for important clinical outcomes. *Health Affairs, 30*(4), 707–715. doi:10.1377/hlthaff.2011.0074

Tuesday tucks me in: The loyal bond between a soldier and his service dog. (2016). Retrieved from http://www.tuesdaytucks.com

Uniform Code of Military Justice, 10 U.S. Code § 47 (1951).

Uniformed Services Employment and Reemployment Rights Act, 38 U.S. Code § 4301–4335 (1994).

United States Courts. (n.d.). Servicemembers' Civil Relief Act (SCRA). Retrieved from http://www.uscourts.gov/services-forms/bankruptcy/bankruptcy-basics/servicemembers-civil-relief-act-scra

United States Department of Labor. Veterans' Employment & Training Service. (n.d.). Veterans' preference information. Retrieved from http://www.dol.gov/vets/programs/vetspref/main.htm

U.S. Army MWR. (2016). Army MWR library. Retrieved from http://www.armymwr.com/recleisure/libraries

U.S. Department of Defense. (n.d.). Department of Defense Education Activity. Retrieved from http://www.dodea.edu

U.S. Department of Defense. (2012, February). *Military deployment guide: Preparing you and your family for the road ahead.* Washington, D.C.: U.S. Department of Defense. Retrieved from http://download.militaryonesource.mil/12038/Project%20Documents/MilitaryHOMEFRONT/Troops%20and%20Families/Deployment%20Connections/Pre-Deployment%20Guide.pdf

U.S. Department of Defense. (2015). *2014 demographics profile of the military community.* Washington, D.C.: Office of the Deputy Under Secretary of Defense. Retrieved from http://download.militaryonesource.mil/12038/MOS/Reports/2014-Demographics-Report.pdf

U.S. Department of Defense. (2016). Military OneSource. Retrieved from http://www.militaryonesource.mil

U.S. Department of Defense. Education Activity. (n.d.). School liaison officers. Retrieved from http://www.dodea.edu/Partnership/schoolLiaisonOfficers.cfm

U.S. Department of Education (n.d.) Military families and veterans. Retrieved from http://www.ed.gov/veterans-and-military-families

U.S. Department of Labor. (2005). *Homeless veteran employment assistance guide for service providers.* Washington, D.C.: U.S. Department of Labor. Retrieved from http://www.dol.gov/vets/programs/hvrp/EmploymentAssistanceGuide.pdf

U.S. Department of Labor. (2008). Your rights under USERRA: The Uniformed Services Employment and Reemployment Rights Act. Retrieved from http://www.dol.gov/vets/programs/userra/userra_private.pdf

U.S. Department of Veterans Affairs. (2010). Accreditation search. Retrieved from http://www.va.gov/ogc/apps/accreditation/

U.S. Department of Veterans Affairs. (2014). VETPOP 2014: Living veterans by period of service, gender, 2013–2043. Retrieved from http://www.va.gov/vetdata/docs/Demographics/New_Vetpop_Model/2L_VetPop2014.xlsx

U.S. Department of Veterans Affairs. (2016). Veterans law review. Retrieved from http://www.bva.va.gov/VLR.asp

U.S. Department of Veterans Affairs. Benefits Assistance Service. (2015). Incarcerated veterans: Can a veteran receive VA benefits while in prison? Retrieved from http://www.benefits.va.gov/BENEFITS/factsheets/misc/incarcerated.pdf

U.S. Department of Veterans Affairs. Health Care. (2016a). Health benefits: Veterans eligibility. Retrieved from http://www.va.gov/healthbenefits/apply/veterans.asp

U.S. Department of Veterans Affairs. Health Care. (2016b). Polytrauma/TBI system of care. Retrieved from http://www.polytrauma.va.gov/index.asp

U.S. Department of Veterans Affairs. Health Care. (2015). Understanding traumatic brain injury. Retrieved from http://www.polytrauma.va.gov/understanding-tbi

U.S. Department of Veterans Affairs. Mental Health. (2015). Military sexual trauma: General factsheet. Retrieved from http://www.mentalhealth.va.gov/docs/mst _general_factsheet.pdf

U.S. Department of Veterans Affairs. National Center for PTSD. (2016). PTSD treatment programs in the U.S. Department of Veterans Affairs. Retrieved from http://www.ptsd.va.gov/public/treatment/therapy-med/va-ptsd-treatment -programs.asp

U.S. Department of Veterans Affairs. Office of General Counsel. (2015). Legal help for veterans. Retrieved from http://www.va.gov/ogc/legalservices.asp

U.S. Department of Veterans Affairs. Office of General Counsel. (2016). Accreditation frequently asked questions. Retrieved from http://www.va.gov/ogc/accred _faqs.asp

U.S. Department of Veterans Affairs. Office of Public and Intergovernmental Affairs. (2016a). Health care for reentry veterans (HCRV). Retrieved from http://www .va.gov/homeless/reentry.asp

U.S. Department of Veterans Affairs. Office of Public and Intergovernmental Affairs. (2016b). Veterans justice outreach program. Retrieved from http://www.va.gov /homeless/vjo.asp

U.S. Department of Veterans Affairs. Public Health. (2015). Veterans' diseases associated with Agent Orange. Retrieved from http://www.publichealth.va.gov/exposures /agentorange/conditions

U.S. Department of Veterans Affairs. Public Health. (2016a). Burn pits. Retrieved from http://www.publichealth.va.gov/exposures/burnpits/index.asp

U.S. Department of Veterans Affairs. Public Health. (2016b). Directory of environmental health coordinators. Retrieved from http://www.publichealth.va.gov /exposures/coordinators.asp

U.S. Department of Veterans Affairs. Public Health. (2016c). Gulf War veterans' medically unexplained illnesses. Retrieved from http://www.publichealth.va.gov /exposures/gulfwar/medically-unexplained-illness.asp

U.S. Department of Veterans Affairs. Public Health. (2016d). Environmental health registry evaluation for veterans. Retrieved from http://www.publichealth.va.gov /exposures/benefits/registry-evaluation.asp

U.S. Department of Veterans Affairs. Rehabilitation and Prosthetic Services. (2016). Guide and service dogs. Retrieved from http://www.prosthetics.va.gov /ServiceAndGuideDogs.asp

U.S. Department of Veterans Affairs. Veterans Benefits Administration. (2015b). *VBA annual benefits report fiscal year 2014 - compensation.* Washington, D.C.: U.S. Department of Veterans Affairs. Retrieved from http://www.benefits.va.gov /REPORTS/abr/ABR-Compensation-FY14-10202015.pdf

U.S. Department of Veterans Affairs. Veterans Benefits Administration. (2015a). Applying for benefits and your character of discharge. Retrieved from http:// www.benefits.va.gov/benefits/character_of_discharge.asp

U.S. Department of Veterans Affairs. Veterans Health Administration. (2015). Vets in crisis get a chance, not a cell. Retrieved from http://www.va.gov/health /newsfeatures/20120216a.asp

U.S. Navy. (2011). *Family readiness groups handbook.* Washington, D.C.: Commander, Navy Installations Command. Retrieved from http://cnic.navy.mil/content/dam /cnic/hq/pdfs/n91_fleet_and_family_support_program/deployment_readiness /DeploymentFamilyReadinessGroupsHandbook.pdf

U.S. Navy Judge Advocate General's Corps. (n.d.). Retrieved from http://www.jag .navy.mil

Veteran's Employment Preferences, Tex. Gov't Code § 657.001-010 (2015).

Veterans of Foreign Wars. (2016). VFW in the classroom. Retrieved from https://www .vfw.org/Classroom

Washington Secretary of State. (2015, March 31). Our prison libraries help inmates to re-enter society [Blog post]. Retrieved from http://blogs.sos.wa.gov/library /index.php/tag/prison-libraries

Watson Institute for International and Public Affairs. (2015). Costs of war: US veterans & military families. Retrieved from http://watson.brown.edu/costsofwar/costs/human/veterans

Weeks, W. B., Kazis, L. E., Shen, Y., Cong, Z., Ren, X. S., Miller, D., ... Perlin, J. B. (2004). Differences in health-related quality of life in rural and urban veterans. *American Journal of Public Health, 94*(10), 1762–1767. doi:10.2105/AJPH.94.10.1762

Yale Law School. (n.d.). Veterans legal services clinic. Retrieved from https://www.law.yale.edu/studying-law-yale/clinical-and-experiential-learning/our-clinics/veterans-legal-services-clinic

Yount, R. A, Olmert, M. D., & Lee, M. R. (2012). Service dog training program for treatment of posttraumatic stress in service members. *United States Army Medical Department Journal*, April–June, 63–69.

Conclusion

The veteran and military communities are made up of a wide variety of individuals who are connected by one characteristic: they have made significant sacrifices as a result of their or their loved ones' military service. As a result of this military service, members of the veteran and military communities have unique and substantial strengths that they bring to the larger community. Veterans, service members, and their families understand how to pull together as a team, how to put the needs of the whole above those of the individual, and how to survive and even thrive in difficult circumstances. However, members of the veteran and military communities also have needs and challenges related to their or their loved ones' military service. They may be experiencing difficulties inherent in transitioning from a military lifestyle to a civilian lifestyle, coping with mental or physical injuries sustained during a deployment, or struggling to help a military child adapt to a new school. Libraries can play a significant role in helping veterans, service members, and other members of the veteran and military communities both overcome their needs and challenges and highlight the strengths that they bring to the local community.

Libraries are uniquely positioned to support the veteran and military communities, in large part because of their mission to serve all patrons. As chapter 1 discussed, there are many members of the veteran and military communities who may not believe that they are truly included within those communities. Because libraries already take a broad view of who they are serving, it is natural for libraries to also take an inclusive approach toward veteran and military-affiliated patrons. This inclusiveness can provide opportunities for marginalized veterans, such as those who received a less than honorable discharge, to receive support and services as veterans, possibly for the very first time. Libraries can also play a significant role in helping veterans, service members, and their loved ones manage the information overload associated with the myriad military and veterans' benefits. And libraries can also make use of their physical spaces to host programs and events that encourage members of the veteran and military communities to engage with the civilian community to share their experiences and to develop crucial connections between these populations.

As chapter 2 illustrated, there are a variety of strategies that all librarians can use to better support the veteran and military communities. The first step that librarians can take to improve their library's support is to learn some of the basics about military culture and the landscape of veteran and military organizations and benefits. By learning the basics, librarians can reduce barriers to engaging one-on-one with local veterans, service members, and their families. This foundational knowledge can also help librarians feel more confident and comfortable in asking questions about the needs and challenges of members of veteran and military communities residing within the local community.

These questions form the next step that all librarians can take to support the veteran and military communities. Conducting a needs assessment, outreach, or other approaches to community analysis can help improve the library's support for veterans, service members, and family members. Once librarians have a good idea of what services and programs are needed, they can identify strategic partners to assist them in developing new initiatives. Partnerships with outside military and veterans service organizations can help librarians ensure that new programming, services, and collections will support veteran and military communities. These supporting programs, services, and collections ideally focus on four primary areas: (1) helping patrons from veteran and military communities feel welcome in the library, (2) connecting them with services and benefits that are available, (3) fostering relationships among members of the veteran and military communities as well as between civilians and the veteran and military communities, and (4) highlighting the service of and sacrifices made by those who are now or who once were affiliated with the U.S. military.

In addition, librarians may interact with different groups within the veteran and military communities, depending on where they work. As chapters 3, 4, and 5 discussed, librarians can apply targeted strategies that are unique to each type of library. Depending on the function of the library and the nature of its users, librarians should consider offering different services, different materials, and different programs. For example, as chapter 4 delineated, academic librarians may focus on providing support to student veterans and service members to help them achieve their academic goals. School librarians may have a slightly different focus; as chapter 5 discussed, school librarians can support the veteran and military communities by helping military children and families during military deployments. And chapter 3 addressed how public librarians can support some military veterans who are particularly at risk, such as veterans who have become disconnected from VA resources. The strategies and focus that librarians take may be different from one type of library to another, but librarians should remember that no matter what type of library they work in, there are ways that they can support the military and veteran communities.

This book was intended to provide a starting point for librarians from all types of libraries. However, neither this book nor its authors have all of the answers about library services for veterans, service members, and their families. Information about programs, services, and organizations for the veteran and military communities can change frequently. Librarians must reach across the boundaries of the different types of libraries to share their success stories and lessons learned about serving the veteran and military communities. By sharing knowledge throughout the library community, librarians can continue to make progress toward better services, programs, and collections for the veteran and military communities. There is also a clear need for librarians to take the lead in researching the information-seeking behavior and the information needs of veterans and service members. By continuing to ask questions about how libraries can develop new and innovative services, programs, collaborations, and collections to support veteran and military service members, librarians can truly heed the call to serve those who served.

Glossary

active duty. Service members who are currently working full-time in one of the five branches of the military (Army, Navy, Air Force, Marines, or Coast Guard).

area of conflict. See **conflict area**.

Armed Forces. The military in general. The five branches of the U.S. Armed Forces are the Army, Navy, Air Force, Marines, and Coast Guard.

battle assembly. See **drill**.

benefits. In the context of veterans, specific types of compensation, including educational assistance, housing assistance, health care, and other assistance that are administered by the U.S. Department of Veterans Affairs at the federal level. Sometimes this term can be used more broadly to include benefits from a state's department of veterans' affairs or other organizations that support veterans and service members.

benefits claim. The process of applying for benefits from the U.S. Department of Veterans Affairs. Benefits claims can be associated with any request for veterans' benefits and are not necessarily associated with a disability. Benefits are administered through systems governed by the Department of Veterans Affairs.

Blue Star Flag. Under 36 U.S. Code § 901, immediate family members of military personnel who are serving during wartime are permitted to hang a service flag in their window to show neighbors that their family member is currently serving. The use of the Blue Star Flag was very popular in World War II, especially when parents had several children serving at the same time. Blue Star Flags can still be used and seen, particularly in military communities where the loved ones are serving in a combat zone.

branch. The U.S. military includes five branches: Army, Navy, Air Force, Marines, and Coast Guard.

cadet (or midshipman). An individual who is in training to commission as an officer in the military, either through a military academy, a senior military college, or via a Reserve Officers' Training Corps (ROTC) program.

caregiver. A spouse, partner, family member, or friend who cares for a wounded or disabled veteran or service member. Caregivers may need to access information to learn about services and benefits for the wounded or disabled veteran or service member or to seek support for themselves.

In this book, this term is also used for the person caring for military children during a parent's deployment.

combat veteran. In its broadest sense, a veteran who has spent time in an officially designated combat zone. Some veterans may define the term more narrowly to refer specifically to those who directly engaged in combat or who received a badge or ribbon recognizing their combat service, such as a Combat Action Ribbon or Combat Infantry Badge.

conflict area (or area of conflict). A place where military conflict occurs.

congressionally certified/chartered. An organization that serves veterans or military personnel and has been acknowledged by Congress. Organizations with a congressional charter are included on a list as part of a code by the U.S. Congress, but not all veteran and military-oriented service organizations are congressionally chartered. The list of congressionally certified/chartered VSOs can be accessed at https://veterans.house .gov/citizens/resources.

county veterans service officer (CVSO). The county veterans service officer works to support veterans and facilitate access to veterans' benefits in a specific county. CVSOs are responsible for communications about veterans' benefits in their area. They often serve as a type of ombudsman in representing veterans in need or in referring veterans to organizations or individuals who specialize in various issues. A national listing of CVSOs is online at https://www.nacvso.org/find_service_officers.

cultural competence. Some advocacy groups have asked those who want to teach people about veteran or military culture not to use the term *sensitivity* because it may suggest that veterans are insensitive or that veterans are overly sensitive about certain things. *Cultural competence* is the term now used, as it is used in teaching other diversity topics, to emphasize that the subject of the training is the unique culture of those who served in the military.

DADT. See **Don't Ask, Don't Tell**.

DD-214. The Department of Defense form 214, or DD-214, is the military's official Certificate of Release or Discharge from Active Duty. The DD-214 serves as a veteran's official proof of service, and it also documents the veteran's discharge type. It is the official form provided to the VA, employers, and other official entities to receive veterans' benefits and privileges.

dependent. Military dependents include the spouse and minor child(ren) of a military service member or any other individual for whom the service member is financially responsible. Dependents of service members or veterans may be eligible for benefits, depending on their relationship to the person with military experience, their age, and the status of the service member at the time they left the military.

deployment. The act of sending military service members to a designated location where they may assist organizations in disaster relief, work with United Nations or other joint task forces to participate in civil affairs activities on behalf of U.S. interests, or engage in the defense of military interests or combat.

disability compensation. Veterans who have physical or mental impairments as a result of their military service can apply to the VA for disability compensation. Eligible veterans are assigned a disability rating based on the severity of their disability or disabilities. Some VSOs help veterans prepare their applications for disability compensation, even if the veteran is not a member of the organization. The VA prefers that only VA or VSO representatives assist veterans with applying for disability compensation.

discharge. A service member's separation from military service. The *discharge* refers to orders from the person's branch of service that specifies the date that the service member is no longer on active duty. Service members may be discharged for many reasons: the end of their contract, a medical condition, retirement, or some type of involuntary separation. Depending on the person's service record, the character of the person's discharge may range anywhere from honorable to dishonorable. The character of a service member's discharge is very important, as a less than honorable discharge may affect future employment opportunities as well as eligibility for VA benefits.

discharge upgrade. A request by a veteran that the military review service records and other data to reassess the nature of their service. This request is made in an effort to upgrade the character of the veteran's discharge from a less than honorable discharge to higher status discharge, such as an honorable discharge.

Don't Ask, Don't Tell (DADT). The 1993 directive that permitted lesbian, gay, and bisexual individuals to join the military as long as they did not reveal their sexual orientation. Before its repeal in 2011, thousands of service members were discharged under DADT. Many of the veterans discharged under DADT may be unaware that they may be eligible for discharge upgrades or VA benefits previously denied due to their character of discharge.

drill (or battle assembly). Members of the National Guard and Reserves typically spend one weekend per month at drill. Drill is the time when all Reservists conduct training to maintain their military knowledge and skills. Reservists who report to drill each month are often described as being in "drilling status," as opposed to being activated to full-time military duty.

eligibility rating/status. Veterans often refer to a disability claim or other form of registration for services by the VA in terms of a level of eligibility. Veterans who receive services from the VA are enrolled with the VA, and they usually re-enroll each year to confirm their eligibility, especially if a medical condition has worsened or they experience unemployment. The benefits they receive are determined according to priority groups that are reviewed by Congress every year to update the status of any underserved groups when necessary. Determination of priority groups, enrollment, and eligibility are legal decisions made only by an authorized representative of the VA. More information about the enrollment process is available on the VA website at http://www.va.gov/healthbenefits/apply/veterans.asp.

enlisted. Service members whose pay grades fall within E-1 and E-9. Enlisted personnel are responsible for interpreting and carrying out the orders of commissioned officers. The upper ranks of enlisted are referred to as noncommissioned officers, or NCOs. Within military culture, there are differences between a person's standing as an enlisted service member as opposed to an officer, though each unit may have some variations on the cultural importance regarding those differences, and both enlisted members and officers take pride in their status.

era of conflict. A wartime period spanning dates that are decided by Congress and reviewed on a regular basis to ensure that veterans who served during the designated eras of conflict receive proper recognition, benefits, and pension according to when they served.

Family Readiness Group (FRG). An officially sponsored network that provides information and support to military families, including spouses and children.

GI Bill. Specifically, the Montgomery GI Bill, a VA educational benefit that was first made available to veterans after World War II. However, the term *GI Bill* is commonly used to refer to the suite of VA educational benefits for which many veterans are eligible. Most veterans currently enrolled in higher education are using the Post-9/11 GI Bill.

Gold Star. Similar in its origin to the Blue Star, the Gold Star is used to indicate those who have lost a loved one during military service.

inactive duty. Someone who has been discharged from the military but is considered to still be in reserve status should a war necessitate that the Department of Defense recall them. For most service members, their service usually requires a total of eight years of combined active and inactive duty. Also commonly referred to as **inactive reserve** or **individual ready reserve (IRR)**.

inactive reserve. See **inactive duty**.

individual ready reserve (IRR). See **inactive duty**.

Memorial Day vs. Veterans Day. See **Veterans Day vs. Memorial Day**.

midshipman. See **cadet**.

military children. The minor children of military personnel. Although some organizations use this term to refer to adult children who are serving in the military, this book does not use the term *military children* in this context. See also **dependent**.

military community. All of those who care for a service member. It includes all family members of a service person, including significant others and children, as well as parents, siblings, and caregivers.

military family. A service member, any spouse or partner of a service member, any children of a service member, and any combination thereof. Although this term is sometimes used more broadly to include the parents of service members, this book uses a narrower definition to communicate services and resources that a library would want to offer to a military family as it is defined above.

Military OneSource. A Department of Defense–sponsored website that connects service members from all branches of the military to resources and services, including counseling, financial resources, and library resources, among many others.

military parents. This term is used in the context of families in which at least one parent is in the military and where the parent(s) are raising minor children in a military environment. Although some organizations may use this term to refer to the parents of military personnel, this book does not use the term *military parents* in this context, though it is important to include parents of military service members when considering the impact of military experience on the overall military community.

military sexual trauma (MST). The sexual assault or sexual harassment of individuals serving in the military. For more information about VA services for veterans who have experienced MST, see http://www.mentalhealth.va.gov/msthome.asp.

military spouse. The husband, wife, or partner of a military service member. A military spouse is considered to be a dependent of the service member regardless of employment or financial status. See also **dependent**.

MWR. Each branch of the military has a Morale, Welfare, and Recreation (MWR) program that is responsible for resources and programming aimed at building morale among the troops and their families. Common MWR resources include pools, bowling alleys, and libraries, among many others.

National Guard. The National Guard has two components, the Army National Guard and the Air National Guard. Each U.S. state has a National Guard that serves one weekend a month and two weeks a year that can be called up by the state's governor to respond to state-level needs, especially natural disasters. The National Guard also functions as a national network that can be called up to active-duty military status to provide federal-level support as a supplement to active-duty troops. This federal-level support has included combat deployments, particularly during the wars in Iraq and Afghanistan.

National Resource Directory. A website hosted by the federal government to provide a directory of VA locations and facilities as well as information about Vet Centers and other veteran resources. It can be a good first stop to learn about veteran organizations in a community, but it is ideal to contact a county veterans service officer (CVSO) or military liaison to ensure that the library is aware of all nearby resources.

officer. There are two types of officers in the military: commissioned officers and warrant officers. Officers are individuals who commission into the military, generally after completing a bachelor's degree, and whose pay grades fall within O-1 and O-9 (for commissioned officers) and W-1 and W-5 (for warrant officers). Some officers are former ROTC or service academy cadets, while others are former enlisted personnel who were educated and trained to become officers. Officers are responsible for administering, directing, and commanding military operations.

orders. Each time a service member is stationed anywhere, permanently or through a temporary deployment, the service member is given orders. These are a written document specifying the time of departure, destination, nature of work, and such other things as whether the individual is permitted to wear civilian clothes or will receive hazardous-duty pay. Other orders may be written to give an award or to specify when someone will undergo training or participate in an exercise.

PTSD. Post-traumatic stress disorder (PTSD) is a mental health condition in which someone experiences long-term issues related to having experienced a severe trauma or life-threatening situation. PTSD can occur in response to both combat and noncombat experiences. For more information about VA services for those with PTSD, see http://www.ptsd.va.gov.

Purple Heart. A military award recognizing a service member who was injured in combat or killed in action. Veterans (or the survivors of veterans) who have received a Purple Heart are honored and eligible for a range of benefits from the VA and other organizations.

rank. Designates a position in the military hierarchy that is usually, but not always, linked to the service member's pay grade. A rank also suggests a form of address, such as "sergeant" or "corporal."

reserve component. The reserve component of the military includes both the National Guard and Reserves. Each branch of the Armed Forces has a reserve component (e.g., Army Reserve, Coast Guard Reserve). Members of the Reserves receive the same training as active-duty military personnel but then return to their communities, where in general they report to duty one weekend a month and two weeks a year for training.

Reservist. Members of the reserve component of the U.S. military. This term encompasses members of the National Guard and Reserves. Reservists typically maintain a civilian job, although some Reservists do work full-time for the National Guard or Reserves. Reservists can be called to active duty by the federal government to supplement and support active-duty troops, including during combat deployments overseas.

retired military. A military retiree is a veteran who served in the military for at least 20 years and is therefore eligible for additional benefits and entitlements from the Department of Defense and VA. Some military retirees may be granted military retirement without completing 20 years of service, often due to medical reasons.

ROTC. The Reserve Officers' Training Corps (ROTC) is a program available on many campuses in which cadets or midshipmen participate in military training while they are in college in hopes of commissioning as an officer in the military.

school certifying official. Colleges and universities that enroll veterans must designate a school certifying official (SCO) who is the person responsible for coordinating VA education benefits.

school liaison officer. Employees of the Department of Defense who are assigned to schools in military communities. School liaison officers are responsible for coordinating and improving understanding by K–12 school personnel about military families, deployments in a military community, and opportunities to assist members of military families who experience hardship.

service member. An individual who is currently serving in any branch of the U.S Uniformed Services, either on active duty or the reserve component.

stolen valor. A claim by anyone who pretends to have been decorated by the military for experiences in combat or elsewhere. Congress passed the Stolen Valor Act in 2013 to make it illegal for a person to fraudulently claim having received an award or any recognition to receive tangible benefits.

survivor. The spouse or dependent child of a deceased service member or veteran. In some cases, this term may also be used more broadly to describe other family members of a deceased service member or veteran as well.

TBI. Traumatic brain injury (TBI) is a head injury that results in long-term chronic health problems. For information about VA services to veterans with TBI, see http://www.polytrauma.va.gov/understanding-tbi.

transitioning. Refers to a service member who is preparing to leave the military and is experiencing the logistical and emotional difficulties of adapting from military to civilian culture.

TRICARE. The health care system provided to active-duty military service members. Reservists and military retirees may also be eligible for TRICARE-based health insurance.

Tuition Assistance (TA). Educational benefits available to service members (those currently serving). Not to be confused with the GI Bill, which primarily supports veterans (those who have already separated from the military).

UCMJ. The Uniform Code of Military Justice (UCMJ) is the legal code that governs all service members on active duty as well as Reservists while on active status.

Uniformed Services. The seven branches of the U.S. Uniformed Services: Army, Navy, Air Force, Marines, Coast Guard, Commissioned Corps of the Public Health Service, and Commissioned Corps of the National Oceanic and Atmospheric Administration.

USERRA. The Uniformed Services Employment and Reemployment Rights Act of 1994 (USERRA) is legislation that protects members of the military from discrimination in employment. USERRA is frequently referenced as the law that protects the civilian jobs of members of the National Guard and Reserves when they volunteer for or are called up to full-time military duty.

Vet Centers. Vet Centers are official VA facilities that provide readjustment services for combat veterans and other veterans who may have experienced trauma during their service. For more information and to find a nearby Vet Center, librarians should visit http://www.vetcenter.va.gov/index.asp.

veteran. An individual who served in the U.S. Uniformed Services, on active duty or in the National Guard or Reserves, for any period of time, regardless of combat service, deployment, or type of discharge.

veteran center. Veteran centers (also commonly referred to as veteran support centers or resource centers) are offices that may not be officially affiliated with the VA but that provide services and programs for veterans. Some college and university campuses may have a veteran center that centralizes services and coordinates benefits for veterans, service members, and other military-affiliated students.

veterans service officer/representative. Someone authorized by the VA to assist a veteran with paperwork and explain benefit eligibility issues. A veterans service officer (VSO)/veterans service representative (VSR) receives extensive training so as to be able to communicate clearly and avoid any legal issues. The VA asks that no one make any promises to a veteran on their behalf unless it is a VSO/VSR.

veterans service organization (VSO). A nonprofit organization whose purpose is to assist veterans or military personnel. May also be referred to as "veterans support organization." A VSO may provide services to veterans or active-duty military personnel and their families or caregivers.

Veterans Day vs. Memorial Day. Both Veterans Day and Memorial Day celebrate the services of the military. Veterans Day honors all who have served or are serving in the military. Memorial Day is a day set aside to pay tribute to those who have lost their lives in war.

veterans' preference. Some veterans may be eligible for preferential treatment in hiring. Title 5, United States Code, Section 2108 covers the regulations for federal government organizations that offer veterans' preference. Not all veterans are eligible for veterans' preference, and veterans' preference is not a guarantee of employment.

VSO. May refer to a **veterans service officer** or a **veterans service organization**.

VSR. See **veterans service officer/representative**.

Index

About the Authors

Sarah LeMire is the first-year experience and outreach librarian at Texas A&M University in College Station, Texas, where she provides outreach and support to student veterans and other military communities on her campus. She was recognized as a member of ALA's 2015 class of Emerging Leaders. Before becoming a librarian, LeMire served in the U.S. Army as an Arabic linguist, including a deployment to Iraq in 2005–2006. She is the spouse of a current Army service member and a parent to two young girls.

Kristen J. Mulvihill is a librarian at the San Diego Public Library. She has taught workshops about military veterans in California and served as a consultant on working with this community since 2011. Mulvihill earned a master of library and information science degree at San Jose State University after receiving a Librarians for Diverse Communities Scholarship from the Serra Cooperative from 2010 until 2012. She also holds a master's degree in Chinese from the University of Oregon. While serving in the military in the early 1990s, Mulvihill earned a Meritorious Service Medal and two Army Achievement Medals.